The Dogs of Bedlam Farm

The Dogs of Bedlam Farm

AN ADVENTURE WITH SIXTEEN SHEEP,
THREE DOGS, TWO DONKEYS, AND ME

Jon Katz

VILLARD  NEW YORK

LIBRARY OF CONGRESS CATALOGING-IN-PUBLICATION DATA

Katz, Jon.
    The dogs of Bedlam Farm: an adventure with sixteen sheep, three dogs,
two donkeys, and me / Jon Katz.
        p.   cm.
    ISBN 1-4000-6243-8
    1. Dogs—New York—West Hebron—Anecdotes. 2. Dogs—
Behavior—New York—West Hebron—Anecdotes. 3. Katz, Jon.
4. Farm life—New York—West Hebron—Anecdotes. 5. Bedlam Farm
(West Hebron, N.Y.)—Anecdotes. 6. Human-animal relationships—
New York—West Hebron—Anecdote. I. Title.

SF426.2.K3824 2004   636.7'009747'51—dc22   2004054966

Photos on pages iv and v by Jon Katz

Villard Books website address: www.villard.com

Printed in the United States of America on acid-free paper

987654321

First Edition

Designed by Susan Turner

Prologue

. . . .

THE JULY SUN WAS BEATING DOWN ON THE PASTURE ON A STICKY
afternoon. Flies and gnats swarmed all over me; the smell of
poop was pungent; and Carolyn Wilki's usually compliant sheep
were getting grumpy, tired of being chased around and eager to
leave their fenced enclosure—which contained dozens of them,
along with me and my troubled and complex border collie.

"Lie down!" I was saying again and again, louder each time,
to no particular effect and in a voice I vaguely and distastefully
recognized but couldn't quite identify. My dog Orson, like many
of his breed, had his own agenda, which bore little resemblance
to mine.

He was tearing around the sheep, crashing into them, grabbing mouthfuls of wool. I waved my crook menacingly; if he'd held still long enough, I might have clobbered him.

I wasn't enjoying this. This wasn't like the Discovery Channel. I was soaked in sweat and covered with bites and welts and caked with unspeakable stuff. Worse, my dog had not lain down, not even once. Orson's notion of herding didn't involve the fabled, exquisite interplay with the herder-shepherd. His idea was to grab the biggest sheep and drag it around a bit.

Carolyn, the trainer who'd pulled this dog and me back from the abyss, chugged over to me on her all-terrain vehicle. She owned this Pennsylvania farm, and she was a formidable presence as always in her slouch hat, which she wore in all weather, and flapping cape. "Leash up your dog," she ordered in a displeased tone, "and leave the pen."

Carolyn had become a close friend; we yakked and squabbled endlessly about life and dogs. Like many professionals in the dog world—vets, breeders, rescue workers, trainers—she'd lost some of her capacity to be tactful or optimistic about the way people handle their dogs.

"Look, Katz," Carolyn snapped. "That wasn't good dog training in there. You're getting angry, talking too much, being too reactive. Face it: if you want to have a better dog, you will just have to be a better goddamned human."

I was surprised; that wasn't what I wanted or expected to hear from a dog trainer. But what she was saying struck home, deeply. She was talking about anger, impatience, impulsiveness, frustration, an inability to watch and listen—enormous problems all my life, still not easy to vanquish in my mid-fifties. Only my helpless love for this screwy dog could cause me to undertake such an overhaul.

Two years after that hot and bothered afternoon in Pennsylvania, though I can't say whether I'm a better human—I'm still working on it, and ultimately, it's something for others to decide—I do have a better dog.

Carolyn was right, perhaps more than she imagined. I've come to see my dogs as a reflection of my willingness to try to improve, as well as an unsparing measure of my frequent failure to do so. Orson is a different dog than the frantic, matted, and terrified creature who arrived in a crate at Newark Airport several years ago. He is calmer, more responsive, more loving—the result, I'm convinced, of my struggle to learn and grow and to be more patient, less angry. For better or worse, I see Orson's progress—and that of my other two dogs—as a mirror of my own humanity, a benchmark of my progress. Or lack thereof.

SOMETIMES IT ONLY BECOMES CLEAR WHAT A BOOK IS REALLY about later on, after it's published, when readers and time and life and memory have done their filtering and perspective brings things into focus.

It's only now, for example, that I realize that two of my books—*Running to the Mountain* and *A Dog Year*—are, despite their differences, about the same thing: trying to become a better human. For me, this lifelong struggle has become enmeshed with dogs, almost inseparable from them. There are many other means, and I didn't particularly choose this path. The dogs, I think, chose me.

When Carolyn yelled that day in the pasture, she wasn't attacking me, just giving voice to a powerful idea: dogs are blameless, devoid of calculation, neither blessed nor cursed with human motives.

Insofar as they have problems, except for genetics or unusual circumstances, it's usually because we either inflict them or fail to correct them. They can't really be held responsible for what they do. But we can.

Dogs have their own identities and personalities, certainly, but they're also living and breathing testaments to our pasts, our families, our strengths and frustrations. They have their own traits and instincts, but to a considerable degree they are what we make them, what we teach them to be.

Dogs that we raise from puppyhood reflect our willingness to know and love and train them properly. Dogs we rescue or inherit are often more complex, and can challenge us even more.

In either case, we are profoundly responsible for them. It's become increasingly fashionable to see dogs as human substitutes, childlike equals, or even, in some cases, superiors. I see our extraordinary relationship with them differently: they are voiceless, so we must be their advocates, their stewards.

Staring in shock that July day at my traumatized border collie, who was frantically trying to please me and to make sense of my confusing commands, I recognized that I had a lot more work to do on myself, though I already had done plenty.

What a different life it's been since that revelation. I can hardly believe to what degree Orson (formerly named Devon) has altered my existence. My two beloved yellow Labs are gone, one of cancer, the other of heart disease, replaced by three creatures who are in most respects at the other end of the animal spectrum: three border collies—Orson, Homer, Rose. The cabin about which I wrote a book (*Running to the Mountain*) is gone, sold and then replaced by an aging farmhouse fifteen miles north, with four decrepit barns, a milk house, and forty-two acres of pasture and woods.

My work is completely different—I write about dogs now. I have new and wonderful friends, and have begun the terrifying and painstaking work of reconnecting with my original family, especially my dear sister, with whom I'd been out of touch for years.

And all of it is the result, directly or indirectly, of acquiring this dog—an animal I briefly had the conceit of thinking I had rescued, but who now seems to have done a businesslike job of rescuing me. I am his rescue human, I like to joke, even as I've come to understand that it's no joke at all.

I have to credit a retired English professor for some of the ideas in this book. Last year, Orson and Homer joined me on a three-month book tour, in a sojourn that took us from New England to Kentucky and into the Midwest. One spring night in Brookfield, Wisconsin, an elegant, bookish-looking woman approached me after a signing. She loved books even more than dogs, she said, and therefore had no questions about puppies, poop, or excessive barking. She just liked my books and offered a brief but knowledgeable critique of several. After we talked a little and she was preparing to leave, she asked, "I assume you'll write about dogs again?"

I nodded; I wanted to write about dogs and the people who owned them until I dropped.

"Then I have a favor," she said, "assuming it doesn't violate your ethics. Write a book in which no dog dies. At my age, it really matters." She shook my hand and walked off.

I smiled most of the way back to my hotel.

So I can safely say a number of things about this book. It is about how several dogs led me to confront my own sense of humanity and challenged me to try to be a better human being. It's about the startling degree to which dogs can enter and alter a human life.

It's about a mean winter I spent on increasingly rebellious legs, in manure-caked boots, on a remote, windswept hillside in upstate New York, with a few lifesaving friends, the usual various ugly ghosts from the past, and more livestock than any suburban rookie should attempt to manage. It's also about the fact that crisis and mystery are, as always, around the corner, rushing toward me.

Finally, and with gratitude to Professor Chernowitz, I am happy to say what while no truthful book about any life is without loss or suffering, no dogs die in this book.

JON KATZ
Bedlam Farm
West Hebron, N.Y.

The Dogs of Bedlam Farm

Chapter One

CITY OF GOD

BEDLAM: a place, scene, or
state of uproar and confusion

Columbia Encyclopedia

FAR IN THE DISTANCE, AS THE MORNING MISTS BEGAN TO CLEAR,
I could see a livestock trailer heading west on Route 30 from
Salem toward the hamlet of West Hebron. From this hill behind
my new house, I could spot visitors approaching from miles away.

There were plenty of farms around this quadrant of upstate
New York, lots of places livestock haulers might be going, but
my guess was that this was Wilbur Price of Bethel, Pennsylvania,
delivering a ram named Nesbitt and the ladies, fifteen "dog-
broke" ewes.

Which meant it was time to walk down the hill. Change was
just around the corner, big change.

For three border collies, there could be no more meaningful event than the arrival of sheep in their backyard. For me, the change was more complex, but a big transition nonetheless, another midlife crapshoot. I was stepping out of one existence and into another, a shift inexorably linked to these three dogs.

We all clambered down the hill as the trailer descended into town. In a few minutes, this farm, known around the county as the old Keyes place—somehow I doubted it would ever be known as the old Katz place—with its listing and peeling dairy barn, an even more askew pig barn, an overgrown chicken pen, and several other outbuildings, would be home once again to livestock. Everyone in the tiny village could look up the hill and see animals grazing, as they had for generations.

I was no farmer, and this place wouldn't really qualify as a working farm. I am a dog lover and writer, and this would be, in part, a dog-centric adventure with my border collies. Even before the animals arrived, in the few weeks since I'd moved in and begun preparations, I could hardly believe the amount of work involved just in overseeing forty-two acres and a Civil War–era farmhouse. I could only imagine how difficult and relentless real farmwork was, particularly in brutal winter. My work would be fractional in comparison, and I wouldn't rely on the farm to provide my family's livelihood—an enormous difference.

Wilbur, a garrulous man in a giant baseball cap and overalls, was indeed waiting at the gravel driveway with his noisy cargo. We shook hands and chatted about the weather and the drive and his dicey encounters with fog en route. Wilbur, I realized, drove sheep and cows around all day and didn't want to pass up the chance for a more satisfying conversation.

I, on the other hand, was eager to populate my farm and get it rolling. After considerable effort and dismaying expense, I had fences up, hay and straw in the barn, and corn and feed stashed in critter-proof containers all over. I was as ready as somebody like me was ever going to be. But I'd learned that country talk can't be rushed. It had to have been a long and lonely ride up from Raspberry Ridge, my friend Carolyn's sheep farm and dog-training center. These ewes were loaners from her much larger flock.

We knew these sheep. My elder dogs and I, frequent visitors and herding students at Raspberry Ridge, had taken them to graze in the pasture countless times in rain and sunshine, in deep night and bright day, heat and cold. We'd moved them around during herding trials, chased them during our lessons, retrieved them from the woods when they wandered, midwifed a few of their lambs. We also knew—and were appropriately wary of— Nesbitt, who'd sent me flying more than once.

I could hear them all shifting and bleating in the trailer, prob-ably hungry and thirsty. I heard an asthmatic-sounding bray, too, which meant that at the last minute Carolyn had decided to send the donkey along with the rest of the crew. The donkey lived alone in a pasture, and Carolyn thought she might have a better quality of life at my new encampment. Carol, the donkey, was a sweetheart, whose affections I'd won with gifts of apples; I wondered if she'd recognize me in this strange new environ-ment.

Wilbur finally sensed that it was time to get moving. He slowly backed the truck a few feet inside the barnyard gate and slipped the latches that opened his trailer.

Carol the Lonely Donkey hee-hawed again, looked around, snarfed down the donkey cookie I was holding out for her, and trotted down the ramp. She did seem to remember me, and in any case appreciated the cookie.

Behind her, fifteen sheep and Nesbitt came charging past me, headed for the lush grass that covered the hill, and immediately started crunching away. Unlike dogs, sheep are not complex in their attachments. Grass is good. Grass is always good.

I shook Wilbur's hand and wrote out a check on the cab of his truck. Bedlam Farm was in business.

My dogs, corralled in their own spacious fenced enclosure a few yards away, sat frozen; they seemed shocked, wide-eyed, ears and tails at the alert. One rarely sees a more focused look on any creature than I saw on the faces of Orson, Homer, and Rose.

The autumn wind was sharp, parting the mists on the hill. I looked up to see a small flock of sheep and a donkey grazing near an old apple tree. I could hardly believe it myself; they looked as if they had grown out of the ground and had been there forever. Wilbur declined coffee and other amenities, saying he wanted to be home for dinner, and after much rattling, banging, and slamming, the truck rumbled off down the dirt road into town, back to the world.

It was one thing to drive out and work with Carolyn's sheep once or twice a week from suburban New Jersey, where much of the time my dogs and I lived an ordinary-looking life with my wife. It was quite another to be responsible for sheep living just outside my kitchen window.

They would need shots and worming and medical certificates from a vet. They would need to be shorn, to have their hooves trimmed. They'd need corn to build up calories for the winter, vitamin supplements when the ewes got pregnant, straw to lie on, and hay to eat once the grass withered in the first hard frost. They needed a continuous supply of fresh water, even in sub-zero weather.

In a few months, their newborn lambs would need to be located instantly, dried, and placed under heating lamps, separate from the rest of the flock. Lambs often required special supplements, and they'd need to be tagged and registered and have their tails docked. And everyone would need shelter from the vicious winter storms that would be arriving in just a few weeks.

All of these things had to be provided when the ice was packed a foot deep on the ground amid waist-high mounds of snow. And I had to—wanted to—take care of almost all those things myself.

When we bought this place, my wife, Paula, had set down three ironclad conditions: no firearms; no farm or other heavy machinery; and the gargantuan 1982 Chevy Silverado pickup I'd bought for hauling hay and other farm chores was not to be driven more than five miles in any direction. She was convinced that it would break down at inconvenient times; I had to be able to walk home.

Anybody who knew me understood the wisdom of these conditions. So while I would need help with barn repairs, drainage ditches, anything involving heavy machinery, the work was otherwise mine to do.

So as Wilbur drove out of sight and I waved goodbye, I was elated but also unnerved. There was no going back.

OUR DAY HAD BEGUN MUCH EARLIER, AROUND FIVE A.M., WITH our new morning routine. Orson, Homer, and the puppy, Rose, had labored up the steep hill behind the house with me, the wind whipping around us, tearing leaves off the trees at the top of the ridge. Even in the forbidding predawn, I could scarcely believe I owned such a beautiful tract of countryside. I could hear the occasional yip-yip of coyotes—"coy dogs," the locals call them—and wondered how soon they would be circling my soon-to-arrive sheep.

To be honest, *I* was the only one laboring up the hill, heading for two Adirondack chairs placed at the crest. The dogs were racing and gliding effortlessly, zipping around in enthusiastic circles the way border collies go everywhere—back and forth, round and round, always somehow keeping me in the center. I'd become used to walking in this odd way, aware vaguely that I was being herded. The two adults, Orson and Homer, had plenty of energy, but Rose positively zoomed, galloping from one corner of the pasture to the other in the time it took me to go a few steps.

Every dog has a story, but Orson's is better known than some. A breeder in Texas had retrieved him from someone she deemed an unsuitable owner, then sent him to me after reading one of my books, in which I talked about my late, beloved yellow Labs. Orson, then named Devon, was a dog in trouble. He was anxious, confused, apt to jump onto passing minivans, herd school buses, raid the refrigerator and jump through windows; we brawled until I found a great trainer—Carolyn—who helped turn our lives around.

He was followed by Homer, as sweet and submissive as Orson was difficult, but a dog who presented challenges of his own. Then a few months ago, our pack had been joined by Rose, the nuclear-powered puppy with strong herding lines who made the other two seem like stone statues. People ask me why I got a third border collie, and the truth is I hardly know. I still can't quite explain why I got the first one.

"Guys, this will be a great day for you," I announced. "Soon there will be fifteen ewes in this field, along with a grumpy ram named Nesbitt and maybe a donkey. You've got to watch out for Nesbitt. He'll nail me."

It had only been a couple of months since I had put my cherished mountaintop retreat—a cabin where I'd written three books and found more peace and beauty than I'd ever known—up for sale. I wanted to buy an old farmhouse with a porch, some land, maybe a barn. Through a series of flukes, I'd gotten more than I'd bargained for, more acreage, a lovelier house, more barns in more advanced stages of decay, along with coyotes, hawks and songbirds, yellow jackets and fleas, feral cats, rats and mice (despite the feral cats), raccoons, chipmunks, foxes, loads of deer, and unconfirmed rumors of two moose and a mountain lion. I also had a sweeping view of a lush valley checkered with pastures, cornfields, and barns.

The classic white Greek revival farmhouse had seen a lot of history. It sat on a hillside above a tiny hamlet of thirty or forty houses, two lovely old churches, and a general store—Bedlam's Corner. The name mesmerized me from the moment I first drove by.

My earlier cabin, a half hour south of Hebron, was a getaway, a private corner for a writer's internal life. I worked there, read, hiked with the dogs. Apart from my wife and daughter and two or three friends, hardly anyone else had ever seen it. That was part of the problem; it was my place and only my place.

As much as I'd loved it, as important as it had become, the cabin had also defeated me in a way. It was so small that there was barely enough space for the dogs and me; it felt crowded when my wife visited, let alone my daughter Emma. I had come to want not a retreat for me, but a rural home for us, with places for Paula to work and Emma to stay, with space for friends—a place for liveliness more than solitary contemplation. I felt ready for a fuller existence, though I had no inkling just how full it was about to get.

I was conscious, as I try always to be, of entering another phase, of marking the transition and pondering how I was going to deal with it. I'd just turned fifty-six. How many more houses would I be buying? How many more dogs could I ever own? How much more time did Paula and I have to be together in a place like this?

I couldn't really afford the farm any more than I could the cabin that preceded it, but I couldn't really afford to wait, either. For several years, especially since the terrorist attacks on New York City, I'd seen people assessing their lives, making changes, seeking property upstate. In another five years I doubted I'd be able to buy acreage. My little cabin, forlorn and ungainly at the time, had been on the market for two years when I bought it. It sold in less than a week, once I put it on the market.

Driving me around the town of Hebron as I looked for the replacement I had in mind, the real estate agent had looked up at the hillside as we passed and pointed at the white farmhouse.

"There's the house you want," she said ruefully. "But it isn't for sale." Three weeks later, it suddenly was. Sometimes houses, like dogs, find you.

What better place to test my notions about dogs and humans than here, with border collies and a bunch of sheep? Could they become happier dogs and more useful partners? Could I learn to be a better human? The four of us and our little band of animals, tucked away on a hillside through a glorious fall, the bitter up-state winter, and a cold, muddy spring filled with lambing, could probably find out.

Two months later, I was here, unpacking boxes and dealing with hay supplies, cranky barn doors, monosyllabic Vermont fence builders, and more. It seemed I had compressed years of activities into weeks and days—selling a beloved home, buying a more complex one, moving out and in, arranging the endless de-tails that would make it possible for me and my assorted live-stock to live here.

In a few hours, I told the dogs, as we puffed uphill in the dark, there would be sheep right out the back door. The an-nouncement wasn't as loopy as it seemed: every mention of the word "sheep" got three heads swiveling. Even little Rose, who'd visited Raspberry Ridge just a few times, was already hooked and showing quite a bit of herding style.

I bought the place for my family and me, but my wife pointed out what I privately conceded—I bought it for the dogs, as well. Owning land you could barely see the end of was wonderful, but owning property that could give dogs a chance to do and perfect what they most loved, what their breed had done for hundreds of years, that was still another dimension.

Perhaps I could finish the difficult and painstaking work I had begun with Orson years ago and finally show him how to make sense of the world. Perhaps I could resolve my long-standing concerns and bring the good-hearted but anxious Homer into the mainstream of our family. Perhaps I could take advantage of the opportunity presented by the astoundingly energetic Rose and, applying what I'd learned researching and writing about dogs for the past few years, not screw up this remarkable puppy.

As our odd little group made its way up the hill, I was leaning on a walking stick to guard against my bad ankle giving out. I'd filled a travel mug with hot coffee to ward off the wind's chill. I was also carrying a copy of Saint Augustine's *City of God*, which I planned to read aloud to sort of bless the farm and our adventure together, officially about to begin. The early Christian writers were spiritual ancestors to me—born a Jew, a convert to Quakerism, still struggling with religious conviction. Saint Augustine and his colleagues also grappled valiantly to make sense of their world, and *City of God* was his brave effort to explain the fall of Rome and the world's plunge into the Dark Ages.

Though I've always struggled with religion, I've never given up on spirituality. It's not always an easy distinction, and I'm not sure the saints would approve of my applying the word "spiritual" to the profoundly loving and complicated relationships that people like me have with their dogs.

I don't see dogs as psychic or telepathic. Nor do I believe that we will meet them in the afterlife, or that mediums can channel their deepest thoughts. But I do believe the human-dog relationship can be deeply meaningful. Dogs have a remarkable gift for entering our lives at particular times and weaving themselves in. It is one of their most endearing traits, a key part of their impressive adaptability.

This morning held that promise. The early walk up the hill had become a ritual for me in West Hebron—navigating the steep and rocky rise with the dogs to watch the sun appear. Was there any finer way to start a day? Afterwards I could fire up the woodstove in my study and have a few good hours to work while the dogs rested from their romp and waited for their shot at sheep.

In their own way, experts that they are at reading their humans, my dogs seemed to grasp the ritual as well. They couldn't literally understand what I was doing, of course, but they sensed that something important was happening.

This morning I could see an eerily beautiful dawn about to break after the classic dark and stormy night, with gusting winds left behind by the weakening and retreating Hurricane Isabel. The mountains that stretch all the way to Vermont were shrouded in mist as the light began to creep up. Living in cities and crowded suburbs most of my life, I could never take the sight of such beauty for granted. I almost felt it lifting me up, soothing and healing and inspiring.

Even my dogs paused in their circling and tilted their heads, noses in the air to pick up strange scents, perhaps brought on the wind from far-away places.

Panting and sore, I made it to the hilltop chairs and flopped into one. Orson hopped onto the other. Homer and Rose chased each other across the field. Orson growled, jumped off his perch, and began to move toward them—he discourages any kind of enthusiasm or horseplay—but I reached out to put my hand on his head, a calming gesture.

"Relax, pal," I said. "Let the kids have their fun. What do you say us old farts sit up and read from this book?" He relented, putting his head on my lap.

Orson and I have been together for less than four years, but it's hard to describe all the two of us have been through, how difficult and rewarding and complicated our relationship is, how much we've come to mean to each other. This dog came out of nowhere to challenge my very nature and alter my life; I think I have returned the favor.

"Look what you've done, pal," I said to this intense and complex creature. "All this because of you." It was true: my work, this farm, many of my friends, much of my life, all were different because of him and the unexpected directions in which he'd led me. If not for this dog, would I have been sitting atop a hill, overlooking a tiny town, waiting for sheep and perhaps a donkey? Would I own this place? Or see this beautiful valley brighten as the sun rose after a passing storm?

I cradled Orson's head in my lap, stroking the side of his nose. He seemed as peaceful as it was possible for him to be. The animal ethicist James Serpell has written that the human-canine relationship is as close as humans ever come to a dialogue with another species, and Orson and I were engaged in that dialogue this morning.

I took in the sight, sat back in the chair, sipped from the coffee mug, and tried to accustom myself to this new, still strange setting. Orson's presence made it less odd, more familiar, part of the continuum of our lives together.

I felt as if we had crossed a portal, entered a serene and beautiful space, strolled together into Augustine's City of God.

My friends often chuckle knowingly when I tell them that I'd decided to read aloud from Saint Augustine to mark the occasion. I had no illusions that Orson understands such weighty prose, but he does love it when I read aloud to him, watching my face for clues, listening to my tone. Probably he's wondering how long it will take me to stop droning on and reach into my pocket for a biscuit.

Still, it was a beautiful moment.

I loved reading about the City of God. I'd carried a worn copy of the book all over the country, reading it in airports and hotel rooms. The City of God wasn't the sphere I usually occupied, sadly, but the place we all strived to reach.

Augustine believed there were two realms, the earthly and the heavenly, and the City of God was the heavenly part, a holy place of rivers, streams, and mountains—just the sort of place I was seeing at that moment, as the light began to glow in the distance.

Augustine was a religious man; my own vision of the City of

God was different from his, more a state of mind, a place of serenity we rarely found in our overstressed lives.

"Since, then, the supreme good of the City of God is perfect and eternal peace, not such as mortals pass into and out of by birth and death, but the peace of freedom from all evil, in which the immortals ever abide, who can deny that that future life is most blessed?" I read to Orson, to whom peace was generally an alien concept. "Or that, in comparison with it, this life which now we live is most wretched, be it filled with all blessings of body and soul and external things?

"And yet, if any man uses this life with a reference to that other which he ardently loves and confidently hopes for, he may well be called even now blessed, though not in reality as much as in hope."

The wind was pushing the clouds across the hills at a quick pace now, and the morning light had filled the valley. I closed my book to watch for the first glimmers of the sun itself. Homer and Rose, tongues dragging, came over and collapsed. Orson's eyes were closed, his head still in my lap as I scratched his ears.

In a busy suburb or on a busy-and-getting-busier farm, moments like this are rare. Soon I'd be yelling at Orson or Homer to stay away from the road. I'd be ordering feed, checking my answering machine, my e-mail and my voicemail. Soon the world would, as it should, begin its inexorable intrusion. Soon Wilbur Price would be here.

The places a dog can take you, I thought. Look where mine had brought me.

BUT SAINT AUGUSTINE WAS NOT A SHEPHERD.

A few days later came a lovely night with a quarter moon. The sparse lights of West Hebron twinkled below.

The sheep, settling into Bedlam Farm, seemed happy, crunching away up in the pasture even after a full day's grazing. I shined my powerful new flashlight—purchased to help me spot circling coyotes—up the hill and saw their eyes reflected in the light.

I had to duck into the pig barn for a second to hook up a hose. It seemed safe enough to leave the pasture gate briefly unlatched. The sheep and Carol, crunching along with them, had plenty to eat, and I'd only be a second.

As I walked into the barn—just twenty feet from the gate—I heard the sound of hooves thundering behind me. My new flock went flying past before I could move, racing down the dirt driveway alongside the house and across the dirt road toward an unfenced meadow.

I remember feeling something between shock and panic. There were lots of woods—and coyotes—across that road, and beyond that, miles of thickets and fields.

What a dumb way to invite catastrophe. What was I thinking? But I would learn many times in the coming weeks that panic is useless in Bedlam, where catastrophes are not rare shocks but an integral part of life. You either learn how to handle them, or you pack up and head back to the Flatlands. There's no dialing 911 up here, unless you're about to be murdered. Help is too far away. A volunteer firefighter visiting me soon after I moved in had offered some advice: "Put some of your valuables in one of the barns, because if there's a fire, your house will burn down before we can get here. We're mostly basement-savers."

So it was me and the dogs. I ran into the house to get them. I couldn't see the sheep, but I could hear them. I had belled two of them, so the clang would warn me if they were running from predators at night. They hadn't gone far.

I had limited options, though. Orson was too excitable to send out. He'd tear after the flock, and the sheep would just take off and scatter. He hadn't yet mastered the difference between herding and chasing. Homer sometimes got excited and gripped the sheep—took mouthfuls of wool—but he had considerable experience taking flocks out to graze. He was my best shot. Rose was much too young. I'd brought her near Carolyn's sheep a few times, and she'd stared at them hypnotically, but the sheep barely paid attention. She was only five months old, and it was risky to work her much; if Nesbitt charged or the ewes stomped her, she could be traumatized for good. Border collie puppies, if pushed too fast or too far, sometimes became too skittish to work sheep at all.

So I grabbed Homer and we headed out. "Homer, find me sheep," I commanded, and he dashed across the road into the meadow. He'd been trained to do an "outrun," to circle the sheep, urging them back to me. But Nesbitt emerged from the mist and charged him, and Homer lost it and broke into a full run, right into the middle of the flock. I heard them gallop still farther into the darkness, spooked by the charging dog and strange environment—or maybe by something I hadn't seen. They were headed for the deep woods.

We were really in trouble now. I called the panting, wild-eyed Homer back to me and hustled him back to the house. He was just too cranked to help, perhaps in too strange an environment himself. This was not the gentle grazing we'd done in Pennsylvania, where the sheep were so familiar with the path that they practically herded themselves. I could hear the coyotes yip-yipping somewhere in the distance, perhaps telegraphing the joyous news that dinner was racing their way.

I felt I had no choice but to turn to Rose. She might not be able to turn the sheep back, but I didn't think she'd freak out. Rose was not lacking in confidence. She already dominated poor Homer and took no guff from the possessive and iron-willed Orson, either. She was lean and fast and had some chance at catching up with the flock. But it was a long shot.

I worried about Nesbitt charging again, about Rose getting lost. The idea of my puppy wandering the countryside at night was even more disturbing than worrying about the sheep, who at least had one another.

But I decided to try. Even at her tender age, Rose exuded a feistiness that made me trust her. She was bred to be a working dog. If I were going to make it on this farm, I had to handle situations like this. And Rose would have to help me.

I took her across the road on a leash, peering out into the inky blackness. Clouds had drifted across the moon, making the night even more impenetrable. All I could see in the flashlight's beam were tree trunks. I couldn't hear the sheeps' bells or bleats any longer. They could by now be miles away.

I took the leash off, understanding that I was probably violating every rule of sound herding training. But my instinct was to trust this dog. "Rose," I said softly, "can you find the sheep?"

Rose spun around and looked at me uncertainly. She knew the word "sheep" from our previous encounters and remembered it. She looked up the hill toward the barn, then across the meadow, so intense I thought she'd lift off the ground. She wasn't sure what she was being asked to do, but she was ready to do something.

I raised my voice. "Rose, girl," I said, a bit desperately. "You're free. Go get the sheep! Find the sheep!"

She paused for another moment, and I stayed quiet to give her a chance to think things over. Who knew what her genes might cause to bubble up? Then she took off like a rabbit into the meadow, moving so quickly I couldn't keep the flashlight beam on her.

Within minutes, my anxiety had grown to terror. Now there was no sign of her *or* the sheep. Had I lost my dog as well as my herd? It seemed I had compounded one idiotic mistake with another.

I ran off in the direction I'd seen her go, finding a trail at the edge of the meadow. I stumbled over holes, stumps, and undergrowth, my clothes jabbed by thorns and branches as I plunged down the path, yelling her name. I was frightened and tired. I

heard all sorts of strange sounds in the dark that I couldn't identify. After five minutes of running, I was gasping and had to lean
over, wheezing and puffing, to get my wind back.

Should I go get my truck and drive up the road, or call a
neighbor for help? But what, exactly, could I ask anybody to do?
And the road led in the opposite direction from Rose and the
sheep.

Suddenly I heard some faint barking ahead. I started forward, calling Rose's name while swatting branches away from
my face. In a minute, I entered a small clearing. The sheep were
bunched right in front of me, their eyes reflecting the light. Nesbitt was out in the front, trying to butt Rose.

She was standing her ground, not intimidated in the least,
barking and nipping at Nesbitt's nose, backing up, charging and
nipping again. He looked ticked off but also a little rattled.

It was quite a spectacle, this twenty-pound pup holding all
these three-hundred-pound animals in a tight clump while staring down an enormous belligerent ram. Between nips, she circled the ewes, keeping them together, bobbing and weaving in a
manner that would have made Muhammad Ali proud. Nesbitt
tried a few more feints, then retreated back into the herd.

It was great that Rose had found the sheep, and miraculous
that she'd held them for me, but now we had to walk nearly a
half-mile and ease them back into their fenced pasture.

I wasn't entirely sure how to proceed, but I knew the nervous
sheep would move toward the safest thing. Of this pair, I was
preferable to the ferociously focused dog stalking them.

Keeping a close watch on Nesbitt—I clunked him on the
head with the flashlight for good measure—I turned and began
walking back up the trail. Rose kept circling, but when I held up
my hand and yelled, "Get back," she dropped to the rear, keeping the group moving toward me. Instinctively, she began
"wearing"—shuttling back and forth behind the flock, a move
Homer hadn't mastered in two years of training.

But Rose seemed to grasp the technique without ever having been taught. She kept the sheep trotting along while I walked ahead with the flashlight. After a while, I could see the farmhouse lights ahead and recovered my bearings. We didn't proceed in a direct line—the herd zigged and zagged—but we kept moving steadily back toward the house.

It took us about fifteen minutes to reach the road. I started walking backward and holding up my hand as Rose circled the herd like a bumblebee. She had a big bark for a little dog. When the sheep saw the open gate, they broke for the pasture as maniacally as they'd left it, Rose in pursuit. She chased them to the top of the hill, then turned and came racing down to me, her tail wagging wildly. There can't be too many dogs who've ever gotten more joyous or heartfelt praise from a grateful owner.

"Great girl, great dog, thank you!" I burbled, as she slurped at my face and squirmed all over. She seemed quite proud of herself, and she was entitled to.

So much for serenity. We headed back into the house. "Welcome to Bedlam," I told her. 🐑

Chapter Two
BEDLAM

O I remember when a lad,
The people here were very bad;
They fought, they swore, they guzzled rum,
And Bedlam it was called by some.

*"West Hebron in Song!" by Lafayette Smart
and the Rev. John Fisher; sung by students of
the West Hebron Academy, March 31, 1874*

The Bedlam's Corner Variety Store sits at the intersection where Route 30 from Salem hits West Hebron and comes to a T.

It's been there for several lifetimes. In 1878, I read in a local history, it carried its owner's "celebrated steel-pointed hand-made potato hooks," along with parlor stoves, agricultural tools, clover seed, and groceries. In 1911, crowds of farmers gathered to see its new electric-powered lights; lemonade and ice cream were served. For a while, the store housed the local post office.

West Hebron (as opposed to North or East Hebron, all of

them part of regular old Hebron) lies about an hour northeast of Albany, the kind of small town that's vanished from general consciousness—but which is full of small dramas nonetheless. The ferocious survival struggles of its embattled and dwindling farmers are wrenching to witness, and so is the inexorable exodus of the town's children. The population of the larger town of Hebron peaked in the early 1800s at about 2,700; it's roughly half that size now.

Bedlam's Corner—gateway to West Hebron—is important to the town, a tiny, dark, cozily atmospheric shop, its front window decorated with an American flag and a neon beer sign.

Inside, the row of counter stools, tin ceiling, and ancient globe lights don't seem to have changed for decades. Its shelves and narrow aisles are crammed with what used to be called "sundries"—milk, local papers, groceries, and chewing tobacco, with a closet-sized hardware department in the rear that sells nails and automotive supplies. You can arrange to have your dry cleaning picked up and delivered, or to have your film developed. You cannot, however, find skim milk, whole-grain bread, or anything containing soy.

The store matters for the obvious reasons—it's a ten-mile drive for a roll of toilet paper otherwise—but it's also the source of almost all important town news and gossip. In the morning, the Big Men in Trucks stop by, leaving their trucks idling while they grab some coffee; if they have time, they plop down at the counter to yak about the weather, hunting, or the trials of raising kids. More than one elderly widow or widower comes in at some point during the day to make a tiny purchase and find some company, which the store's staff generously provides.

This is the sole surviving business from West Hebron's heyday as a thriving commercial and agricultural center. Newcomers like me, inquiring into its history, are startled to learn that a century ago this crossroads and its immediate surroundings supported seven stores, a hotel, an opera house, three blacksmith shops, two mills, a railroad depot, a power plant, a cheese factory, a meat market, wagon and harness shops, and two barbers. Hence the nickname, which lingers years after the reasons for it have vanished.

The name Bedlam comes from Bethlehem, specifically the Hospital of St. Mary of Bethlehem in London. Originally dedicated to treating the poor, it began to admit the city's growing number of "lunatics" in the late 1300s.

Bethlehem got shortened, over several centuries, to Bedlam. In the late 1600s the hospital became a bizarre tourist destination, as audiences came to witness the spectacle of the mentally ill. By the eighteenth century, visitors paid a small fee to enter the building and laugh at the patients, many chained in their cells. The crowds grew so large and unruly that Bedlam came to stand for chaos and disorder.

There's nothing chaotic in the hamlet these days, a tribute to the impact of the automobile, the decline of the family farm, and the way jobs migrate to coastal and urban areas.

But the sleepiness has its appeal, at least for people like me, who aren't looking for work. West Hebron sits along the Black Creek, a meandering stream fed by a potent waterfall. I count about fifty buildings now, stretching in a line from the store: modest old millworker houses, a few grander Victorians, the two churches, the town clerk's office and the headquarters of the Hebron Volunteer Fire Department, a few trailers and shacks.

From my farmhouse porch on warm fall Sundays, I can hear the hymns wafting up from the Presbyterian church below, and see the volunteer firefighters converging when the siren sounds. I missed the town's bedlam period, but I've imported some of my own.

MY THREE PUREBRED BORDER COLLIES CAUSED QUITE A BIT OF discussion at Bedlam's Corner, where they often waited outside in the truck as I picked up a few cans of dog food or (Sundays only) *The New York Times*. People admired their sleek beauty and, thanks to cable television, often had seen dogs herding. But they were a curiosity in a town where dogs lived very different lives.

Ellie, for example, a shaggy brown Disney-cute mutt, was the West Hebron town dog. She wandered from one house to another, escorting an elderly couple on their morning walk, greeting visitors, monitoring traffic in and out of the variety store. Sometimes she napped in the middle of Route 30. People here make a point of tolerance—what you do in public is everybody's business, and what you do on your own property is nobody's. But there was an understanding about Ellie: when she dropped by, you were expected to be hospitable, to offer food and water and a warm place to spend the night. You also understood that she would never stay. She belonged to everyone and no one, a Ruby Tuesday of dogs.

Ellie reminded me at the outset that the dog culture upstate is very different from the one I knew back in New Jersey. Almost all Hebron dogs are mixed-breeds, and I've never seen one walked on a leash. People often let them out when they leave for work in the morning and bring them in when they come home at night. Dogs are never trained in the formal sense, at least not beyond housebreaking; they learn as they go. When they misbehave, they can generally expect a swat or kick in the rear.

Missing from the lives of local hounds: gourmet treats. Doggie day care or playgroups. Agility classes. Obedience trials. Competitions of any sort. The whole idea of a "fulfilled" dog. Even, sometimes, basic veterinary care.

People in town comparison-shop when their dogs are sick enough to need a vet—and mere lameness, vomiting, or droopiness doesn't qualify. "The vet in Salem wanted a hundred and seventy-five dollars to neuter my dog," a mechanic explained to me. He found a clinic in Granville that would do it for $125, so he went there. A lot of people wouldn't have bothered at all.

It isn't that Hebronites don't love their dogs; they do. But their view of animals in general, and dogs in particular, is more philosophical. Dogs are sweet, but they come and they go. They live at the periphery of family life, not at the epicenter. They aren't best friends or soulmates, and they are definitely not children. They may not even sleep indoors, or want to.

Backyard doghouses are common, and one brown mutt— maybe part wolfhound—would only sleep in the back of his owner's red pickup, no matter how cold it got. "We feel bad," confessed his owner, "but he goes crazy inside the house. If it's below zero or raining or snowing, I make him a sort of lean-to, with a sawhorse and a tarp. Sometimes when I come out in the morning, the whole thing's covered in snow." The dog didn't seem to mind.

There are some serious breeders tucked away here and there, but purebred dogs are still exotic, a city guy's way to acquire a dog. When people in town want a dog, they call the county shelter, or find a stray at the back door one day, or pick out a puppy when a farm dog has a litter.

For all these differences, Hebron has plenty of dogs, and they look both happy and healthy, if on the scruffy side.

I'm sometimes embarrassed when I open my pantry cupboard and see the stacks and bags of bones, biscuits, and dentally approved rawhide chews that my dogs gnaw on, supplementing their diets of lite dog food. My crowd, admired as they were, came from a different solar system, from the planet Flatland.

IN THE WEEKS BEFORE WE COULD MOVE IN, I'D BEEN BUSILY preparing, meeting my neighbors, finding the helpers I'd need, from vets to handymen, laying in supplies.

I'd need a farm truck, for instance. You wouldn't want to befoul your primary vehicle with hay, sheep poop, or (if bad luck hit) carcasses. So I was on the lookout for something sturdy and—mindful of my wife's admonitions about the state of our finances—cheap.

On a drive to Argyle, down a long dirt road miles from anywhere, I came across Sheldon's Used Trucks, a two-trailer complex with several trucks in various stages of decay, three of which had goats tethered to their bumpers. They ranged in price "from $886 to $4,823," as Sheldon explained to me when I stopped, intrigued. He explained his marketing strategy: "You put a round number, like three thousand, on it, people think it's expensive and give you a hard time. But you put a real specific price on it, then they think there's gotta be a reason." He seemed proud of his technique.

Sheldon's newest truck was a 1993 Dodge Ram with no front tires. The others had broken axles, cracked windshields, scraped paint, and a crayoned slogan on each windshield: "We Are Negotiable!"

"Just out of curiosity, if you don't mind my asking, how many trucks do you sell in a year?" I asked, noticing the empty acreage on each side and the sparse passing traffic.

Sheldon, his big belly bulging out of a T-shirt, a John Deere cap framing his ruddy, bearded face, gave me an appraising look. "Marlene," he yelled toward one of the trailers. "There's a guy here who wants to know how many trucks we sell in a year."

"Is he from the IRS?" came a voice from the inside.

"You from the IRS?"

I told him I wasn't.

"He says he isn't," Sheldon yelled. "And he's got some of those sheep collies in his truck." There was a giant satellite dish behind the trailer. Another Discovery Channel watcher, I guessed.

"If he's from the IRS we sold four trucks last year," the voice answered. "If he isn't, we sold five." I wrote Sheldon's phone number on a scrap of paper, but decided to broaden my truck search.

Next on my scarily long list of things to do/buy/contract for before Bedlam Farm was operational: fencing. You couldn't have fifteen sheep wandering around town. I solicited names.

Some of the best craftsmen lived just across the border in Vermont. I was still learning how to talk Vermont. As when I called Shane Becker, a highly regarded fence builder near Bennington.

"Yuh."

"Is this Shane Becker?"

"Yup."

"My name is Jon Katz, and I just bought a farm over in West Hebron. I need to fence about ten acres for some sheep."

Silence.

"Do you do sheep fences?"

"Yup."

"Could you do mine?"

"I guess so."

More silence.

"So, what's the process, Shane?" I ventured. "How does this usually work?"

Silence for a good ten seconds as he digested the question.

"Well, the way it works," he said, "is I build the fence, and then you pay me."

"Okay," I said, giving up. "Whenever you're ready." Apart from a chat about sheepdogs, this was the longest conversation Shane and I would ever have.

On my own side of the state border, getting anything done is likely to involve the Great Rolling Conversation—a.k.a. Country Bullshit. Even the simplest tasks involved a ritualistic series of exchanges: information gathering, anecdote relating, strategizing, reminiscing, arguing. I loved it, and was getting good at it. To me, bullshit has always been an art form, a skill to hone and celebrate, one of the few gifts I've had from childhood.

Take hay. It might seem a simple thing to order enough hay to see a small flock through a tough winter, when the grass could no longer provide nourishment. It wasn't.

Step One in getting the Great Conversation rolling: you either stopped in at the nearest Agway farm-supply store, or raised the topic over sweet-potato fries at the Burger Den in Jackson, or went early in the morning to any Stewart's coffee shop/gas station/convenience store, the favorite stop of the Big Men in Trucks.

Country Bullshit encompasses many issues, from weather to trucks and guns to tales of silly Flatlanders moving in from New York and doing stupid, inexplicable things.

"Get your deer yet?" is one way to kick off plenty of bullshit during hunting season. Among my other favorite sayings is, "It's been here long before you were born and it will be here long after you've gone." An all-purpose phrase, it came up a lot while I was trying to figure out how to prop up my flock's future shelter.

It seemed to me that my tottering barn, which *was* here before I was born, would stand until it didn't—which could happen at any time, and I didn't want to be inside it when it did.

But that kind of sentiment is dismissed as Flatlander anxiety. Country Bullshit values calm and stability; it takes the long view.

To find hay, therefore, I started the process at a Cambridge coffeehouse called Bean Heads. I loudly told Bill, the proprietor, that I was looking for hay. Before he could respond, three customers were already sidling over, chiming in.

I was grateful for advice. People upstate have spent a lot of time explaining things to me. The trick, I'd found, was to concede ignorance. If you admitted you were clueless and threw yourself on their mercy, the locals were happy to help out. To do otherwise was to be branded arrogant and hopeless, and then you were on your own.

"Not so fast," said a grizzled farmer, evidently dragged away from Stewart's by his coffee-loving son. He'd sized me up instantly as a dumb-ass Flatlander, and he was eager to get things rolling. "You want round or square bales? First or second cut? How big is your barn? How many can you store?"

An argument instantly broke out about whether I needed the big round bales or the smaller square ones. The round bales lasted longer, but they were impossible to move around without a tractor. "First cut" meant the hay of late spring, "second cut" meant hay from late summer (and sometimes there was a third). "More nutrients by far in the second cut. Hold out for that," the farmer announced. Disagreement, though, erupted from the other two guys. Bill, who used to sell farm equipment, muttered that he'd never found two farmers who agreed on anything. The discussion soon ranged far afield to include the dietary habits of dairy cows and the outrageous price of everything, feed in particular. The talk left me and my hay far behind, so I took my coffee, slipped out, and drove over to Stewart's, just down the road.

The farmer and his son pulled in right behind me. In seconds, about a half-dozen men in trucks had mysteriously convened and were peppering me with questions: How many sheep? How big a barn? What other feed was I thinking of buying? Oats? Corn? Did I have water access near the barn?

People coming out of Stewart's joined in, recognizing people in the crowd, adding their own horror stories about bad hay or wet hay, the dangers of ordering too much or of getting caught short and having to scramble. Soon, to my amazement, a truck pulled in stacked with hay, as if summoned by the gods of bullshit, and the farmer offered to sell it to me on the spot and drive it "right on up to Hebron."

But the old farmer wouldn't hear of it. "What? You gonna sell him first-cut hay for sheep?" And he was clearly skeptical of this hay, anyway. He pulled a handful from a bale, pinched it, chewed on a few strands. I could almost hear him thinking that this Flatlander was just foolish enough to go for it. I politely declined.

The consensus—it had been an hour and a half since I mentioned hay at Bean Heads—was second-cut square bales, and Danny Thomas on Center Cambridge Road was the clear favorite for the best hay.

Like many Washington County farmers, Danny Thomas was much too busy to be reachable by telephone. He was up before dawn, out till dark, and early to bed. I called countless times and finally left a handwritten note in his mailbox saying I wanted four hundred square bales of second-cut hay, and if he couldn't provide them, would he please call. Knowing how business is done in the county, when I heard nothing back I could safely assume I'd get good-quality hay delivered on time.

Which still left the matter of a farm truck. Paula and I were spending our last bittersweet weekend together in the cabin, something we'd done too rarely in the years that I'd owned it, when I found a likely candidate.

We were driving down Route 22 when I swerved over to an auto-body shop, mesmerized by the sight of a giant red truck with yellow running lights and a FOR SALE sign.

Ernie, the owner, had been spray-painting an old Corvette but materialized speedily.

The Silverado, he said, was a classic, vintage 1982. He was asking $3,500 for it. It was a beautiful thing, massive and strong, with two gas tanks, a lost farm truck in need of a farm. Paula, sitting out in my Explorer while I talked to Ernie, was undoubtedly groaning about another $3,500 when we could hardly afford the farm itself, the hay, Shane's fence, and the other Bedlam Farm expenses gouging deep holes in our financial stability. I loved the truck, though. It was the mother of all pickups. It would haul rocks, hay, firewood, and trash, and it would sit proudly like a beacon announcing there was serious stuff going on at Bedlam Farm. Only a serious man would have such a serious truck.

Ernie invited me into his inner sanctum.

"That your wife out there? She don't look too happy."

She wasn't, I explained. Money was . . . an issue.

"Well, she's special." He was talking about the truck, of course. "She won't let you down. You can have her for three thousand."

We shook on it and I said I'd be back once I registered her in Ft. Edward, the county seat. Paula was now walking around and peering suspiciously at the truck, scowling. Ernie wiped his hands on his T-shirt and offered to help. "I know how to talk to women," he said.

A brave, if foolhardy, man, he strolled outside. "Listen, honey," he told her. "It's a good truck. You can trust her."

She shot him a look that could have bored a hole through his skull, but all she said was, "Looks like some rust on the fenders."

"Well, it *is* an '82," he said, retreating quickly.

"She's a tough one, isn't she?" he muttered to me, preparing the paperwork. Yes, I said. She was.

WHEN MOVING DAY CAME, IN SEPTEMBER, I COULDN'T SHAKE A sense of dread, of flailing in waters over my head.

On that foggy day, the farm and its pastures were shrouded in mist and rain. The house, vacant, was eerily quiet. I heard creaks and groans, strange sounds from the basement and skittering in the ceilings.

The house carried an air of history and gravity. It was a working place, with lots of mementos left behind—a pit for slaughtering pigs, rusting metal collars that once held dairy cows in place, a tiny milk house, where cans were left for pickup. You had the feeling of much hard labor there, many lives lived.

I'd spent a restless night with the dogs, staying with kind friends in Vermont, and now, waiting for the moving van, I started to panic. What was I doing there? If we could barely afford the cabin I'd just vacated, how could I possibly afford this vast empire of decaying old buildings, new fences, and all the other alterations I still urgently needed to make for the flock of sheep soon to arrive?

Orson, Homer, and Rose had no such anxieties. They were in

dog heaven, tearing happily through the barns and pastures, down the wooded trails, pursuing an apparently robust population of rodents.

But anxiety was hitting me in waves. Paula was back in New Jersey, Emma working in New York, and I was alone on this vast property, watching swarms of bees pour out the open windows of the pig barn. I had really done it this time.

I could hear some sort of beeping alarm coming from the house—to do with that elaborate water filtration system in the basement, maybe. I also noticed the basement door, swollen from summer humidity, banging in the breeze—but I couldn't shut it.

I felt paralyzed. I couldn't shut the door, couldn't figure out what was beeping. I just paced, mumbling nervously, realizing I'd made a mistake, another of my reckless moves, another lunge at change for change's sake, rather than accepting my middle-class destiny.

I could just put the place up for sale, I thought, and get most of my money back. Paula would be relieved, even delighted. I just wanted to go home and see my wife and kid.

I was interrupted by a green pickup pulling up the driveway. A barrel-chested man climbed out and walked up the porch steps: Don Coldwell, a retired millworker who now made Adirondack chairs and did carpentry. I'd stopped at his workshop to buy the two chairs on the hilltop behind the house.

I didn't recognize him immediately, but I remembered his convincing handshake, his calloused fingers and steady gaze. This, I thought, was one of those men who go off and hold the line for people like me in places like Vietnam. Don was, in fact, a proud former Marine (the Corps flag flew in front of his house in the hamlet). He had the air of a man you'd want beside you when trouble came.

We had spent a few minutes talking when I bought my new chairs. "You'll like it here," he'd told me. "We keep our doors open and our guns loaded."

What were the guns for, I asked, if the doors didn't need to be locked?

"City people and coyotes."

Now he was on my porch, giving me a piercing stare and asking what was wrong.

Startled by the question, I mumbled something about waiting for the movers. "Why, do I look bad?"

"You look a little funny," he said. "Disoriented, maybe."

He asked what the beeping was, went inside, and located a smoke detector in need of a new battery. Only then did I realize just how discombobulated I was: I've replaced smoke-detector batteries a million times in New Jersey. Why didn't I recognize the same sound here?

Over the next few minutes, Don took charge. He took the basement door off its hinges and put it in his truck bed, saying he was taking it home to plane it and would bring it right back. When he returned in twenty minutes, he brought me a melon and some soup, in case I was hungry. (I was.)

Then he patted me on the back. "Take it easy," he said. "This seems strange now, but it will be okay. Just give it a few weeks." I decided to believe him, and thanked him about twenty times for stopping to buck me up.

He shrugged and moved toward his pickup. "Hey, we're a small place in the middle of nowhere," he said. "It means something to be a neighbor here. If you need anything—anything—you call me and I'll be here." And he drove off as the moving van came lumbering up my dirt road.

IN A FEW DAYS, I WAS ONE OF THE LOCALS STOPPING AT THE Bedlam's Corner Variety Store with my dogs. Two sisters, Mary Zeller and Barb Worthington, own the place. There's a FOR SALE sign in the window, has been for years. Everyone in town would love Mary and Barb to stay put, but they're resigned to the store's changing hands one day.

They are strong-willed women. Shortly after I moved in, the town was stunned by an armed robbery. A guy in a mask walked into the variety store brandishing a handgun.

Mary, alone in the store, was less scared than furious. She gave the guy some money, then pulled the mask off his face, recognized him, and chased him out, noting his license plate as he sped away in his too-colorful-for-anonymity pickup. In the following days, almost every male in Hebron stopped at the store to scold Mary for taking on an armed criminal. But the robber, arrested the next day, was awaiting trial. "I just got mad," Mary explained.

Now when I drove down for a paper, coffee, or a can of dog food, everyone in the store knew who I was the minute I walked in.

"Hey, you're the guy who bought Jesse and Ralph's place. You're the dog guy," said one of the Worthingtons one morning, shaking my hand.

"How did you know that?" I asked, surprised as always.

He chuckled. "Who else could you be?"

Another morning, an elderly woman having coffee smiled and said, "You were up early this morning, walking those sheep around. Your little dog is coming along real good." I must have looked nonplussed. "Oh, I can look up and see the sheep from my kitchen window," she said. "It's great to see animals up at the old Keyes place again."

When she had time, I sat down at the counter and had a cup of coffee with Nancy Fortier, the sole employee, who seemed eager to hear tales of the dogs, donkey, and sheep. But, then, she heard a lot of stories each morning. While we talked, the Big Men in Trucks pulled in, wisecracking with her and one another.

Though I was an obvious Flatlander, they were unfailingly friendly and generous. "You a religious man?" one big man asked me one morning.

"Not really all that religious," I said carefully. "Why?"

"You will be soon," he said. "Every time you drive down that hill in the winter, you'll be saying a prayer." Everybody in the store cracked up.

Though I was not a Big Man in a Truck, I played one in my red Silverado. I registered it at a shockingly friendly Motor Vehicle office in Ft. Edward, put on my new plates, then put the three dogs in the giant backseat and pumped the gas pedal. It rumbled to deafening life. The radio was set to a country music station, and the first lyric I heard was, "You can watch your movies, I'll take my NFL."

I went roaring into town, the other men in trucks tipping their caps as we passed, the dogs sticking their heads out the windows.

The truck was a behemoth. It took a long time for the brakes to check in, and the roar from the engine was guttural. But it was great blasting along Route 30, windows cranked open, the dogs of Bedlam Farm taking to the road.

I stopped at the Stewart's in Salem to fill up the left gas tank, which cost $36. I decided to wait a week before filling the other one. 🐑

Chapter Three

. . . .

DOG DAYS I

"Why, not to put too fine a point on it, this is Bedlam, sir."
Charles Dickens

THROUGH THE OPEN BLINDS I SAW THE FIRST HINT OF AUTUMN light creep up the valley below the house. There's no way to see dawn flare in my New Jersey town. I wondered sometimes how I lived without it, though I did for most of my life. Even in the pale gray, I could make out a stand of trees on the opposite hill so yellow it appeared on fire. I couldn't recall seeing anything more beautiful than my new front yard on a crisp fall day.

Closer by, I saw a tiny pair of wolf eyes inches from my nose, watching me intently. Rose had gotten out of her crate again. Either I'd fastened it poorly or she'd nosed aside the latch. She never really slept, at least not that I could see. I didn't think she'd figured out how.

I rarely saw Rose truly at rest. She preferred to move toys and bones from one room to another, to industriously dig holes in the yard, to wait at the base of trees for careless squirrels. Even sitting quietly in her crate, she was simply pausing, waiting to go to work, fetch a stick, chase a sheep, greet visitors, hop into my lap. Like sandpipers on the beach, she did everything rapid-fire.

As soon as I stirred, I'd be showered with licks from both sides. Orson, who stays by my left side, was nestled in the crook of my legs; Rose was on the right, awaiting instructions. Homer was off somewhere—he generally slept alone—but would report for duty shortly, alerted by the others' activity.

I loved the affection, but I didn't think it was aimed totally at me. Mostly, it signaled the start of a new day, things to chase and run circles around. In Border Collie Land, a human merely putting on shoes generated joy and excitement.

I'd come to terms with dog love. I didn't need to kid myself; the reality of it was enough. We loved them to pieces, imagining an unshakable bond; they loved whoever fed them and paid attention to them. Their love was no less pure or meaningful for that, and I struggled against the temptation to make it more than it was.

Homer appeared, melting into the room quietly, and headed for the foot of the bed. Homer's life, it sometimes seemed, was accommodating Orson, like a worshipful kid who could never get his older brother to give him a break.

Orson glowered him away from the bed. I could command Orson to lie down, but I couldn't prevent his giving Homer the evil eye every time he approached me. Ever since Homer arrived, Orson tried to enforce a no-fly zone around me, so Homer had learned to come close only when Orson wasn't around.

This seemed a point we couldn't get past, one of those inalterable attitudes dogs form. Trainers believe that any dog can be trained to do just about anything—a sound general principle, but I wasn't always so sure. I believed Orson would rather starve than allow other dogs easy access to me. I had no idea of his motives, but his implacability was very real. No amount of training, crating, scolding, imploring, or treat-scattering had induced Orson to share me willingly. So Homer skulked off.

Unwillingly, however, Orson had learned to tolerate Rose. When he tried to stare her away, she either nipped him on the nose or hopped blithely over him to land on my chest and slurp my face. Nothing intimidated her.

I staggered out of bed, threw on some jeans, a flannel shirt, and boots. I'd come back to shower after our walk and barn chores.

Although there was a daunting list of things to attend to before winter—fixing gaping holes and broken windows in the barn, moving my hay into the loft, stacking the huge pile of firewood—the animal care seemed easier than I'd expected. Several years of herding at Raspberry Ridge, including lambing seasons, had given me some familiarity with sheep. Apart from my watching for health issues like bloat, worms, and diseased hooves, I let them take care of themselves pretty much. There was enough grass in the pasture for them to feed themselves. An artesian well, which never froze, provided water all year. Assuming the testy Nesbitt had done his work and the ewes were pregnant, I brought them corn and supplements each morning to strengthen them and build energy for the winter.

Still, it was astounding how many details arose on even a tiny, one-man farm like this, with so few animals. Repairs, maintenance, supplies—I felt I could never keep up, or even get close. All I could do was what I could do, day by day.

From the paddock around the barn, I heard Carol braying happily in anticipation of her morning cookie—an alfalfa-barley-carrot concoction. Whenever I came out of the house, Carol was waiting by the gate, greeting me. I'd come to love her raspy call. It trumpeted a new day, much as my tying my shoes did for the dogs.

Carol rushed up, tail swishing, as I swung the gate open. I offered the cookie, felt her warm mouth move expertly around my hand.

I'd grown increasingly fond of Carol. Her peaceful, steady sweetness seemed almost spiritual. She was calmer than the sheep, more connected to people, and smarter, too. She knew her name and came when I called.

Sometimes she ambled over to put her head on my shoulder while I fed her cookies or carrots. She loved to have her forehead and ears scratched. Like dogs, she was driven by food and attention, not by human-like attachment, but she'd surprised me with her mellowness and affection. Sometimes we'd do lunch: I brought out a sandwich and gave her a bucket of oats and we sat in the barn together. "Munch and crunch," I called it.

On the way around the pasture—we walked the fences each morning, stretching our legs and looking for holes or loosened posts—I called the dogs off the sheep. Reluctantly, they moved away. Letting all three dogs near sheep at the same time would cause pointless panic. So the dogs quickly fixated on other things, and began chasing small meadow creatures, running and digging in one spot, then another. The hill and woods teem with wildlife, and little of it went unnoticed. I loved the dogs' enthusiasm; it had drawn my attention to things I might not have noticed, from butterflies to hawks.

"Walking the fences" is a country expression, sometimes called "walking the line," as in property line. Farmers do it all the time to make sure everything is in order, the animals where they should be, the fences all solid. It was maybe a quarter-mile up this stretch of hill, and a steep climb. It took several weeks before I could make the top without having to stop and catch my breath.

The sight from the hilltop was striking, no matter the weather or time of day, a Currier and Ives diorama with steeples popping out of the trees, barns and cornfields spread below, the

Green Mountains of Vermont looming in the distance, blazing yellow and red.

Pausing before I followed the fence line to the left, I watched the sun rise and gave thanks for my good fortune, for this place and my dogs and the spectacle before us that lifted my heart every time. Sometimes I focused on the hawks riding the wind currents overhead, sometimes on the shifting light or the clouds skimming the mountains.

At the top of the hill, Rose challenged Homer to play. At first, as usual, he looked uninterested; then he glanced warily at Orson for permission. Eventually Rose wore him down and the two of them went tearing off. With Rose, it was play or die. Homer, as always, chose the path of least resistance. Orson disapproved of this rowdy behavior, but I held his collar and scratched his ears; he seemed to be getting the idea that it was none of his business.

It's too easy to slip into attributing human emotions to dogs, but Orson did seem to be slowing down, quieting. When he arrived those few tumultuous years ago, I'd thought he didn't know what peace or stillness were. Like me, he now appeared to appreciate them. Like mine, his legs were probably sore.

I missed Paula, more than on previous separations and adventures. She was a reporter, so our work often took us separate ways, as it had for thirty years. But it was never easy, and she was never out of mind. Perhaps as I grew older, I felt more vulnerable when I was alone. I suspected she did, too.

I try not to envy anybody else's life, but sometimes I met couples around Hebron who'd plotted, schemed, and worked half their lives to buy a piece of land and move to the country. My only marital regret was that we hadn't yearned for that together. Still, I honored her choices, as she honored mine.

Even if we never had the same dream, that didn't mean we didn't have a great marriage. Paula loved writing and, more recently, teaching, and she was doing both based in New York.

She had friends in the city and felt connected to our New Jersey town. I'd been less lucky in friendship and had less to leave behind. Yet the connection I did have there—Paula—was the most important of all.

So, therefore, the tug and the pull. When I was here, I wanted to be there. Back there, I needed to be here. I loved the solitude here. Some things are heard only in deep silence. To me, space and quiet meant freedom. But I also needed to talk with my wife each morning, once or twice during the day, again before bedtime. We were on the phone a lot.

I felt confident she'd be up more often than before, but maybe never as much as I wanted. And with my flock to care for, it was harder for me to shuttle back and forth than it was from my mountain cabin. It made the farm bittersweet. When I thought of Paula so far away for so long, I sometimes ached. I knelt so that one dog or another could lick my face. It was comforting. No one with good dogs is ever truly alone.

Dogs go only so far, but we were on this trip together. Not to put too fine a point on it, this was Bedlam, sir, and we were its inhabitants. The framed print of a mill, which the farm's former owner had left on the living-room wall as a sort of benediction and house-warming gift, even came from the attic of an old psychiatric hospital called "Bedlam Hall." Jesse had discovered the print when she worked there thirty years ago, stored among the "cage beds" and "lockdown chairs" once used to restrain patients, and smuggled it away. Now, she said, it seemed to belong here.

We belonged here, too, maybe to learn humility. I wouldn't be the least surprised if soon people started paying admission to watch us bumble around. We'd see how far a balding, semicrippled middle-aged man and three good working dogs could get on a real farm in the real country, where grocery shopping required a forty-mile round-trip.

When Orson arrived in my life, he challenged me in an elemental way. He opened doors and walked out of the house, jumped through a leaded-glass window (twice) and over fences, launched guerrilla attacks on neighborhood barbecues. He rarely listened to me, let alone obeyed. No creature on earth had ever been more attached to me, and I loved him ferociously. Yet I couldn't begin to recount how he'd frustrated me, how many times I yelled commands at him at increasing decibel levels. A few times I even threw things at him, from choke chains to shoes. I had never felt so provoked.

When I began the serious process of learning how to really train him, with Carolyn at Raspberry Ridge, what I saw in chilling relief wasn't a bad or rebellious dog, but an angry and impatient man. Rage, smoldering throughout my life, was never far from the surface, and much as I adored this dog, he had a genius for flushing it out. I didn't like the voice that sometimes came out of my mouth when I tried to train my dogs. It was, a psychiatrist friend helped me recognize eventually, my father's voice: critical, scolding and judgmental.

My father loved me as much, I'm sure, as I love Orson. Perhaps he never realized that he was causing damage. In any event, he couldn't help himself. Whereas I believed I could help myself, and I wanted to. This reform was one of the most basic unfinished tasks in my life, and the dogs represented my best chance to evolve. Perhaps that's what I was really doing at Bedlam Farm.

THERE WERE A MILLION TASKS ON THE FARM, BUT NOT MANY involved dogs yet, which was probably a good thing. Orson was too crazy to herd, Rose too young, Homer too unpredictable in close quarters.

My herding needs weren't complicated. I needed a dog that could go out to the pasture and bring the sheep down to the barn at feeding time, or at night, or during a storm. I needed a dog to keep the sheep from storming me while I was toting buckets of corn and feed. I fantasized about a dog that would even help me take the sheep out of their fenced pasture to the lush meadows higher up the hill or across the road. A dog like that, however, would require more herding skills than I'd been able to impart in three years.

Herding is a complicated undertaking, even with storied border collies. To be useful at all, the dogs needed to learn how to approach the sheep at a wide distance—an "outrun" that took them around a clump of sheep without stampeding them. They needed to learn how to lie down on command, instantly, to anchor the flock with their presence, and to "stay" there. And to understand "come by," moving around the sheep from the left, and "away to me," moving around to the right. They needed to keep a healthy distance, so the sheep felt safe enough to graze. They needed to use their eyes and bodies to intimidate their wooly charges, not their teeth. The dog had to learn to work with the herder, too, moving in relationship to the human. A trained border collie was always maneuvering to keep the sheep between him and the shepherd.

Yet none of these skills was really natural to a dog. The border collie is a close cousin of the wolf, a predator whose instinct is to chase and eat sheep, not to lie patiently alongside a grazing flock. My cranky knees could testify to the persistence, the months and years required to get these dogs to do what looked so natural on TV. Our herding was complicated by the donkey, who was protective of the sheep—I was counting on her to help ward off coyotes—but didn't like to be herded by dogs or anybody else.

My goals for each dog were different. With Rose, I had to first let her get comfortable with sheep, then train her slowly and positively. Orson, as always, needed to learn how to follow commands and not knock the sheep around. Homer got into a frenzied state around sheep, sometimes even a dangerous one, though he's normally a good-natured, somewhat timid soul.

In our canine constellation, Homer had always been the easy dog, especially compared to the intense and excitable Orson. Homer was the sweet one, the one who wanted no trouble, the one who loved kids and whom kids loved to cuddle; with him, I didn't need to be so watchful.

Maybe that's why Homer had quietly become less attached, as I'd noticed over the past several months. He rarely stayed in the same room with Orson, Rose, and me. He lagged behind on walks, and didn't come as promptly when called. For a while, because he seemed listless and lethargic, I feared he might have some physical problem. The vet checked his heart, his joints, his thyroid. He was healthy, she said. That left, by default, a training problem. With three dogs, one a puppy, it had been tough to make time for Homer's issues. But I had to. He was a great dog, and I owed it to him.

For the moment, the dogs' major job was to race around the woods and fields, after which I combed through their coats for stickle-burrs and ticks, both plentiful. But I also took each dog to work with the sheep, briefly, each day.

One such afternoon as we approached the barn a beat-up old Chevy pickup pulled into the driveway. It had the unmistakable signatures of a farm truck: it reeked of manure; its paint had flaked almost completely off; its bed was stacked with rusting tools and bits of machinery; clots of hay and mud clung to the tire wells.

Jay Jeffers was, in fact, a farmer, who lived down in Argyle. He showed up complete with weathered face, faded baseball cap, and the deliberate walk of a man with stooped back and battered knees. He'd just come from milking his "girls," he said. He'd been doing it for thirty years and, like most of his fellows, he didn't expect to be in business much longer. Small-farm life was dying fast, and nothing spoke to that decline more than the arrival of people like me.

"Saw your collies, just wanted to stop by and see them

work." He leaned over to pat the circling dogs. "Beautiful dogs. I could sure use one. Wonder if they could move calves."

I sent Homer tearing off after the sheep so Jay could watch. Homer plowed into the middle of the flock, rather than circle around it as border collies were supposed to. Still, the sheep, accustomed to working with amateurs, turned and hustled toward the barn. Homer got the job done. Jay whistled appreciatively.

"Ever think of getting one?" I asked.

He shook his head. "Nope," he said. "Couldn't afford one and don't have the time to train one. Don't want to pay all those vet bills, either." By now, I knew what that meant. Farm dogs had better stay healthy. Repairing a broken leg could, in a bad month, make the difference between profit and loss.

Jay was the first but not the last farmer to stop by. As the weeks passed, quite a few pulled their pickups over to watch me work with the dogs and the sheep. Their appreciation for the dogs was heartfelt, but no one expected ever to have one himself. They all said almost exactly the same thing: they'd love to have a dog like mine but couldn't afford the money or the time. It made me increasingly uncomfortable.

Real farmers all had barn dogs—mutts—to keep down the rodents and chase off predators. But only émigrés from Boston and New York had herding dogs. And, of course, we were the ones who didn't truly need them. For us, herding was a pleasure, a hobby. Jay had no hobbies. His "girls" needed milking twice a day, every day.

Like most of the men who came by, Jay was in his late fifties or early sixties. He knew his time was coming. They all expected soon to be dealing with knee and hip replacements and, if they were lucky, retreating to Florida for the winter. They also wanted to keep some home base around Washington County, so they could stay close to their kids and grandkids. Dogs were not in the picture.

· · ·

THESE FIRST DOG DAYS WERE SWEET AND EASY, EVEN A BIT formless. The dogs dozed in the front yard, lounged in the fenced area out back, raced after critters. We wandered the trails around the house. Otherwise, my days were spent on the phone and meeting with workmen, trying to get the barns and house ready for what was ahead.

This regimen would become a pleasant memory when winter arrived. I'd spent some part of the previous six winters in my cabin, and had helped Carolyn through several lambing seasons—which often seemed to coincide with blizzards—at Raspberry Ridge. I had some sense of what was coming. Maybe we'd luck out and have an easy winter.

But even if we did, all the sheep's nutrition would have to come from me, tossed down from the barn loft or carried over in buckets. I'd need a dog's help. I'd had a small training pen built within the fenced pasture, for practice.

For Rose, the first task was to be comfortable and calm around sheep. An Irish border collie trainer with whom I'd struck up an e-mail friendship over the last few years suggested I stand back and give Rose time alone with sheep, to make sure she wasn't intimidated.

"Let her solve some problems," Wink advised. "It will build her confidence. If she gets too excited or nervous, take her out, but otherwise let her alone for a bit each day. She'll get easier about it by the week."

Good advice. I stood by the pasture fence and opened the gate. "Get me sheep," I ordered as Rose rocketed up the hill. Nesbitt stepped forward and stomped the ground, but Rose just barked and feinted until Nesbitt, unnerved, backed down. As I would soon learn, confidence was not an issue for Rose. Nesbitt could scare off the easygoing Homer, but not Rose (or Orson, either).

My other training efforts with Rose were also paying off. By hand-feeding her, I got her to focus on me in a way that made training easier. She certainly knew her name, as I repeated it every time she gulped down a mouthful of food. I made training a game as much as possible. "Rosie, come!" I'd shout, scattering the ground with liver treats. In a few days she learned to come roaring out of the woods and down the hill whenever I said "Come," without my ever raising my voice.

She was a star student. I used a crate to housebreak her, a process that took no more than a few days. I also made sure she had a lot of quiet time. Dogs often know how to go nuts, but not how to stay calm. For every hour spent herding or romping, Rose spent an hour in the crate. The breed can be plenty hyper, and there were times when Rose could be, too. But I needed quiet hours for writing, and keeping me company was as much her work as chasing sheep. She seemed to understand this. When the computer went on and I started clacking away at the keyboard, she went to her crate and cooled out—at least for a while.

We did basic obedience training, too, for a few minutes both morning and evening, plus scattered lessons throughout the day. I held bits of hamburger up over her head until she sat down, and when she did, I praised her: "Good sit." I held food on the ground in front of her until she lay down. "Good lie down." I'd never forged such a positive and simple, not to mention effective, relationship with a dog.

It was astonishing to see how pleasant—for owner and dog—positive training could be, and how quick. It mostly depended on how patient, hardworking, and enthusiastic I could be. The dog was happy to oblige, especially for some liver treats, just as Carolyn was always insisting; she saw positive training as the basis for the human-dog relationship.

Within weeks Rose was coming, sitting, and staying more or less reliably, and I'd only resorted to my exasperated voice a few times. I wish I'd known how to do that when Orson and Homer arrived. Orson didn't seem to care much, at least not after a while; but I knew my sloppy, testy training had rattled Homer.

Orson, a former obedience show dog with a troubled history, was still too berserk to guide sheep. Whenever he entered a gate, he became a different dog, excited, overaroused, almost out of control. He'd tear off after the flock and scatter them. I was going back to square one with him. We would approach the training pen and walk slowly around it as I dropped treats on the ground whenever he stayed calm. Then we'd lie down next to the sheep and I would brush Orson, scratch him, sometimes even sing to him, just to keep him steady. He might never herd, but at least he could learn to walk quietly by my side while I took care of the sheep.

Oddly, it was Homer who was having more trouble. Circling some sheep in the meadow, one crisp morning shortly after their arrival, he let one break away. Instead of cutting the ewe off, Homer went roaring after it and, ignoring my shouted commands, gripped its knee, opening a small wound. When the ewe finally broke free, panicked, she ran straight into a fencepost.

This stunt would have been more than enough to get a dog disqualified at any herding competition, and it was very upsetting. No more herding for Homer until we started our training over, I vowed as I bandaged the ewe's leg. He could have seriously harmed one of the animals he was supposed to protect. Wink had one unbreakable rule: Don't hurt the sheep. It was my rule, too.

By chance, Dr. Amanda Alderink, a large-animal vet from Granville, was scheduled to come by that afternoon, to check out the sheep and give them their inoculations. As soon as her truck pulled into the driveway, Carol disappeared, sneaking through the barn and rematerializing a few minutes later, high up in the pasture under the apple tree. Dr. A. laughed. "Donkeys are wicked smart," she said.

But she had come that day for the sheep. She came into the training pen where I had gathered the sheep, dispensing a seminar on sheep care along with the animals' shots. I asked her to check the ewe's bitten knee to make sure it would heal well.

We flipped the ewe on her side—sheep become immobilized and docile when they can't look down at the ground. "Whoa," Dr. A. said. The ewe had a gaping bloody wound in her abdomen, an awful sight—but one hidden by her thick fleece, so I had missed it. She'd probably ripped herself open on the fencepost while running from Homer's assault, Dr. A. thought, and she would need surgery to clean and close the wound.

A few minutes later, I was lying on the ground, holding the anesthetized ewe while Dr. A. probed and stitched. She worked quickly and quietly, but the operation still took much of an hour, involved large quantities of blood, and took place, as the sky darkened into an icy drizzle, during the first freeze of the year. The wetness seeped down my shirt and up my pant legs. Welcome to Bedlam Farm. I didn't know what made me more uncomfortable, the cold and gore or the fact that it was a result of my own dog and his obviously inadequate training. Homer, chagrined and perhaps anxious, avoided me for the rest of the day.

To stop working sheep with Homer, even for a few weeks, could be a serious matter. It left me without a working dog I could really trust. But for the moment, knowing that the ewe would recover, I was more concerned with barns and hay and the floating heaters that would prevent the animals' water from freezing on January nights.

Meanwhile, we savored a string of sunny autumn days, a riot of colors, long walks at dawn and dusk, and endless amounts of Country Bullshit.

THE FIRST SUNDAY AFTER THE SHEEP ARRIVED, I WAS WALKING up the pasture to open a gate to the adjoining field. Nesbitt, I thought, was a safe distance away. He wasn't. The Rams, it turns out, is a very apt name for a football team. Nesbitt charged me from behind and drove me forward five or six feet, into a cedar fencepost. I saw the proverbial stars. My glasses and cap flew off. My hands and shirt were bloodied, apparently from a cut on my forehead. From the ground, I glanced around and saw Nesbitt rearing back for another charge; I scrambled to my knees and creamed him across the forehead with the plastic grain bucket lying nearby. He seemed startled and I remembered (too late) Carolyn's oft-repeated warning: Never turn your back on a ram.

I wouldn't have gotten butted that way if Orson had been in the pasture. The first time Nesbitt rammed me in Pennsylvania, Orson jumped the barnyard fence, grabbed Nesbitt by his tender parts, then pulled him over on his side. Nesbitt hadn't bothered me since. But now Orson was down in the dog pen behind the house, barking furiously. He could see what had happened but couldn't get out. Homer and Rose were my only defenders—and Homer, ignoring Nesbitt, was once more blocking out my shouts and tearing after the ewes, who scattered and ran. Rose, however, quickly zeroed in on Nesbitt and went after him.

This was a bad move. Border collie puppies can be unnerved for life if they're challenged by aggressive sheep before they've developed confidence and experience. And suddenly a 350-pound Tunis ram was heading right for Rose. She backed away and hid between my legs, then regrouped and went into a rope-a-dope, bobbing and weaving, circling and barking.

Nesbitt edged away—he wanted no part of this intense little dog—then focused once more on me, a much bigger and easier target. I had meanwhile forgotten about Carol, until three ewes fleeing Homer plowed into her and she began braying and kicking.

Dogs, ram, and ewes were all converging around me; the sheep were turning to me for safety from the dogs, the dogs impervious to my shouted commands, Nesbitt pawing the ground and contemplating another attack. Things were out of control.

This had become a case for Orson, still yapping frantically down in the pen. For all his eccentricities, he was a dog you could call on in a pinch, especially if the pinch involved chasing something large.

Without my glasses, I couldn't see very far, but I hobbled down the hill to free the Helldog. As I rushed toward the gate—bucking donkey and charging ram close behind—I noticed a few cars and trucks pulled over on the road, their occupants transfixed by the spectacle.

Great, I thought. I've been here three weeks and already I'm an object of ridicule. They'd be having a few good laughs at the variety store the next morning, chuckling over the sorry Flatlander and his out-of-control menagerie.

I slammed the gate closed behind me, rushed to the pen and freed Orson, who began pinwheeling with excitement. "Let's go, boy," I gasped. "I need your help."

Opening the gate, I released him with his three favorite words in the universe: "Go get 'em."

He certainly seemed to grasp the spirit of the moment—my desperation, the chaos before us. He lit up at the sight of Nesbitt, raced up the hill at blinding speed, and plowed right into him. Then he circled around for another charge. But Nesbitt turned and fled downhill in my general direction. As he neared me, I brained him with the bucket again.

"You want a piece of me?" I yelled. "Come on! Come on!"

Had I had a spare moment, I might have reconsidered the wisdom of a fistfight with a ram. But with Orson about to torpedo him once more, Rose circling from the other side, and me screaming and waving a pail, Nesbitt ran up the white flag. He turned and raced through the open barn door into the back paddock.

Orson then intercepted the zooming Homer, who stopped, startled, and seemed suddenly to notice my commands to lie down. Once Homer cooled off, I was stunned to see, Rose smartly veered in a wide outrun around the sheep, collected the fifteen ewes in a tight clump, and held them together with calm authority.

It was an impressive display, at least until Orson plowed into the group—his herding style resembles a bowling ball scattering pins—and the ewes also broke for the rear paddock. Carol quieted and found some grass to munch. At least the field was clear, and Orson had cleared it.

I limped down the hill, holding my smeared glasses in one hand, my cap and the bucket in the other. My clothes were muddy and fragrant from sheep droppings, and my suspenders were hanging down from my pants. As I staggered to the gate, a man and his family got out of their pickup and came up to me, applauding.

"That was amazing," he said admiringly. "How do you train dogs to do that? It's like on TV."

I wiped my hand on my shirt and shook his hand. "Thanks," I said. "It just takes a few years of training."

Chapter Four
....
TEAM BEDLAM

I HEARD A ROAR AND FELT A RUMBLE; THE DOGS WENT NUTS the way they do back in New Jersey when a garbage truck thunders by. Adam Matthews, my closest neighbor, went roaring past the house on his shiny yellow and green John Deere. An auto mechanic by trade, with a repair shop in nearby Rupert, Vermont, Adam had agreed to do some "caretaking" for me. It was an increasingly popular job in places like Hebron, where city people were buying property they needed help with.

To guys like Adam, trucks and tractors aren't weekend toys. They're almost extensions of their bodies, a part of their beings. These guys—who talk bolts, gears, and trannies (transmissions) all day—live by a different set of natural laws; they have a way with machines that sometimes seems to border on recklessness. Over time, though, I came to see they aren't careless, just confident.

Hills, trees, snowdrifts—these aren't fixed objects, but things to be rearranged, taken down, or pushed back (except during hunting season, when the machines get a breather). Landscapes are transient. If runoff rainwater is overflowing a drainage ditch, you just dig a deeper ditch. If underbrush blocks the path to the well, you rip it out and haul it elsewhere. If mountains of snow barricade the barn, you move them.

In fifteen minutes, as I watched, Adam cleared away an incipient forest behind the barn, gouging out weeds and bushes and saplings, clearing a path so that the sheep and I could walk easily to the artesian well. Under his hand, the tractor danced around the barnyard like a skilled boxer. Adam offered me a turn at the wheel, so I could put the tractor in gear and drive forward and backward. I was tickled to move the huge thing, but also wary of pushing my luck. After a few minutes I hopped down and Adam finished up.

IT SOMETIMES DOES, IN FACT, TAKE A VILLAGE. LITERALLY.

I needed assistance from a lot of people these days, more than I'd imagined or required in the past. I was still incredulous at how many wonderful helpers mysteriously appeared.

Adam was first, the grandson of the couple that had owned my farm for more than a generation, brought up four children there, chose the multicolored floral wallpaper in the living room, raised crops and animals. When Adam's grandmother, who now lived in a nursing home in Glens Falls, sold the farm, she reserved a ten-acre plot on the top of the hill for him. It was a gift to me, too. When you're living alone on a windswept farm, Adam is the person you want living nearby.

Like many Vermonters, he is a man of much action but few words. He'd grown up, in part, in this very farmhouse and knew the property well. Discussions were brief. If Adam said he'd handle something, that was the last you spoke about it, no elaboration required.

We didn't actually speak in person for weeks. I simply left messages on his cell phone: I need to get the barn ready for sheep, I need to take down a dead tree, I need someone with a snowplow. Adam loved doing things, but wasn't especially fond of kicking the details around with people from New Jersey. Even if, like many skilled craftsmen, he was partly earning his living from Flatlanders, that didn't mean he had to take their guff. He told me in one message that he would do things cheap and right, and so he did.

When I finally met Adam, he was much as I had pictured him: in his early thirties, handsome, built like a boulder. He was legendary for death-defying snowmobile runs, disdained overcoats and gloves.

I learned—not from him—that he'd built the lovely, nearly completed house up the hill virtually with his own hands. He was reputed to be a hell of a shot, too. Like many men in Hebron, he was already talking about hunting season—the one time he couldn't handle things, even if the farm burned down.

ONE OF THE FIRST THINGS ADAM DID WAS HIRE ANTHONY Armstrong. It was a great move. Anthony was Natty Bumpo and John Wayne all rolled into one. Adam was a friend of Anthony's father, another hardy Vermonter, and the two had known each other all their lives.

The first time he pulled up the driveway in his black Toyota Tacoma, Anthony wore a snug Saratoga Raceway cap, a pencil lodged behind his ear, a vest over a cotton shirt. He was skinny, all muscle and sinew. The truck bed was stacked with ladders, plywood, and an arsenal of tools and hardware. He set a boom box on the hood to provide a country music sound track as he set to work.

He gave me a discreet but appraising stare, taking in my Yankees cap, L. L. Bean walking shoes, and polo shirt. I suspect he was considering several labels that were not compliments: "Flatlander" was the most politic, "yuppie" was worse. Although I had only come from an adjacent state I might as well have journeyed from Neptune. I'd never hunted, driven a snowplow, replaced a tile, or raced a snowmobile.

But then Anthony's eyes went right to Homer, Orson, and Rose, and he sunk to his knees to greet them, wanting to hear all about them. "I love my kid, but I could not live without a dog," he told me.

Soon, in the way of dog people, we were chatting about our dogs, their habits and foibles. We hung around talking dogs for an hour while he sawed and planed a sliding door for the barn and told me about his Cleo, an English mastiff the size of a small pony.

The things that hit you first about Anthony are his watchful gaze, his quick smile, always close to the surface, and his electric energy. He carries a piece of paper in his wallet that he got from an Air Force sergeant: "Integrity is doing the right thing when nobody's looking." He lives by it. Yet there's an elfin quality about him; he exudes mischief, and is fearless about speaking his mind.

It was good to have Anthony around. The laws of gravity were different for him. I never felt older than when watching Anthony, twenty-seven, bound over a gate I struggled to unlatch, toss hay bales around effortlessly while I huffed and puffed, or tote heavy armloads of firewood like matchsticks.

Anthony could fix almost anything—leaky faucets, cracked windowpanes, dangling doorknobs, stalled engines. For now, he liked to work on the "small stuff," the tasks people couldn't get contractors to do. But the big stuff didn't seem to phase him, either.

Even before I'd moved in, he'd put in Plexiglas to cover the gaping windows in the barn, hauled out tons of moldy hay and farm debris, fixed a balky electrical outlet, shored up sagging walls and floors. His work ethic was simple but rare: attack continuously and ferociously until the job is properly done. I soon nicknamed him "Rocket Man," because minutes after I'd leave a message on his machine, or with his wife, Holly, his pickup would come flying up the driveway.

He doted on his fourteen-month-old daughter, Ida, whom he brought along on jobs whenever he could. In fact, one reason he'd become a handyman, he said, was so that he could spend more time with her. Descended from many generations of farmers, Ida toddled all over the farm, passing fearlessly through the barn, among the sheep. She had already logged many hours on snowmobiles.

"Ida, honey," I heard Anthony warn one night on the phone, "please don't eat the shotgun shells. The gunpowder isn't good for you." Anthony's rule for injuries was: "If it's not bleeding, don't bother me." But that was just tough talk. If Ida got too close to a donkey's rear legs, Anthony would zoom over to pluck her out of harm's way.

Like many gifted kids who couldn't quite fit into the conventional educational system, Anthony was a born teacher. He loved inducting a Flatlander into some country ways—how to read animal tracks or stir the hay feeder, how to shoot safely.

Like my other neighbors, he shared the conviction that I would need a rifle at some point. "You better have a gun," the Agway driver told me. "Believe me, there are things that go bump in the night out here, and when one comes after you, your dogs, or your sheep, you don't want to be standing there with just a flashlight and your bedroom slippers." He got my attention, since I could hear such things almost nightly, and they weren't far away.

Although I was reluctant, the presence of some aggressive feral cats, and those coyotes, convinced me to buy a .22 rifle, just in case. A .22 is a small-caliber gun, used mostly for target practice. Still, it was a gun. In New Jersey, only the bad guys had guns. In Hebron, everybody I liked had one, or several.

In a former life I'd been a police reporter; I had seen what bullets could do. And I'd promised Paula—no firearms. But it was odd, the difference between herding sheep and owning them. I felt an enormous responsibility for these animals. They faced real dangers here, and there was no one to protect them but me. I told myself nothing was going to hurt them, not on my watch.

Anthony gave me several lessons, showing me how to hold the rifle and sight it, to always assume it was loaded, to check for unseen buildings or people behind any shot, to use the safety each time and to check the chamber whenever I was done. The seriousness with which he took safety stuck. We drove to a re-mote junkyard where he set up some targets about a hundred feet away. To my amazement, I shot well.

I had no intention of using the gun, and no desire to hunt. But I found I also had no qualms about using it if I had to, and I practiced on empty cans at the top of the pasture. Shockingly, considering that the last time I'd used a gun was in basic train-ing with the National Guard, thirty-odd years ago, I hit almost all the targets. Afterward, I put the rifle in its holder and hid it in a closet, stashing the ammo in a cupboard elsewhere in the house.

WHO KNOWS WHY PEOPLE BECOME FRIENDS? ANTHONY AND I could hardly be more different; yet the friendship we struck up that first afternoon—another gift from my dogs—is one of the most important things that's befallen me in Hebron.

Like me, he's never had a lot of friends, relying on his family and dogs for companionship. Unlike me—and I'm amazed, maybe even envious at his clarity—he sees his life quite accurately, even at so young an age. "I need to work for myself and stay close to my family," he told me one warm afternoon in early fall. It had taken me a couple of decades to figure that out.

He's figured out other things, too. "I've got three rules when trouble comes," he advised me one day when I was, in his words, "freaking out" about some farm crisis or another. He had learned to ignore me when I got excited.

Anthony Armstrong's Three Steps:

Number One: Take your head out of your ass.

Number Two: Calm down!

Number Three: Pay attention.

As somebody who'd spent much of a lifetime with his head up his ass, this seemed like promising counsel. I typed up the rules and taped them to my computer.

We talked for an hour or two that first afternoon, a rare thing among men. As he realized how late it was and began to pack up the truck, Anthony turned to me. He had heard, he said, that I knew a lot about dogs. He was thinking about getting a "ride-along dog." His family didn't think he needed another dog, but seeing the look in his eyes when he talked about Cleo, I knew it would be only a matter of time.

I hadn't heard the term before, but I would hear it a lot upstate. "Ride-along dogs" accompany the men in trucks everywhere, as they go to work, go hunting, plow snow, stop for coffee with other men in trucks.

You see them around Hebron, these proud and lucky dogs, dozing in truck beds or sticking their heads out open windows, working dogs in the most literal sense. They accompany busy but sometimes lonely men and women on tasks that make the world run. Because they are with their human companions so much, they are usually calm and well-trained dogs. They couldn't be ride-along dogs otherwise, exposed as they are to strangers, tools and noise, new places.

Anthony was thinking of adopting a dog he'd seen at the

Shaftsbury, Vermont, animal shelter, a mixed-breed husky-shepherd puppy. Would I consider driving with him to take a look? In the past few years, I've spent endless hours researching, thinking about, and talking with people about their dog choices. It's an endlessly fascinating topic—why people select the dogs they do, why they love the ones they love—and one with enormous consequences.

In my experience, dogs get into more trouble because the wrong dog was chosen for the wrong person at the wrong time than for any other reason. These are the dogs left untrained, grown neurotic and aggressive, returned to shelters. Dogs chosen out of impulse, because a kid saw one at the mall or an adult saw one in a movie. Or because parents didn't realize their cute little Christmas gift would soon become a rambunctious, furniture-devouring sixty-pounder.

A shepherd-husky mix didn't necessarily strike me as the best ride-along dog, I told Anthony. Possessed of an independent streak, Anthony bristled a bit. Like many locals, he didn't believe in paying money for a dog. Almost everyone he knew had gotten a dog from a shelter or a neighbor's litter. He didn't particularly cotton to purebreds; he thought they were goofy and obnoxious, prone to health problems like allergies and hip troubles, likely to pile up big vet bills. Still . . .

"I don't think it's a good idea," I told him. "We ought to talk about it first."

"Why not?"

"Because it's probably a great dog that deserves a home, but that doesn't mean it's the right dog for you."

The last thing I wanted was to deprive a shelter dog of a good owner, but the dog Anthony wanted would need to possess some very particular traits. This was probably the most important decision in the life of any dog and human, and Anthony, I feared, was on the verge of a common mistake.

For all the noblest reasons, he wanted to save a spirited

puppy—one, the shelter said, that didn't get along well with other dogs. But a shepherd-husky mix combined two very active, restless breeds, while its future job required, instead, a dog that was patient, genial, and trainable.

A ride-along dog has to wait quietly for hours in the truck while his human works. He'll encounter all sorts of strangers every day—people old and young, other dogs and pets, farm animals. He has to stay where he's supposed to stay, ignoring temptations and intrusions. Dogs love routine, and for Anthony's ride-along dog, the routine would be constant change and stimulation.

Give me a couple of weeks, I asked. This could be a great home for the right dog, complete with a devoted owner, a dog-crazy family (Anthony's wife, Holly, loved dogs as much as he did), and the thing so many dogs crave, company 24/7.

I started calling shelters and vets, explaining what I needed, describing Anthony. The vets and I all had the same thought: a Labrador, or a Lab mix. Bred to hang out quietly with hunters in forests, hour after hour.

Because Labs have gotten so popular—and so many are inbred and poorly trained—it's easy to forget the extraordinary temperament of this working breed. Properly bred and trained, they are good-natured with people, accepting of other dogs, eager to please, capable of great calm. They wouldn't be much help with my sheep, but I greatly missed my yellow Labs, Julius and Stanley.

After two weeks of calling around, I heard from Dr. Mary Menard, a great vet—smart, warm, direct—at the Borador Animal Hospital. A breeder in nearby Shushan, she reported, had a beautiful, mellow, black Lab puppy; if Anthony didn't want him, she just might take him herself.

The dog, a male, was ten weeks old. When I drove over to see him, the dog waddled over and crawled into my lap. He was striking-looking, perfectly proportioned, with as sweet a disposition as I'd ever encountered. He was so trainable that I got him to sit on command after only three or four attempts. I even tried driving him around Shushan in my truck, where he contentedly gazed out the window. I could picture this dog spending happy years toodling around upstate New York and southern Vermont with his handyman owner, visiting hardware stores and homes, then setting out on weekend hikes and swims and hunting expeditions.

It wouldn't be an easy match, though. Anthony and his friends and family see Labs as elitist, obnoxious, Baby Boomer dogs, symbols of the Flatlands.

Some people argue that it's wrong to ever purchase a purebred when so many dogs languish in shelters, but while I sympathize, I can't agree. There are plenty of abandoned children in the world, too, and adopting one is a wonderful thing, but we still like to have our own kids. The dogs I know tend to fare best when their owners do some homework and find the right dog for them, wherever it comes from.

The other problem was that a purebred Labrador is expensive. Anthony didn't have that kind of money, and would resist spending it on a dog if he did. Yet this seemed as fine a dog-human fit as I'd ever seen.

I thought about it, called Anthony, and announced that I'd located the perfect dog. But it would cost some money, I warned—as much as two hundred dollars.

"It's a runt," I lied. "Ugly. You probably won't want it." I could hear he was intrigued. We agreed to go to Shushan the next day.

Then I told the breeder I had the perfect owner, but would she tell Anthony the dog only cost two hundred dollars? Of course Anthony was too savvy not to figure out that this wasn't a two-hundred-dollar dog, and way too proud to let me pay the difference, but we could sort that out later. My strategy was to put him and the puppy together and see what evolved.

Driving over the next day, he was excited and curious, peppering me with questions about the dog. He had a roll of twenties in his jeans pocket. This was just a dry run, I reminded him. This dog had already been in several homes, I said, and might be beyond redemption. Only a serious dog nut would be interested.

As we pulled up to the small red farmhouse, even before we got out of the car, the Lab mother and this pup, last of the litter, came bounding out.

It was almost as if this dog had read the script. Anthony, confused, perhaps thinking that his ugly runt had yet to appear, kneeled down to see the puppy, who bounced into his arms. You could almost see the bond between these two, it was so instant and palpable. What sight could make any dog lover happier? In five minutes, the two of them were rolling around on the ground. I started writing a check to the breeder, who beamed.

Anthony and the breeder exchanged papers and information, he handed me his roll of twenties, and the three of us—the dog was named Arthur on the spot—climbed into Anthony's Toyota. On the way back, Anthony berated me for tricking him, though he allowed as how he'd suspected there might be a Lab involved. "This dog didn't cost any two hundred dollars," he said. "You'll tell me how much, and we'll work it out through labor." Done.

Now, when I hear Anthony's Toyota pull up the driveway and see Anthony climb out with his tools and radio, Arthur follows right behind. He sniffs around a bit, then stakes out a spot near Anthony as he works. Nothing fazes Arthur—not the passing traffic or my dogs chasing after sheep. He has found his place, and his place is right by Anthony's skinny side. I wish as happy a life for every dog.

ALTHOUGH SIX YEARS OF SPENDING TIME IN WASHINGTON County has taught me more than I used to know, I still can't easily grasp how a lot of things work. I can operate a Phillips screwdriver now and hammer a nail into a wall; I can deal with mice and minor plumbing issues. But the mechanics of how things work, how they're taken apart and put together—I still haven't come much closer to understanding that.

Paula's prohibitions all made sense for me, even though I'd already violated rule number one (and hadn't told her about it yet). I could shoot my foot off if I had a gun. Power tools were dangerous and finicky, heavy farm equipment way beyond my abilities, and that truck was already proving balky. I'd pledged that I'd do all the animal care myself—tasks relating to dogs, sheep, the donkey and their well-being. But on other scores, I was grateful for Team Bedlam, even though their help also made me feel I needed a testosterone patch.

Like many people with animals upstate, I spent a lot of time at an Agway farm-supply store. After my fourth or fifth visit to the Salem store, an employee asked me if I wanted to join the weekly Agway Farmers Call List.

Each week Agway called farmers around Salem and Hebron to ask if they needed feed or other supplies. A truck came by a few days later to deliver them. Apart from the fact that I was delighted not to have to haul around heavy sacks of corn and feed, I have to say my chest puffed up at the idea of being on the list. It was one of the few clubs I'd ever been invited into that I was actually eager to join.

Still, I know I'm considered testosterone-deficient, and I can't really argue otherwise. I spoil my animals, for instance, lavishing what many of my neighbors consider a ridiculous amount of attention on dogs, sheep, and donkey.

Take that sheep surgery, for example. Afterward, I took a lot of guff from neighboring farmers who heard about the operation and pointed out that I was nuts to spend $150 dollars patching up a sheep worth $60 at market in a really good year. Several volunteered to shoot her if it happened again. They weren't being cruel; these men lived on the economic margins, struggling mightily to keep their farms afloat. It was illogical, even indulgent, to spend two or three times as much to heal an animal as it could bring in revenue.

I explained that the animals were different for me. I wasn't sure it was in me to shoot my livestock. This kind of moral ambiguity was the blessing and curse of our generation, but no sheep or dog or donkey was going to suffer or die pointlessly if I could manage to prevent it.

"I'd love to be one of your sheep," one farmer guffawed. I'd been called a sissy before, by classmates and, most frequently, by my father. But this ribbing didn't carry that sting. These guys liked me, got a kick out of me, were always there to help. They accepted the differences between us, even found them interesting.

I found the situation pretty interesting myself, although it often made me squirm. I was getting a small taste of just how hard their lives were, why they couldn't afford my sentimentality. I'd hardly have blamed them for resenting me; instead, I was touched by their generous spirits.

Still, Nancy Fortier and I laughed about the testosterone gap many mornings when I went to get a cup of coffee and a newspaper at the Bedlam's Corner Variety Store. She worked there weekdays, after moving up from Westchester, and had become a keen observer of local culture. "Wait till hunting season," she cautioned.

I was already hearing plenty about it. Weeks ahead of time, every man I talked to seemed to be riding around in his pickup, scouting for deer tracks, feverishly readying his hunting blind or camp. Guys were cleaning their guns, readying scopes and ammunition, taking nightly practice shots.

Hunting season was a big thing in Hebron. It was a father-son ritual of the kind lost to many American dads and kids; it was also an expression of friendship. Much of the planning and preparation and intensifying Country Hunting Bullshit was not about deer at all but about the chance to get together, away from family and work, and have a few beers with your buddies. It was also, for better or worse, an immersion in nature, a reinsertion of men into the woods.

On opening day, starting at three A.M., pickups began creeping up the road in front of my house, heading into the hills. I waited until daylight to walk the dogs and kept a close eye on Rose, who is wont to bound off after anything that moves and can cover a lot of ground before I can open my mouth. Some people only walked their dogs on leashes during the season, or put orange collars and vests on them. I just walked mine in the open meadow across the road, avoiding the tree line.

The gunshots started just before dawn. Unlike the sharp ping of my .22, they made loud booms, a strange and discordant sound.

The second morning, Adam's green pickup pulled into my driveway. He'd been up in his stand for an hour or so when an unruly buck wandered in front of him. Did I want to come up and see? We bounded up the hill in Adam's truck, over spaces I wouldn't have considered trails, let alone roads. We found the buck in the woods behind Adam's house, hopped out, picked up the body and maneuvered it into the back of the truck.

Adam was pumped, to say the least, recounting the shot and the kill. Back at his house, he whipped out a knife and went to work, positioning two buckets below the truck bed. He gutted the buck, carving out its internal organs; one bucket filled with blood, the other with body parts. I held the deer while he worked, and he tossed me the fatal bullet, which he found near the heart.

Then he cut the heart out, dropped it into a plastic bag and asked if he could store it in my refrigerator (no electricity at his new place yet). Good for eating, he said.

He was exhilarated and I was mesmerized by how exciting and important the hunt was to people. I called Paula and said I had a deer heart in the fridge. I also told her I lacked the grit to kill a deer and hoped I could still live up here. It was a joke, sort of.

. . .

THOUGH MAYBE NOT. I SUPPOSE I ALWAYS SUSPECTED THAT I might use my rifle, I just didn't know how soon. Three weeks after I got it, we went out walking just after dusk and Rose darted off. In seconds, I heard a bloodcurdling shriek. I ran to the front of the house, Orson and Homer rocketing ahead of me; there was a dreadful racket from under the porch. Suddenly it subsided, and Rose dashed out toward me, a nasty gash under one eye. Orson, too, was bleeding from the nose. Up ahead, in the flashlight beam, I saw a huge black cat with a stubby tail loitering in front of the barnyard gate. Orson spotted him the same time I did and charged, and the cat hopped the gate—slowly— and stood unperturbed on the other side while all three dogs barked and lunged in a frenzy.

There were two feral cats in my barns, maybe more, and they were quite welcome to stay. They stayed away from the dogs and me and kept busy controlling the population of mice and rats. But I hadn't seen this black one before. He'd inflicted some serious damage on Orson and Rose, missing her eye by a fraction of an inch, and then hadn't skittered off; he was behaving oddly.

Next morning, local vets and the county animal welfare officer I called said cats that stand their ground are often sick. That left few options. Trapping them and dropping them off elsewhere is cruel to them and unfair to the animals and people living where they're dumped. But I didn't want them around my place, either. Their droppings could make the sheep ill, and they could, everybody said, inflict serious damage on dogs. Meanwhile, every time we went outside, the dogs were now on the lookout for the cat, charging the porch, rushing the barn, sometimes racing right across the road. Rose was especially at risk; she wouldn't back down, but she was too small to win the fight—the cat was her size, if not larger. And Orson, when challenged, went nuts.

"There is no feral cat rescue up here," the county agent said, choking back a laugh. "They can't be domesticated. I'd suggest the five-cent solution." A bullet, he meant.

I didn't like the idea. But the cat kept reappearing. Once or twice, he was waiting by the back door, then backed off slowly as the dogs lunged. His eyes, I could see, were rheumy. Maybe he *was* sick. But I held off taking any action, hoping he'd move on.

Then came the afternoon when, talking on the phone, I heard a strange high-pitched yowl coming from the first-floor bathroom. I couldn't imagine what could make such a sound. When I investigated, I found the cat staring at me. The door that led to the cellar was open, and the bathroom floor was a mess. I grabbed a broom and charged, and he retreated into the cellar. There, I discovered a window pushed open, and an unspeakable, smelly mess on the dirt floor.

Deliberately, he hopped up onto the sill beneath the open window and made his exit. "You better get the hell out of here," I yelled, swatting at him with the broom. He had clawed Rose. Who knew what he might do to gentle Homer? He was driving all the dogs berserk; even if he didn't maim or infect them, they could get hit by a car or truck while in pursuit. I was feeling an unfamiliar but visceral response: this creature had invaded my house and threatened my animals.

Once he was gone, I released the dogs from their backyard pen to bring them inside. But they blasted off toward the side of the house, where I heard barking and more yowling. I ran to look and saw Orson and the cat rolling around on the ground, the cat biting and clawing him, Orson alternately yelping and lunging but refusing to back away. Rose and Homer were circling them, Homer barking, Rose nipping. This was insane.

I sprinted into the house, grabbed the rifle, rammed in the ten-shot clip, made sure the safety was on, and ran outside. Orson had cornered the cat behind a trash can. I screamed to the dogs to get back. Rose and Homer did, but Orson was too enraged; I had to grab him by the collar and drag him into the house, and the others followed.

Outside, the cat hadn't moved. In fact, he stepped away from the trash can, inching toward me. "Get the hell away from here!" I yelled. "This is your last chance." If he ran off, away from the house and barn, I'd give him a chance to go elsewhere.

But he didn't. He made for the front of the house and his usual cellar-window entrance. He broke into a run, and I shouldered the .22. There was nothing but open meadow behind him, so I pushed the safety off and peered into the scope. Just as he was about to round the corner of the house, I squeezed off a shot and he flipped over. I rushed over to where he lay and shot twice more, to be sure he was dead and wouldn't suffer longer than necessary. Inside, the dogs were throwing themselves against the window.

Then I got a trash bag and gloves, gathered up the cat's dead body, and drove to the vet for rabies testing. My hands were a bit shaky. I never imagined I would shoot a living thing, I told the vet.

"You had no choice," she said, unperturbed. She'd seen this before. "You had to protect your dogs and your farm."

I had no regrets, either. The other barn cats are still there, seldom-seen but welcome citizens of Bedlam. But if I had it to do again, I would pull the trigger in a second. Maybe the farm had changed me. Nothing that I could stop was going to hurt my little kingdom, and nothing was going to hurt my dogs.

Anthony and Adam—and pretty soon the whole village—heard of my five-cent solution. They empathized, even congratulated me. For a Flatlander, they said, I was a decent shot. That, and membership on the Agway list, might spare me the testosterone patch yet.

HAPPILY, NOT EVERY RECRUIT TO TEAM BEDLAM WAS FOCUSED on guns, trucks, and hunting season. I met Jacob Worthington at Bedlam's Corner one weekday morning. He was twelve, the son of Barb, who co-owns the store. Jacob didn't say much, but I noticed him staring out the storefront window at my dogs, who were sticking their heads out the truck window, taking in the scene. I gave him a handful of biscuits and over the next ten minutes watched the dogs fall in love with him. Homer loves everyone, but Orson is picky about who he associates with, while Rose loves sheep more than most people. I liked Jacob's way with animals, his quiet, easygoing manner.

I asked if he might like some part-time work visiting Carol—she ought to be brushed and petted if she were going to continue to be fond of people—and doing some barn work, like mucking out the sheep poop and donkey dumps, of which there were already a prodigious number. You might have thought I'd offered him a flight to Disney World.

Life gets continually stranger. My daughter had left home four years earlier for college; now that she'd graduated, she was living with roommates in Brooklyn. Although we were close, I only saw her every month or two; she was going about the business of building her own life. This was the way life was supposed to work: if we did our jobs, they moved on and didn't look back much. But I missed her, of course. The dogs filled some of that void, but while dogs are wonderful, they aren't kids.

So I had reconciled myself to a now childless life. Back home in New Jersey, I knew some great neighborhood kids I would have happily taken to the movies or a baseball game once in a while, but urban and suburban communities like Montclair have become phobic about kids spending time with older men. It's just not done.

A year earlier, in one painful reminder, I found myself with an extra ticket to a Yankees game. It was a great seat, and I immediately thought of inviting my eleven-year-old neighbor, a baseball fan I had seen nearly every day for years. He played with my dogs. His school-bus stop was right outside my house. Of course I asked his mother first, expecting her to be delighted, but she looked uncomfortable, and apologetic. "I'm sorry," she finally blurted out, "but our school suggests that we never let our children go anywhere except with family members. It's a safety precaution." I'd read the same headlines she had, so I understood her concern, but it was a wounding reminder of why so many people turn to dogs for companionship. We find it harder to connect with humans sometimes.

So I was cheered that Jacob, a natural farm kid, began coming by after school to brush Carol, feed her cookies, and help me move hay and manure around. I sensed that life wasn't simple for this kid. His parents had separated earlier in the year. His favorite sport, he told me, was chess.

Out in the barn, though, his shyness seemed to melt away and we yakked happily about my dogs and his, and the odd treasures—old tools, a rusty cowbell, ancient feed sacks—he found in the loft.

Because of our age difference, and all the dreadful stories about older men and kids, I kept our initial contacts outside. Friends in New Jersey reacted with horror or concern when I told them about this new friendship. "Are you crazy?" demanded one—a lawyer. "You should never be alone with this kid. You've got to protect yourself." It was probably the same advice I might have given if the shoe were on the other foot, but I wasn't about to send Jacob away.

Being around the farm and having this two-dollar-an-hour job seemed important to him. It was to me, as well: I liked having him around. Besides, I needed the help. There aren't many people who love brushing donkeys and mucking out barns. So Barb dropped him off in the late afternoon, then picked him up an hour or so later.

But as it got colder and sunset came earlier, it was hard to maintain this arrangement, difficult to relegate Jacob to the barn and the pasture. By November, the temperature dropped sharply by four-thirty. Jacob, who didn't believe in jackets, insisted on wearing an Old Navy sweatshirt out in the barn. I couldn't go inside and work, thinking of him out there in the dark and cold.

So I decided not to yield to the tenor of my time, and I yelled for him to come inside. My own personal referendum: I was voting for the kind of world I'd prefer to live in, the kind of community I wanted to become part of. Oblivious to all of these complications, Jacob sauntered inside and was shortly munching on microwave popcorn and watching the first *Lord of the Rings* movie on DVD.

The relationship took on a life of its own after that. Jacob arrived, called out that he was there, grabbed a fistful of donkey cookies, greeted my dogs, and headed for the barns. He stayed outside, working or exploring, then came into the house when he was finished with his chores and forays. He could hardly have been more at home. He named the sheep, rearranged the cans of donkey and sheep feed, and presented me with an ancient pot and bits of crockery.

We played chess, too. I could usually beat him, but he was good. I bought him a chess book and, unfortunately for me, he read it, and each game got a little tougher.

Orson particularly loved Jacob, felt intuitively at ease with him, and would plop his head in Jacob's lap while we played. The ever-busy Rose would pause from her indoor duties—monitoring the sheep through the living room window, chewing rawhide, moving her toys from one end of the house to the other—and leap up to lick Jacob's face. Homer soon recognized the sound of Jacob's mother's car in the driveway and would wriggle delightedly as he walked up.

I told Barb about the DVDs and chess games and asked her if she felt in any way uncomfortable about them. She and Mary, Jacob's aunt, had come by several times to check out me and the farm before Jacob started working here and they seemed easy about our arrangement, but this was a new wrinkle. But Barb had no objection; in fact, she was grateful. The last year had been tough on Jacob, and he loved having this job.

A neighbor later explained that such issues were treated differently in Hebron. "Things like that are never, ever discussed up here," he said, meaning child abuse. "Besides, if anything happened to a kid, somebody would just shoot the guy on the spot."

As the fall turned to winter, I was always happy to see Jacob pop in through the back door, yell "Hey, Jon, it's Jacob," and head into the barn. Sometimes we didn't speak at all during his visits, especially if I was working. He seemed able to tell when I was not in the mood to talk, and I could usually see when he was blue and just wanted to watch TV and relax. Other days we yakked over the chessboard like old geezers at the park. I'd ordered more DVDs online, and as the days shortened, they were considerably brightened by the sight of this kid absorbed in an Indiana Jones movie while I clacked away on my computer at the other end of the house.

Once, after a period of prolonged quiet, I came out to see what was going on, and found that Jacob had turned off the TV and gone into the adjacent room that would one day be Paula's office. It looked out over the barnyard, and Jacob was sitting at the little wooden desk, silently sketching one of the barns with a pencil and pad I'd gotten him. The next week, he presented me with a watercolor version: the red barn, an evergreen, a contented-looking donkey. I kept it propped by my computer, right near Anthony's Three Steps. 🐾

Chapter Five
THE DONKEY LADY
OF BELCHER

INFORMATION, LIKE COUNTRY BULLSHIT, FLOWS IN AN END-
less loop upstate. At the Agway or at Stewart's or at the Volunteer Fire Department's prodigious roast beef dinners, the
weather updates get passed around continuously, especially in
winter. You hear about traffic accidents, farm failures, marriage
failures. Postal workers, the plugged-in staff at Bedlam's Corner, traveling farriers and vets—everyone has news, stories, and
advice.

If you have a horse, you hear about horses. If you have sheep,
you hear about sheep. ("You need to talk to old Bill Watkins
over on Chamberlain Mills Road. He had sheep for *years*.")

And if you have a donkey, which rather few of us do, then sooner or later you'll hear about the Donkey Lady.

Cows are common, and there are several local sheep farms; lots of people keep a few goats or chickens. But you rarely hear about donkeys. Although they've been domestic animals for thousands of years and were once a mainstay of agricultural life, they're perceived to have lost their utility.

Nobody rides a donkey anymore, outside of a petting zoo. Pickups and four-wheelers and ATVs have taken over their farm jobs. You can't sell donkeys' meat or their hides. They're what farmers call "money holes"—they eat a lot, so cash flows down the drain, but nothing comes the other way.

Mostly, they stare balefully at the world, perhaps reflecting on their diminished place in life. They do take eating seriously and attach themselves to people who carry cookies and carrots. Carol had X-ray eyes that could spot a carrot inside a coat pocket from a hundred yards. She studied hay like an art student touring the Louvre, sniffing deliberately over each blade, munching happily for hours.

Personally, though, I found the contemporary view of the donkey's uselessness both unfair and untrue. Carol not only kept watch over the sheep, rushing in the direction of any strange animal that approached, she comforted me as well.

All the more reason to look up the Donkey Lady of Belcher—she sounded like a character out of Chaucer—a somewhat mysterious figure. People had been telling me about her for weeks, yet few had actually ever met her, a rare thing in a town where everybody knew everybody.

She was said to be a political activist—another rarity hereabouts—who bred and loved donkeys. Beyond that, nobody in Hebron knew much about her, or even her name. She was just the Donkey Lady of Belcher. (Belcher, one of seven hamlets within greater Hebron, makes West Hebron look like midtown Manhattan.) It was our vet who told me the Donkey Lady's name: Pat Freund. I looked her up in the phone book and left a message, asking her to call me. I was eager for some donkey talk.

I'd never expected to care much about donkeys in my life, but I was finding them fascinating. Much like dogs, they form real connections with humans; they're very loving. But they also possess an almost supernatural calm. They've been perfecting this aura—their "donkeyness," as Pat Freund calls it—for thousands of years, a combination of affection and gravitas they have down pat.

Carol sometimes reminded me, in fact, of a Labrador: deep, sad eyes; the patient ability to ponder nothing with extraordinary purpose; a love for people. I joked to Paula that Carol was the reincarnated spirit of my departed yellow Lab Julius, his peer in soulfulness. I never walked into the barn or the pasture without Carol making an appearance, nuzzling me, checking my pockets, and then observing the activities at hand. I heard her now-familiar hee-haw greeting me in the morning when I got up, at night when I climbed upstairs to bed. We'd bonded as if by Krazy Glue.

Yet I didn't know much about her. She was about sixteen and had come to Raspberry Ridge from a nearby farm. I'd first seen her there while grazing Carolyn's sheep. At first she'd shared a pen with a few goats, but when they learned how to hop over the fence and escape, Carolyn tethered them elsewhere, leaving Carol alone.

If it was cold or raining or snowing, she'd huddle under a stand of trees. In the way of many dog lovers, I quickly began to anthropomorphize her: she was needy and sad, Carol the Lonely Donkey. Maybe it was so. She always came trotting over to the fence to say hello, and after a while I brought apples and carrots with me whenever I went herding. She loved my treats; crunching away, swishing her tail as I scratched her ears and neck—she was clearly a social creature. I rarely had much time to spend with her, as I went roaring by with dogs and sheep, but I was always sorry to leave her.

Nobody likes to speak poorly of their own dogs, and I dearly love mine, but there's a streak in the border collie breed—bred to work alone or with a solitary herder—that is neither generous nor sociable. Their prickly independence may be one of the reasons I'm so drawn to them, but it also makes them less than empathetic.

The plight of a lonely donkey stuck out in a pasture with no company, seeking a chunk of apple or a scratch behind the ear, meant nothing to them. They charged at Carol's fence and barked ferociously when she reached her head over to say hello. My Labs Julius and Stanley, may they rest in peace, would have behaved better.

Carol accepted such slights philosophically, simply lifting her head when the dogs charged, approaching me again when they moved on. She persevered, accepting these affronts as a part of life.

Carolyn sent her to me in Hebron because she thought she'd benefit from companionship. And Carol did settle into Bedlam Farm almost immediately, attaching herself to the sheep as if she were one of them, grazing and even sleeping with them.

I supplemented her diet with oats from Agway, not something a donkey needs, but something a sort-of-farmer feels good about providing. Watching Carol happily munch her oats was one of the day's sweet spots.

At first the dogs continued to harry her, but if they aren't always sweet, border collies aren't stupid. Homer, who was conflict-averse, kept his distance, while Orson, who never backed away from any cheeky creature, got fresh and nipped her. Carol just flicked her left leg and booted him a good ten feet, bouncing him off of the barn wall. He got up, shook himself off, and never seemed to notice her again. Rose also considered taking her on, but when she got too close, Carol lowered her head and swept it back and forth. Rose got whacked this way once or twice, took the point, and the two have maintained a friendly and respectable association since. I was impressed that Carol had tamed two dominant, strong-willed creatures with a minimum of fuss.

But I wanted to know more about these creatures, and to make sure I was taking good care of her. I needed some expert advice, and the Donkey Lady seemed the most promising source.

Pat, it turned out, was indeed a political activist, but also a self-described "Jewish donkey spiritualist" who'd studied and written about the symbolic significance of donkeys, their place in the ancient world, and their profoundly spiritual natures. Both Jewish and Christian religious history is filled with biblical and other references to donkeys, she pointed out. Carol—like Pat's donkeys—wore a cross on her back, a pattern of dark hair behind the shoulders.

Pat could cite numerous references from the Old Testament. In ancient times, donkeys were the trucks and tractors, performing myriad agricultural and mercantile tasks, essential to commerce and daily life. "The donkey," Pat wrote in one of her essays, "remains throughout [history] a symbol of mobility and wealth, an appropriate emblem for wandering peoples." In the Old Testament, Samson was reported to have killed a thousand Philistines by wielding the jawbone of an ass. In the New, Mary rode a donkey to Bethlehem.

Pat's belief about donkeys struck me as powerful and true. I'd never seen more affectionate eyes, or encountered a sweeter, more patient soul. During daily herding lessons, Carol sometimes came up alongside me and put her head on my shoulder.

And she was crafty, too, with her uncanny ability to distinguish a farrier's or vet's pickup truck from anyone else's—and to take off up the hill the minute the former pulled up the drive. "It happens all the time," the farrier said with a shrug. "They just know."

.   .   .

SADLY, I COULDN'T WORK UP THE SAME ADMIRATION OR affection for my sheep. I liked them best when they were grazing happily, peaceable things, incapable of harm. Otherwise, I couldn't feel much connection.

Partly it was their flocking nature. Sheep by definition lack individuality; their survival depends on group behavior. They move like schools of fish, each keeping a wary eye on all the others. This is good news for border collies, who quickly learn they can control the many by intimidating a few. But it doesn't touch me. Some shepherds I know adore their sheep, giving them names, spotting distinctive personality quirks and traits. I couldn't tell most of mine apart. The only exceptions were the hefty, rambunctious Nesbitt, an unusually wooly ewe whose curly fleece inspired me to name her Paula, after my curly-haired wife, and Minnie, an elder ewe who moved slowly. Otherwise they seemed interchangeable.

"Wait till lambing season," other sheep raisers keep telling me. I hoped they were right, but I doubted it. Unlike Carol, the sheep seemed utterly uninterested in me unless I was carrying food, in which case they'd bowl me over in a second to get to it. I'd come to see them as digestive systems with fleece: stuff went in, stuff came out, the quantities were impressive, but the process wasn't terribly interesting. Besides, they had lifeless eyes, a contrast to the donkey's soulful gaze.

We coexisted. I took as good care of them as I possibly could. They had high-quality feed, the finest second-cut hay in Washington County, shelter in the barn, an artesian well that flowed winter and summer. Not to mention acres of pasture, a solid fence to keep predators out, and a donkey to stand guard.

But the truth was, I doubted I'd ever love sheep, mine or anybody else's. One possible explanation came from Carr, a retired farmer who lived nearby and stopped off sometimes to watch

Rose herd and to offer advice on the care and maintenance of a small farm. My estrangement from my flock didn't surprise him one bit.

"Of course you don't love the sheep," he said, chomping on a chunk of Red Man. "Because of the dogs. You see the sheep from their point of view. And they don't like sheep. They got nothing but contempt for them. So there's your problem." Carr was a wise man.

CAROL, HOWEVER, HAD BECOME VERY IMPORTANT TO ME. ON the phone, I asked Pat if Carol needed anything I wasn't giving her.

"Another donkey," was her prompt reply. Carol had been living alone or with sheep for so long that Pat doubted she even knew she *was* a donkey. "You have to bring out her donkeyness," she said. "She doesn't understand who she is."

Her donkeyness. Even for me, this was a strange idea.

Next morning, the dogs and I headed down Route 30 for Belcher, and Pat's beautiful old farm. We drove down one dirt road and turned onto another, finally glimpsing a restored red farmhouse. In an adjacent pasture, a dozen gray donkeys, some the size of horses, eyed us silently.

Pat was waiting for me outside, and we strolled along, looking at her neat, well-kept buildings and talking about donkeyness. Then she steered me across the road to a clean, spacious barn where another score of donkeys, many still babies, were chewing hay. A couple came over to sniff and nuzzle us. One sweet young thing, a miniature in a lovely shade of taupe, with wide brown eyes and long lashes, seemed a bit shy at first, then put her head in my hand. I gave her a cookie and she took it gently and gratefully.

She seemed the perfect companion—small, well-tempered, nonthreatening—to help Carol rediscover her donkeyness. I bought her on the spot, christened her Fanny after an aunt on my mother's side, and Pat made arrangements to bring her by.

But the next day, when we let her trot into the pasture, she was not welcomed. Carol went nuts, racing around in circles, bucking and kicking a bit, rushing to protect the sheep. A few minutes later, the two of them were standing together way up in the pasture, Carol's ears back, staring at the newcomer as if she'd fallen from the sky.

I wasn't quite sure whether Carol, who'd been either hanging out with sheep or avoiding rampaging border collies, had ever seen another donkey before. Pat said Carol would have a rough few days as she discovered what species she was, and her consciousness changed forever.

I wasn't sure what to make of all this donkeyness. Pat sounded like those dog mystics, channelers, and spiritualists who don't want to see canines as animals but as some sort of magical domestic elves. That wasn't my view of dogs. Why should I accept it in a donkey?

Besides, Carol didn't appear to be having a very spiritual time over the next several days. Rather, she seemed traumatized, kicking and lurching whenever little Fanny came near her or her food. Carol raced to and from the sheep for hours, suddenly confused about where she belonged. Then she disappeared into the barn for forty-eight straight hours. Fanny meekly followed her around, no matter the abuse.

On the third day, though, when I came out of the house and saw the sheep high up in the pasture grazing, Fanny and Carol were standing by the barnyard gate, hee-hawing for me together. It was a happy sound and a sweet sight. Finally I saw what Pat was talking about: Carol seemed a transformed creature, happy to stand alongside Fanny, completely at peace with herself and— except for the bucket of oats she still jealously guarded—at peace with Fanny. She remained protective of the sheep, but apart from them, not part of the flock. She did, in fact, seem to have discovered her donkeyness, and I had seen it happen.

Carol and Fanny came from very different places. Carol was a somewhat beat-up old farm donkey, overweight and shaggy-coated, never taking food for granted. Fanny, well bred and used to Pat's clean, well-appointed barn, was more graceful, with a glossier, more even coat.

They both carried the same cross on their shoulders and shared the same heritage, however. And from that moment, the two were inseparable. Carol and Fanny sometimes visited the sheep; if stray dogs or other presumed dangers approached, they circled the flock, kicking and braying. Who said donkeys weren't useful? It would take a brave coyote to challenge this pair.

When Fanny came near Carol's hay or oats, Carol lowered her ears and nudged or kicked the little donkey away. Otherwise, the two were never more than a few feet apart. At sunrise and sunset, they experienced a bit of donkey madness, racing playfully back and forth across the pasture.

Rose wanted to get in on the fun and tried to herd the baby donkey. That didn't work, but they sniffed, nose to nose, and Rose once in a while deigned to give Fanny a lick. They were almost exactly the same age—seven months.

However good-natured, the donkeys were no angels. One night in late November, on the eve of the opening day of deer-hunting season in New York State, I came out to make my final rounds. It was so dark I didn't notice that I hadn't latched the gate properly, and when it swung open quietly behind me, Carol and Fanny, who'd come out to greet me in search of a cookie, made a break for it.

I'm afraid I took this personally. What more could these two want than a daily bucket of oats, gourmet donkey cookies, a pasture full of grass, and, lately, fresh hay every day? But like dogs, they had alien minds. I doubt I'll ever know what beckoned to them out there, but both donkeys hustled past me toward the road. I tried to get ahead of them but Carol just brushed me aside. Here was their famed stubborn streak in action.

This was a particularly terrifying time for donkeys to be running around loose. The following dawn the woods would fill with men with guns, and any large animal bounding along at sunrise had a good chance of getting shot. Meanwhile, they were cantering up the road.

Orson would just tear after the donkeys and most probably get kicked; Homer had been ignoring Carol for weeks, so why would she pay him the slightest attention now? Once more I turned to the puppy. Rose was faster than the others, and tireless, always ready for work, great in a pinch—and here was another pinch. So I sent her off after the renegades, and she loped around in front of them before they could disappear into the darkness.

Donkeys are independent-minded, but they don't like trouble. Carol looked down the road, into the forests beyond, then turned her head and spotted or sniffed the cookie I was waving around. She turned back and Fanny fell in behind her, just as a truck came barreling down the road. I waved my flashlight and the driver slowed. "Good Rose!" I yelled. The Queen of Bedlam Farm.

Despite the breakout, I was grateful to Pat Freund. The donkey pair enriched our little encampment. Though I never asked mine to haul firewood or carry me to town, they served other functions. For months, I heard coyotes, but never—knock wood—saw one. The donkeys might very well have been the reason.

And every night before bed, reeling from fatigue—I was sore all over from herding, barn mucking, hay toting, and other aspects of animal care, not to mention housekeeping chores—I staggered out to the barn for "munch and crunch," which quickly became a ritual.

I stuffed a granola bar into my pocket, went into the pig barn for two buckets of oats. Sometimes I also brought along a boom box. When I turned on the feeble overhead light in the barn,

Fanny and Carol were always happy to see me. I'd sit on a bench by the barn door. Across the driveway I could see Orson, Homer, and Rose staring unhappily from the window, but this was my moment with the donkeys.

It was an unlikely love fest. I played them all sorts of music at night, from Sinatra to Missy Elliott, but our mutual favorite was the last CD the great Johnny Cash had recorded before he died. We were fond of listening to "Give My Love to Rose," "Bridge over Troubled Water," or "Personal Jesus" as we had our night-time snacks, my donkeys waiting for their ear-scratching.

After a while, I turned the music down low or turned it off, and sat in the quiet, munching along with Carol and Fanny. Then I'd give them each a pat, collect the buckets and wrappers, gather up my boom box, and head back to the house, where a joyous reception from three anxious border collies awaited.

Chapter Six
. . . .
DOG LOVE

LAURIE HARRINGTON WAS SMILING FROM THE BACK ROW AT A book reading in Hubbard Hall, the lovely old opera house on Main Street in Cambridge, New York. She appeared a bit apart from the other people in the room, uninterested in them, locked onto my dogs, especially Orson, whom she'd read about in my first dog book. She was eager to meet him, she later told me; he'd been through so much; he was such a great guy.

She was the last in line to get her book signed—not, I suspected, by chance. With everybody else gone, she'd have more time to talk, more time to get down on the floor and hug Orson.

I would have recognized her almost anywhere as one of the

Dog People. There are innumerable subcultures and enclaves within America's vast, complex dog universe—breeders, hunters, rescuers, trackers—all in their own canine worlds, talking on their own mailing lists.

The Dog People are a group that tells more about us than about dogs. They live a life as bounded by dogs and other Dog People as possible, as emptied of everybody else as they could arrange. "If I could buy gas only from dog people, I would," Laurie once e-mailed me. "I don't really want to deal with anybody else. I don't fully trust people who don't love animals."

People like Laurie—mostly, but not all, women—have become familiar to me, to anybody whose life or work centers around dogs. They attend dog adoption fairs and dog book readings, lots of events. Though they have human friends, those friendships are usually connected to dogs. They are curiously interactive: obsessive phone talkers, Net trawlers and messengers, list subscribers and e-mailers. But most of their computer use also relates to dogs—their rescue, care, adoption, and well-being.

Laurie was clearly one of their number. She had wavy hair dyed brown, and wore faded jeans, a T-shirt celebrating a local rescue group, and battered running shoes. Her canvas bag was stuffed with dog treats and snacks, and she was carrying a dozen faded snapshots of her dogs, living and dead.

Her face displayed a panoply of emotions as she displayed her photos: Bear was hit by a car in 1986; Wimpet was killed by a pack of marauding Rottweilers; Angela lived to be sixteen before dying of cancer in Laurie's arms. "My dogs don't die in vet's offices on linoleum floors," she explained. "They die with me at home."

When Laurie talked about how much she loved her dogs, or how much they loved her, she was radiant, her face suffused with joy. Yet I felt ill at ease with her; she made me nervous. Perhaps she seemed too intense, a bit odd. She appeared to have crossed some line, in her love of dogs, that I didn't want to cross.

She had e-mailed me a number of times before the reading,

inviting me to come see her. She lived on a four-acre strip near Argyle, with eleven dogs, six that were "mine," five that might not be, she didn't know yet. "Some people might feel my life is a sad one," she had e-mailed me, "but I feel it is a beautiful life. I am happy, happier than I have ever been, and dog love is why. It's hard to explain it to people, hard for others to understand."

She *could* tell me, though, and I did know. That, of course, was why she invited me out to her place; that's what bound us.

LAURIE WAS EAGER FOR ME TO MEET HER DOGS, FOUR OF whom were outside in her van right now. These were her "traveling troupe," who went everywhere she went—to the market and the doctor's office and the Rite Aid. She had asked to bring them into Hubbard Hall and had been rebuffed. But when I left the reading, she was waiting outside to introduce us.

Her van had seen a lot of miles, judging from the worn tires, the grime, the scratches and dents. The seats in the back were permanently folded down to support a cozy nest of blankets, strewn with bones.

I started to smile at this rolling dog crate until I remembered that the back of my pickup cab was configured exactly the same way, with quilts, fluffy sheepskin, and rawhide chews.

Finding her waiting out in the parking lot long after everyone else had left, I had another twinge of discomfort. Laurie was perfectly sweet, the very embodiment of harmless. And yet . . .

This seesawing became a part of my relationship with Laurie and people like her. It involved a sense that they were different from me, and a reflexive idea that they were frankly a bit weird. Yet simultaneously, I felt a fascination, a desire to get closer and know more, a nagging sense of kinship that meant we might not be so different after all. Laurie would probably understand how I felt about my dogs, how much I loved them, what they meant to me. She wouldn't have to be told, wouldn't think it strange.

She radiated pain, and increasingly over the years I had come to see pain around the periphery of the love between dogs and humans. Sometimes, pain was the source of dog love, the reason for it. I knew that was the case with me; I suspected it was the case with Laurie. Maybe that was our connection.

Outside, telling me her dogs' names, Laurie asked me again if I wouldn't stop by her place, meet her other dogs and her friends.

Any writer knows to be a bit cautious on a book tour. Readers sometimes assume they know you better than they do, or they attach to a character you've described, as Laurie had with Orson. Few authors go visiting people they've just met at a reading. Somewhat to my surprise, though, I accepted the invitation.

The truth is, I wasn't very interested in Laurie's dogs. I don't love many dogs beyond my own; I avoid playgroups and playdates, activities like agility and obedience classes. While I'm drawn to sheepherding, I dislike the tension of herding trials. In fact, large gatherings of people and dogs are rarely fun, for me or my dogs.

"I'll come by," I said, "but to be honest, my motive is probably to write about you." She shrugged; that seemed as good a reason as any.

Though I wasn't particularly curious about Laurie's dogs, I was interested in her life, and especially in how much her life reflected my own. Were we really part of the same phenomenon? I'd come to this remote corner of upstate New York without my family to spend extended periods with three border collies—how different could I be?

LOOK FOR THE BIG GRAY BARN OFF ROUTE 40, LAURIE HAD told me. There's an ad for a restaurant painted on the side. Take a left down a dirt road. There's a picture of a golden retriever painted on the mailbox. If all else fails, turn off the engine and follow the barking.

A din erupted as I pulled alongside her house. The yelping and shouting wafting from indoors gave me pause; it wasn't going to be a quiet evening. I pulled the three take-out pizzas I'd brought from the backseat and headed toward the door. "Just stand out there for a second," yelled a voice I recognized as Laurie's. "We'll do this in stages."

The door opened a crack and three or four dogs came tumbling out and plowed into me. A white blur—a bichon frise—followed and, as Laurie screamed a warning, lunged for my ankle.

"Darryl," Laurie shouted. "Get back in here, now!" She scolded the dog, but didn't apologize, simply assumed that I understood this was part of the package. The bichon retreated, growling peevishly. A retriever jumped up into my crotch, and a nasty tussle erupted between a shepherd mix and a terrier. Laurie and two other women came running and separated them, dragging them to crates in different rooms.

Together, we all moved inside.

I saw and smelled what Laurie meant about not wanting non–dog people to come over. This wasn't a house for everybody. It wasn't dirty, but it clearly reflected the presence of many dogs, some not yet housebroken. The odor was overpowering, even oppressive: dog food mixed with animals and accidents. Fur rose in clouds from the carpets and chairs.

Laurie had a soft spot for the often-unadoptable mixed breeds from shelters. Her troupe—all but one rescues—currently included shepherd-husky mixes, pit bulls, and terriers, plus Heinz 57s of indeterminate parentage. Along with health problems like hip dysplasia and arthritis, their behavioral issues were prodigious, mainly aggressiveness toward people and other dogs. Some couldn't be touched or bathed. Most had come from the South, where, Laurie told me, more dogs are available for rescue than in the Northeast.

The biters were housed in crates and kennels in what once was a family room, separated from the rest of the house by toddler fences. A couple of dogs were sweethearts who rarely caused any trouble, but the shepherd mixes were in nearly continuous riot, knocking down the gates, challenging me and other visitors, terrorizing the smaller dogs.

Laurie was unable to monitor the continuous movement—the squabbling, peeing, eating, and playing of all these dogs. No single person could have, really. Her relationship with the dogs was, by necessity, reactive. She was constantly shouting warnings or commands—"Ben, don't chew that table leg! Sophie, get back into your kennel. Hannibal, stop growling!" Sometimes they listened, sometimes not.

So we were different, weren't we? My dogs weren't encouraged or allowed to play in the house. They chased sheep and geese, went for multiple walks, visited parks and forest preserves, pursued balls and Frisbees just about every day of their lives. But inside, the house was mine. I needed quiet, partly because of my work, partly due to my nature. Inside, my dogs were as calm as Labs. Outside, they could be as crazed as safety and circumstance permitted.

I herded separately with each dog, often had separate training sessions besides. At night, the dogs took turns visiting me, jumping up on the sofa for a pat and a scratch. In my experience, some of the strongest relationships occur when dogs spend lots of time with their owners; it helps the dogs feel secure, and means somebody is around to correct bad behavior and reinforce good habits. None of that was really possible in Laurie's house.

I waited, as you sometimes do in homes with rambunctious small children, for Laurie to quiet everything down so we could have our pizza. Instead, she and her friends—not one of them introduced herself—intervened in one squabble after another. Laurie did ask if I was hungry. But there was no table—the dining room was filled with crates and grooming tables—so we ate our pizza slices standing at the kitchen counter. Fran and Dana

(I learned their names later), two Dog People from nearby Cassayuna, had several dogs of their own they were planning to bring inside from their cars after dinner. They needed some playtime, Dana said, more socialization.

"It can get pretty raucous in here," Dana cautioned.

But no such explanation was necessary. As we ate, more free-for-alls erupted, dogs jumping for the pizza, barking and whining at one another and at us.

"They're excited," Laurie said a bit apologetically. "They'll calm down a bit."

I made some excuses and left quickly, the mayhem too jarring compared to my quiet farmhouse. I said I'd be back the next week.

While Laurie adored her dogs, her knowledge of them was skewed, limited; she saw them mostly in terms of their perceived emotional lives. Sophie was aggressive because she had been abused. Ben had separation anxiety because he'd been abandoned by a roadside. Several had been days or hours from euthanasia for their health problems. All had been kept alive by her devoted, selfless care.

Most of the dogs seemed to know their names, but none seemed to have been trained, nor would it have been possible, given how time-consuming it was to take care of them. Stacks of pills, bandages, and food supplements overflowed the kitchen counter.

It would be difficult, almost impossible, for Laurie to live this way in a suburb in New Jersey, or most places. The barking and whining would disturb the neighbors; the aggressive dogs would bring lawsuits and probably the authorities. It would be too expensive to find a place with enough space. But here, wooded hills and vast farms were Laurie's neighbors. Even if somebody discovered how many dogs she had, nobody had any reason to care.

· · ·

OUR RELATIONSHIP WAS, FROM THE FIRST, BOUNDED BY DOGS. I visited Laurie almost weekly and spent long stretches on the phone, talking her through some of the innumerable crises that beset her household. Yet she never asked a single question about my wife, my daughter, or my work beyond my life with dogs. She never volunteered anything about herself that didn't relate to her dogs, either, unless I asked.

These visits were always both compelling and troubling. They inspired—no, required—me to look more deeply into my own evolving ideas about dogs.

Writing about dogs for some years now, experiencing intense ups and downs with a complex and troubled dog, talking almost daily to dog lovers on the street, at parks, and online, the more disquieting implications of dog love were something I still hadn't really come to terms with.

One thing Laurie and the other Dog People understood was the depth of my feeling for my dogs, the sense of overwhelming affection that came over me—and them—at certain moments. I can hardly describe how much Orson had come to mean to me, and with Laurie, I didn't have to. She understood, too, that pain is often the genesis of dog love.

Though I write about the intense interactions between people and their dogs, I had a sense that I was ducking the truth. I value self-awareness; the psychoanalysis I underwent for most of a decade was one of the more penetrating adventures of my adult life. So what was I hiding from? If dogs are often a vehicle through which we reenact powerful needs and dramas in our lives, as I believe, then what were mine?

This is the dark side of dog love, the part that sappy dog-story spinners, trainers, and breeders and rescue people never mention. I can't blame them; I don't want to talk about it either. But part of my upstate sojourn was a search; Bedlam Farm was an intense, round-the-clock laboratory in which to explore the roots of my love for dogs, why I needed them, and whether I had crossed some boundary into unhealthiness.

Like many of the Dog People, part of Laurie's dog love seemed to flow from a growing conviction that vets and dog-food companies were engaged in a greedy conspiracy that threatened dogs' welfare. The Net had fueled this view: much of her information about canine health came from Internet mailing lists suggesting miraculous alternatives to traditional veterinary care. Laurie had grown almost paranoid about commercial foods and medicines, refused to give her dogs their recommended shots, wouldn't feed them kibble or canned food. Vets were useful only in dire emergencies—broken bones, savage bites. Otherwise, Laurie and her friends firmly believed in herbal remedies and holistic diets. Many of her dogs would be dead, she told me, if not for the alternative approaches the Dog People shared.

This *was* a significant difference. The vets I've met are serious, sympathetic, highly skilled, and quite dedicated despite their profession's grueling hours, emotional intensity, and relatively low pay and status. I rely on their counsel and have rarely regretted it. My dogs have always thrived on store-bought kibble, and I'm not interested in baking them organic treats. I understand that all companies are interested in the bottom line, yet I'm hard-pressed to believe that it's in the economic interests of pet-food manufacturers to poison dogs.

Laurie—again, like many Dog People I knew—had fantasies about eventually running some dog-related business that would enable her to buy more land, thus have still more dogs. She dreamed of hundreds of remote acres with hundreds of dogs, a literal sanctuary where they could all live out their lives with room to run and no end of loving care.

I doubted she'd find that mythical place, and I think she doubted it, too, but the fantasy kept her going. Perhaps one day she could underwrite the plan by marketing her organic biscuits nationwide. For now, she baked them at home for friends. (Without preservatives, they had to be consumed quickly or frozen.)

It didn't surprise me that Laurie identified with the complex and mercurial Orson, because he was something of a rescue, although I've become uncomfortable with that term, overused as it is. She saw the same thing I did in this dog: a great and loving heart that had every right to be angry and hard, but wasn't.

Her own life, past and present, was difficult, a litany of abuse, bad luck, and hard times. Like Orson, though, she had made a choice; she had chosen to love. Like him, she could easily have been bitter and resentful; instead, however battered, she had chosen a caring life. There was something stirring in that.

But she had also made a fateful decision: she had largely abandoned humans, even the idea of human companionship. "I had a choice," she said simply. "I chose dogs. They saved me."

I didn't want to make that choice.

Laurie was in her early fifties. Ten years earlier, she'd finally summoned the strength to end a nightmarish marriage that capped a brutally difficult childhood. A nurse by training, she'd worked for years in hospitals around Philadelphia, until she wearied of bureaucracies and suffering; her work with humans had proved less rewarding than her work with dogs. She'd waited for her three children to grow up and scatter around the country, then scavenged everything she'd been saving for years and moved upstate into her charmless but affordably low-maintenance split-level. She struck me as sad; yet she insisted she was finally happy.

She'd been swallowed up by dog love, and judging from her e-mail—she got hundreds of messages a day from her various lists—she was far from alone. I hated to think what her life might have been like without dogs.

She barely knew any nondog people any longer, nor would she have much to say to them. She rarely read a paper and had little time for TV, although she often had Animal Planet on as she tended to her brood. Yet she read every book about dogs that she could afford, and, as she put it, "many that I can't."

There was even a Dog Person economy. Laurie bartered goods and services—housepainting, dog-sitting, plumbing, and maintenance, sometimes even food—with other Dog People living nearby. "When somebody gets sick, one of us takes care of their dogs. If there's a frozen pipe, we all come and clean up. We grow vegetables and share them. We buy our food together at co-ops. It's the only way we can live."

Only Dog People could truly understand other Dog People. Most people—including her own children and grandchildren—didn't feel comfortable visiting, so they didn't. "And I understand it, I do," Laurie admitted. "Who wants a dozen dogs, some of them out of their minds, around little kids? My house is smelly. I have allergies—I know how bad the hair is—so I'm on medication all year. It's not a good thing, but I accept it. It's the price, and you know what? I'll live with it."

Her statement stuck with me. I was also paying a price for this dog adventure. It was costing lots of money, much more than I expected. It sometimes got lonely and strange. I missed my wife and daughter constantly. The responsibility of caring for so many animals weighed on me, and there was never time enough to do all the things that needed doing. The border collies required plenty of care in their own right—exercise, feeding, training, grooming. With Rose, I had a rare chance to train a great new dog right, to show real patience, tolerance, affection; I was determined not to screw it up. But I was also doubtful.

The reality of middle age had hit me hard at the farm. My knees ached; my bad ankle throbbed continuously; my skin cracked and bled as the weather turned. I was almost always cold or wet, bitten by bugs or choking on dust from hay; I wore Band-Aids all over to cover blisters, welts, cuts, and burns. I dreaded the arrival of true winter. Even five years earlier, country life wouldn't have felt so hard. Now, many times it seemed beyond me.

It took almost three hours just to drive to the nearest supermarket, shop, return, and unpack everything. Sometimes it was easier to just stand at the kitchen counter with a bowl of cold cereal for dinner. When I crawled into bed, I had to remember to take off my glasses before I lay down, otherwise they'd still be on my face in the morning.

How did real farmers survive, I kept asking myself. How did Laurie? Strenuous as I was finding it to care for the sheep and donkeys, overseeing eleven screwed-up dogs was probably no simpler. Yet she saw herself as having traded misery for nirvana.

"I miss my kids . . . a lot," Laurie confessed once. "But at the same time, I see them as part of my past, to be honest. Some people would be horrified. I mean, I am a mother. But the dogs are my kids now."

She'd moved upstate because her old working-class row house didn't have much of a yard and she wanted to be able to take in the "dogs from hell," as she put it, the dogs that nobody else could handle. They truly needed her, calling on every nurturing gene in her body, and that was enough.

She haunted local vets' offices and shelters and trawled Internet mailing lists looking for sick, abandoned, and abused dogs. When she found them, she took them in, loved them, "fostered" them, fed them special diets, and tried to find them homes—sort of. Some of her dogs were far beyond adoption, and she knew it. But she and her friends maintained an unwavering "no-kill" policy. No dog Laurie took in would ever be put down, no matter what it did. If she couldn't retrain or re-home a dog, Laurie kept it.

She'd steeled herself to accept these gains and losses. Some dogs died of health problems, one or two escaped, and every now and then one got killed by another. Yet she couldn't, it seemed, be busier, more engaged, or more fulfilled. She was wedded to her dogs for life, for richer but mostly for poorer, in sickness and in health.

I WAS CONSCIOUS FROM THE BEGINNING, OF COURSE, THAT SHE reminded me of my sister.

Jane is two years older than I am. We have loved each other all our lives, but we were especially close when we were young, thrown together in tough times.

Our family was falling apart and she was descending into a life marked by pain, emotional troubles, and crisis. My parents, like most, did the best they could, but not nearly enough.

As her life spiraled into a series of breakdowns, obsessions, and addictions, we mutually recognized that it had simply become too painful for us to talk to or see each other.

When I moved to the farm, I hadn't seen Jane in more than a decade and might not have recognized her if I'd run into her on the street. We hadn't even spoken much by phone in years. She had only seen my daughter a handful of times, though each reminded me of the other in their humor and intelligence.

Witnessing her near-destruction, her struggles to care for her children, her collapsed marriage, her valiant but unsuccessful effort to become a doctor, her complete immersion in serial obsessions from punk rock to Catholicism and now dogs—plus my own estrangement from the person I'd been closest to—was the tragedy of my life.

Watching her disintegrate was something I've never figured out how to surmount. I'd seriously considered all the enduring clichés—forgive your parents, let the past go, move on with your life. But I never could, not completely.

My fruitless efforts to get Jane help left me troubled, isolated, estranged from almost all authority—familial, religious, educational. I suffer, of course, from many of the same ills that have afflicted her—anxiety, depression, anger. Although she had in many ways moved beyond that awful drama, I never fully have. In my mid-fifties, I doubt I ever will.

I feel that loss—the loss of my sister, the destruction of our family—every day. It surfaces in the way I relate to my own daughter, in the way I respond to other children, in every encounter with siblings who move through life loving and worrying about one another. For lucky people, family is the one thing you can always count on. For Jane and me, it was the thing you never could. With time and a great deal of effort and help, I've begun to write a different family story for myself. But even as I struggled to do that, I could never fully escape the one I was born into.

As Jane began to recover and put a life together, I was vaguely aware that she'd become deeply enmeshed in dog rescue. My life had taken a somewhat similar turn, also relatively late in life. I had published ten books before I thought to write about dogs; Jane was well into her forties before she got her first rescue dog. But her involvement had grown considerably more consuming.

When Jane did communicate with me from time to time, it was to e-mail me pictures of her latest dog or to relate another's humorous adventure. She told story after story about a dog behaving adorably or idiosyncratically.

Those stories always felt oddly discordant, given our own now-distant relationship. Rarely did she ask about my family or my work. But I understood that this was what allowed her to survive, and her being alive at all was a miracle. And so it was left, for years.

Jane lived somewhat like Laurie, happiest in the company of other Dog People, somehow rebuilding or reworking her own mangled life through the lives of sick, needy creatures. She loved them powerfully, creating special diets, soothing them through grievous illnesses, enfolding them in love and attention. You didn't have to be a shrink to notice that she was giving her dogs the kind of life she'd never been given herself. But if she sensed the connection, she didn't want to talk about it. This was the happiest she'd felt in years. Why pick at it?

"It's why I didn't go and get a gun and shoot somebody," she told me once. "We all get by the best we can. This is how I get by."

She spoke so passionately about her dogs that it sometimes made me uncomfortable, even resentful. Had she moved past all her pain to lose herself in dog love, while I refused to forgive the world for what had happened to *her*?

We barely spoke, yet she had unlimited time and affection for strange dogs that weren't even hers. She'd never suggested coming to see me, but routinely drove hundreds of miles to pick up some Newfoundland with heart disease. She'd never shown much concern about my problems, yet there wasn't a troubled mutt she wouldn't open her home and heart to.

This was unfair. I knew my sister loved me. I knew she was doing the best she could. I even knew dogs were saving her life. Like Laurie, she took in the lost causes of the dog world—the biters, the misanthropes, the crippled. As she had moved away from me, she had moved toward them.

I missed Jane, as I sometimes ached for Paula and Emma. Our family crises had taken her from me, and I had let her go; now, after she'd survived, dogs were keeping her away all over again. People often told me how dogs presented a wonderful way for humans to connect with other humans. I wondered. Often, I feared that dogs were a way for humans to leave other humans behind.

Like Laurie, Jane had left a husband and kids behind. Like Laurie, she missed her children and wished they were part of her life, but was prepared to live with the possibility that they never would be.

When my sister talked about her dogs, she became animated and chatty, describing their histories and misadventures. But when the conversation drifted away from dogs, she grew restless. She didn't seem to grasp that I was less interested in her dogs than in her. "You've got to see Pudge," she told me several times. "You've got to meet them all."

I didn't really want to meet them. When we began talking regularly again after years of near-silence, just after I'd moved to the farm in the fall, she told me how eager she was to drive to Hebron with her dogs. My heart sank at the thought of my intense border collies with her herd of Newfies and others. I was nearly overwhelmed struggling to care for the dogs and sheep and donkeys. If there were one more animal spewing waste on the farm, I sometimes thought, it would sink and so would I. How could my sister not sense my fatigue, even panic? But it seemed inconceivable to her to go anywhere without bringing eight or nine dogs.

I loved my own dogs dearly, and my work now centered on writing about dogs. But I don't want them to occupy so central a role. My wife and daughter, friends and books are more important to me. I don't want to see dogs the same way I see people; I don't want dogs to replace or supplant them. There are some holes even dogs can't fill.

To me, dogs offer a chance to keep working at the issues that prevent me from attaching to other human beings—impatience, judgmentalism, intolerance, anger. I hope dogs lead me toward, not away from, people. One reason I hope they help me to become a better human is so that I can apply those lessons to life *with* humans.

But in my initial discouragement over this aspect of my relationship with my sister, I'd forgotten that relationships can change, and that change takes effort. I'd also almost forgotten what I loved about my sister in the first place. Over the next few months, her sensitivity, humor, and raw intelligence led us into an ongoing conversation—though only on the telephone—about our lives and the place dogs had taken up in them.

When she got laid off from the software-development job she'd had for many years, I urged her to consider moving out of the Boston area, to a place with some land—like Laurie, whom I told Jane about. Jane, too, could have room for her dogs, a cheaper and therefore less stressful life, and the kind of community she'd been seeking much of her life. She could perhaps even make a living from working with dogs, as Laurie and her friends were more or less managing to do. It wouldn't be easy. Life in rural areas could be discouragingly harsh, as I was learning. But it was possible, and this was the perfect time to consider a move.

We also began to talk about human-animal attachment,

something I'd been studying for some years now. She seemed to me to be reworking earlier traumas through her dogs, I told her; to some degree, I probably was also. But I confessed that her perspective concerned me, that dog love might have thrown off the balance in her life.

If she really wanted to connect more with humans, as she claimed, then shouldn't she consider how caring for numerous sick and troubled rescue dogs, which hemmed her in, might make that more difficult? Didn't she realize, for example, that I felt overwhelmed at times on the farm? That showing up with a van full of Newfoundlands wasn't a way for us to reunite? Repeatedly, Jane had offered to come help me on the farm. Yet her suggestion didn't seem real to me, tied as she was to her dogs.

This was an astonishing conversation to be having with my sister. During her worst troubles, it wasn't possible to talk with her. Now, she was listening intently, groping toward change, welcoming my interest.

It was a hallmark of our family life that no one ever helped anyone solve anything. Bringing your problems to the family just made things worse, sparking guilt, hysteria, or recrimination.

So I was amazed when Jane called me one night and quietly told me that she was buying a house on three acres in upstate New York, several hours west of Hebron. She'd found the place online through another dog person. A woman who had as many dogs as she did would sell the house—already marked by scents and stains—only to another dog person. They'd talked on the phone, and Jane had made the long drive to look at the house. Dog People from adjoining towns and farms—women much like her, with similar pasts and similar packs of dogs—came to meet her, tell her about the area, introduce their dogs.

"I realized when we sat down to dinner," Jane told me, "that it had been so long since anyone had invited me to dinner that I couldn't remember the last time." She couldn't see my eyes tearing. "These people, these dog people, they were my new community, my friends. I felt completely at home there."

And the new house, perfect for her dogs, opened onto a lake, was surrounded by woods, and had a roomy fenced yard.

Jane further surprised me a few weeks later when she called to say that she'd decided to find new homes for two of her smaller charges that were aggressive with other dogs and difficult to care for.

She had thought a lot about our talks. Dogs were the center of her life now, she said; that was true, and she wanted to keep it that way.

"But you don't see that dogs are the reason we are talking," she pointed out. "Taking care of these dogs has opened me up, forced me out of myself. I have lots of work to do, still, but the dogs aren't taking me away from people. They are bringing me to people like you, and maybe one day back to my kids as well. If I can learn how to love and care for them, then maybe I can bring that to my other relationships."

Still, she agreed that it had grown too difficult to care properly for nine or ten dogs, too hard to maintain balance. Over the next months, she intended to relinquish a couple of others. Life in a new place with five Newfoundlands would be plenty interesting enough. When she told her shocked comrade in dog rescue that some of the dogs needed to go back, her friend chided her for letting the dogs down.

"Sorry," Jane said. "I love the dogs, but I come first."

I thought it was one of the healthiest things she'd ever said, and I was overjoyed to hear it and to have played any role in her decision. It spoke to the power of dog love, of the need to find perspective and fit it into our lives without drowning in it.

SOME PEOPLE ACQUIRE DOGS FOR THE SIMPLEST, MOST UTILI-tarian reasons—to hunt birds, to guard warehouses. But people who see their dogs as integral, vital parts of their families often feel that way for reasons buried deep within their own histories. People who've been hurt, who know suffering and helplessness, who've felt powerless in their own lives, are drawn to these dependent animals, who they believe love them unconditionally. Caring for dogs, feeding them, healing their wounds, is somehow healing for people, too.

Dog love is powerful stuff. Dogs are voiceless, so we are free to project any sort of thought and emotion on them. They are helpless, so they touch our innate and visceral need to nurture— which can arise because we were nurtured and know how to do it, or because we weren't and are drawn to the chance to rewrite our pasts. We think we can make the world a perfect place for at least one creature.

Beyond that, we perceive dogs as being unwaveringly loyal and devoted. We rarely perceive other people as that dependable, so we are grateful. Dogs give back, provide attention, affection, and comfort.

But sometimes, people can come through for you, too. It was miraculous for me to finally be able to help my sister, even a little. I would come see her, I promised, when she moved into her new place on the lake. 🐾

Chapter Seven
THE GOOD DOG

ROSE WAS STILL TOO YOUNG TO WORK SHEEP REGULARLY—THE conventional wisdom said she was a year or two away from serious herding—and Orson too excitable. So in the days after the livestock arrived I usually took Homer, my most experienced herding dog, into the pasture. He needed more training, but I expected him to help me get by until I sorted things out.

It was odd having my own sheep; as with my dogs, I felt ferociously protective of them. I was vigilant about their welfare, tossing out more feed and hay than they really needed, scanning the horizon for enemies, checking the fences daily. I evaluated everything around me—bugs, animals, weather—as either good for the flock or not. I had belled two of the ewes, so if the flock started running for any reason, day or night, I'd hear the noise and check things out. At Carolyn's, she and her horde of herding dogs were always around to provide backup. Here we were on our own.

Homer, who'd spent the most time around sheep, seemed my best shot as a helper. I planned to train Rose to herd by myself, a long and complex process that would require more research, patience, and experimentation than I could usually muster for a task. I respected trainers, and had gotten much help from several, but I wanted to see what I'd learned. Come spring, Rose would either be learning to herd sheep, or not.

My own frustration and anger were my worst enemies. To a great extent, Homer had already paid the price. He had his own problems and issues, but my barked commands and short temper had made him anxious and confused. When a border collie gets anxious around sheep, bad things happen.

Rose, I had sworn, would have a different history. If she could learn to herd well, I would know I'd made progress. If I could make it fun for her, if I could encourage her gifts, she'd do fine and would teach me much more than I could teach her.

But that could take years, and meanwhile Bedlam Farm was up and running—a shocking reality, considering the very idea was just a few months old.

I had limited needs for herding, initially. Mostly, I had to move the sheep from one paddock to another, and to keep them at bay while I put down corn and feed. But with a testy ram and two donkeys roaming around—and all these creatures always hungry—things could quickly get chaotic and, if you weren't paying attention, dangerous. The peaceable ewes turned avaricious when a bucket of corn appeared, and their table manners were not refined. They could stampede. In fact, if they could knock you over and grab the bucket from your hands, they would.

A dog was also necessary to drive the sheep out of the corners of the barn or the training pen for vet visits and other maintenance—hoof-trimming, worming, shearing.

People who watch the process on cable don't realize how predatory the relationship really is between dogs and sheep. To a young border collie, sheep are lunch, writ large. The dogs therefore do a lot of racing around and lunging early on, whereas a border collie who knows his stuff will glide easily around the sheep and turn them quickly.

That's why developing a calm, practiced herding instinct and the ability to work with a herder takes so much patience, endless repetition. The dogs are so intense, with such drive and energy, it often seems they'll never slow down enough to listen. That had been my problem with Homer. From the first, though, Rose had watched me like a hawk and moved gracefully and professionally around the sheep. The contrast was confusing. Had I screwed Homer up? Or was he just a different dog? Perhaps some of each.

Still, I thought Homer could handle most of our rudimentary farm tasks, especially if I continued our training. He had a pretty good recall (meaning, he usually came when called) but he got excited quickly. And because he was square and low to the ground, he couldn't move as quickly as some border collies could. So he sometimes compensated by running and gripping, using his mouth to move the sheep, rather than his eye or body movement.

I was determined to do better by Homer here. With sheep out the back door, we could learn and improve together. We'd begun going out for short runs around the training pen.

But then came that crisp day when Homer drove a ewe into a fencepost, necessitating emergency surgery in a freezing drizzle.

Experienced border collies are always aware of where the herder is, eager to keep the sheep between themselves and the shepherd. At its best, herding is a beautiful, synchronistic ballet. A herder should be able to walk with his sheep for miles without even turning around, knowing that they're right behind him, with the dog trotting right behind them.

But Homer had been so aroused that day, he seemed to have forgotten I was there at all. Wild-eyed, he'd been moving too quickly, more like a missile than a sheepdog making a curved outrun, ignoring my commands, grabbing the errant ewe by her left knee until, in a panic, she shook him off—only to run straight into the post.

I was startled and horrified, screaming at Homer, who was far too aroused to hear me.

This wasn't how I'd wanted to treat any of my animals, not how I'd wanted to begin life at the farm. Homer was here to move and protect the sheep, not to attack them. How could a border collie not know that? As his ears went flat back and he backed away, abashed, the answer was as simple as it was unpleasant: he had not been trained properly.

It was an unhappy reminder of my continuing conflicts with Homer: we had been herding together for two years, and despite all our lovely afternoons grazing Carolyn's flock, I still couldn't get him to come, lie down, or stay when I needed him to. I understood all too well that this said much more about me than him, but still, it said a lot. I was frustrated and disappointed, in myself and in him, in what we still hadn't been able to accomplish together.

WHEN TRAINERS GATHER AT TRIALS AND SHOWS TO JOKE AND banter among themselves—they have volumes of "you-won't-believe-this" tales—among the stories they most love to share are the tales of the "good dog," the sweet one, the dog introduced invariably as the model citizen.

The good dog is usually presented in sharp contrast to a troublemaker peer. Unlike the problem dog—ironically, often the most loved, to whom his or her owners are most attached—

the good dog does what's expected. He or she is obedient, appropriate with people and other dogs, causes no trouble.

Invariably, this is the dog the trainers keep a cautious eyes on.

"Whenever I hear somebody tell me about their 'good' dog, I think, 'Uh-oh,' " a trainer friend told me. The problems of the bad dog are obvious, much described. The good dog flies under the radar. Since he demands no attention, he usually gets little. He either has troubles nobody notices, or he causes troubles other dogs get blamed for. "The 'good dog' is the one nobody's paying attention to, that people have forgotten about," my friend said. "But more often than not, sooner or later there's a problem."

I'd come to understand that. On the farm, I was playing out the drama of the good dog.

Homer was *my* good dog, and everyone else's, too. He's one of those dogs—unlike Orson—who fits most people's image of what a great pet should be. He doesn't chew things he isn't supposed to chew or mount strange canine females. He isn't overly needy or intrusive, doesn't jump or slobber.

In other words, he does few of the things that most dogs naturally love to do. Submissive, wary, and good-natured, he was sent to me in the first place because his breeder believed him to be one of the few dogs who could live peaceably with his temptestuous housemate. This turned out to be true, but it cost Homer a lot.

Studies of submissive dogs show that they often adapt by becoming background pets, living on the periphery, staying out of the way, waiting to edge toward the food bowl, or daring to chew their biscuits. They do what they need to do to stay out of trouble. This is what Homer had learned, what I had allowed to happen.

Trainers and behaviorists know, of course, that the good dog (like the bad dog) is a myth. Dogs are neither good nor bad; they are shaped by all sorts of factors: their mother's feeding and nurturing habits, life in the litter with their siblings, their first few months in the world, their owner's instructional methods.

They adapt to their environments depending on training and circumstances and on varying degrees of luck, instinct, and skill on the part of human beings. "Good" and "bad" are human constructs with relatively little meaning to dogs. As people come to see animals as part of their families, however, it follows that they begin measuring them in human terms of being obedient, well behaved. I didn't want to do this to Homer. This wasn't a case of his being good or bad, but of how well I'd taught him to live in our world, or hadn't.

Like the shy, awkward kid growing up in the shadow of a more charismatic older sibling, Homer lived entirely in Orson's shadow. Orson was the hero of my first dog book. Orson was the one about whom a movie would be made.

You couldn't help loving Homer, of course. A profoundly amiable creature, he would collapse with joy at the sight of the mailman, his favorite UPS driver, and every other kid getting off a school bus. Each morning, he braved Orson's possessive wrath to hop onto our bed and wrap himself around Paula's head for a snuggle. He and Paula were crazy about each other, seeing in each other the stability, predictability, and sanity so often missing around them. Unlike Orson, a pest in his affections who never knew when to quit, Homer was gentle and discreet, crawling up to offer a few licks, then skittering away.

While I did love Homer dearly, I'd known for a while that in some ways our relationship was incomplete, troubled. Although it is heresy to say so, we don't love all our dogs the same way, any more than we love all people equally. Nor do dogs love us in the uniform, unwavering way often depicted in dog lore. When I first picked Homer up at the Albany airport, he cringed and backed away from me. We'd gotten much closer, but I'd never completely shaken a sense that he didn't really know what to make of me. It's a feeling I've experienced many times, though usually with humans.

Perhaps because we know that we are supposed to, we pretend, even to ourselves, that we do love all our dogs the same. In such cases, dogs' lives grow even more complicated, since the problems—like the elephant in the living room—are rarely acknowledged and thus rarely addressed.

I should have paid more attention to certain idiosyncracies. Homer was the first dog I ever had, for instance, who rarely stayed in the same room with me. When I was working in my basement study, Orson was always Velcroed to my leg. Rose, more independent and less needy, came and went, but continually touched base and checked up on me. Homer usually went upstairs to doze until the next walk or meal. When I sat on the family-room sofa, I often had to elbow Rose or Orson aside. But Homer almost never hopped up alongside me.

Some of this, I knew, was the result of our chaotic years with Orson, who for a while had glared and glowered whenever Homer came near me. Orson was a powerful, dominant, and possessive creature, Homer a docile, submissive, and cautious one. Some of it, I was repeatedly told by trainers, was the result of my inadequate or haphazard training.

But some of it, I also believed, belonged to that peculiar realm of chemistry. At the core, I was no longer sure I was really the best owner for Homer; I also wondered if he was the right dog for me. My other dogs and I seemed almost eerily in tune. Things didn't always go smoothly, but there were few places I wanted to go that didn't involve Orson and Rose, and vice versa.

How ironic, given that Homer had generally behaved impeccably. Orson raided the refrigerator, opened screen doors, jumped through windows. He roared off after long-haired shaggy dogs he thought were sheep. He herded bicyclists and skateboarders and scarfed food from babies' strollers. He escaped over, under, and through fences. I love him beyond words. Homer did none of those things, yet our relationship seemed a struggle.

Increasingly, Homer lagged behind on walks, left a room if Orson and I were in it, and showed poor name recognition and eye contact, despite hundreds of dollars spent on beef and liver treats. He did not seem—something that only someone who knows and loves a dog well can see—a happy dog.

Since Homer so rarely misbehaved, there hadn't been reason to pay close attention to him, so I hadn't. For a long time, I didn't focus on the fact that Homer couldn't really distinguish between my yelling at Orson and my yelling at him. Bit by bit, he'd detached himself from this raucous process, which he correctly judged had little to do with him. He grew up a dog apart, without a leading role in the main drama. Orson went berserk if left alone in our early years, and he never permitted Homer to play with me. At the sight of a ball or tug toy, he would give Homer the border collie eye and Homer would retreat to the corner of the yard.

Could I have trained our way out of this? Sure, especially knowing what I now know. But I didn't then. Orson took too much time; or perhaps I wasn't motivated enough.

HERDING WAS THE THING HE MOST LOVED, AND THERE WAS NO more companionable grazing dog. Homer quivered with excitement whenever we pulled into Raspberry Ridge. When I said, "Let's go get the sheep," Homer exploded with glee and rushed to the barnyard fence. We'd walk Carolyn's two hundred sheep down a forested path to the pasture—they knew the way so well a stuffed dog could have moved them—where Homer and I would sit for hours listening to the herd's munching. We'd take the flock out late at night, in the predawn hours, in the heat of the day.

Sitting with Homer and the sheep, I came to understand why there were domesticated dogs in the first place, why we'd invited them into our caves and tents millennia ago. Homer had little instinct for actual herding—he was always prone more to chasing—but he did take to keeping watch. He would never quit on a job, digging sheep out of the woods for hours, inefficiently but energetically, then panting in the hot sun while they grazed.

At times, his instincts were nothing less than heroic. One spring evening a ewe broke off from the herd and ran into the woods—strange behavior. Homer followed her, and when I located them, a newborn lamb was nuzzling the startled Homer and the ewe had taken off to rejoin the flock. It took the better part of an hour to identify the proper ewe and bring her and her baby back into the barn for nursing and warmth.

Meanwhile, the lamb had imprinted on Homer and tailed him for weeks. Homer looked unnerved, but kept an eye on the little guy.

We'd shared another sheep adventure the previous winter. Carolyn was sick, so I was staying at Raspberry Ridge with the dogs to help out. A blizzard blew in one night, earlier than predicted, trapping the sheep far out in the pasture. Suddenly faced with bitter temperatures, howling winds, and thigh-high snowdrifts, I feared for the vulnerable lambs who might be born in such harsh conditions, but when I ventured out to check on the flock, shrieking winds drove the freezing ice and snow into my eyes and the dogs'. Orson tried to plow through the snowdrifts, but he soon began limping, as balls of ice formed on his legs, feet, and belly, weighing him down and making it hard to walk. I had to bring him back inside.

It was up to me and Homer, who went to work with a purpose and focus that could never come from training, only from instinct. He knew where the sheep were and made a beeline for them. I had to stop every few minutes to scrape the ice off his coat and free his eyes, which were nearly frosted shut with ice and snow. He ploughed over and under drifts, often disappearing from sight, only to pop up fifty yards ahead of me. Even in a furious storm, I could see his tongue hanging out; he gobbled snow to keep from dehydrating. I worried this was too much for a sweet little dog.

But we were out all night, Homer and I, and he located every ewe and every lamb, and helped me dig them free. He barked and nipped until the half-frozen animals started walking toward the barn. Two lambs had already died, frozen to the ground, by the time we found them. But we finally marched all the others back to the barn, put the ewes and lambs in their heated stalls, working for hours to make sure that all the right moms and lambs were together. I thought more than once what his effort would have meant to a farmer a century ago.

Away from sheep, however, our troubles persisted.

At some point in the successful training of a sheepdog, the dog and herder understand that they are doing this work together, a team working in harmony. That's the beauty of sheepherding; that's what had happened with Rose and me almost from the first day. While Homer loved to be around sheep, we struggled to do it together, to stay in sync. The sheep excited him so much that our training problems seemed to worsen. Out in the pasture, he paid even less attention.

Carolyn had pointed out many times that my "good" dog had problems. When I called his name, Homer often didn't respond. It took three or four shouts to get him to focus on even basic commands. It sometimes seemed almost as if I were invisible to him. Looking back with distress, I now understood that that was precisely how I'd trained him to behave.

Yet it was easy to overlook these problems most of the time, because we had such nice experiences together. I drove to Sandy Hook some weekends and beamed while Homer diligently herded the Atlantic waves for hours. He brought me to herding. And in those moments when I crated Orson or left him outside, Homer and I could almost furtively play and cuddle.

Unlike Orson, Homer was not a dog who would fight for attention or affection. Paula was his champion, his safe place. At night, while she read or watched TV in her favorite chair, Homer crept alongside and hunkered down. They were sweet moments, but also sad, with the aura of a dog seeking comfort and protection, not pleasure. At readings, while Orson barked and scouted for biscuits and stuck his paw and head in everybody's lap, Homer was often dozing quietly behind the podium.

Without really acknowledging it, I had given up on the idea that this would change. The notion that Homer was off in his own world was quietly becoming ingrained in all of us.

ONE REASON I DECIDED TO GET ANOTHER PUPPY WAS TO GIVE Homer a playmate. Orson didn't really play much; he just wanted to be with me. He needed to learn to be calm, to see a crate as a safe place of rest, and to relearn every obedience command there was. Rose, I reasoned, could lighten Homer's load, give him a companion to play with and his own submissive dog to push around while Orson got more time to hang around with me. Everybody would be happy.

It was—as Carolyn had warned me—a mistake, at least for Homer. I was getting another dog before I had resolved the problems with one I had, a common and classic blunder. Carolyn had urged me to set aside three months to train Homer for an hour each day, working on name recognition and basic obedience, generally strengthening our relationship. She believed any dog could be trained through its problems.

Though I did eventually undertake more intensive training with him, I'd also increased the pressure on this docile creature by falling for the easy and pleasurable solution—get a puppy. And this puppy was not about to take orders from her elder brothers. Rose dragged Homer all over the yard by his ruff, trying to induce him to play. Sometimes when he did, Orson—now possessive of this new female as well as of me—would jump in and intimidate him into stopping.

Rose was an extraordinary dog—smart as a whip, confident, possessed of boundless energy and instinct. Training her was almost irresistible, pure joy, free of all the distractions, errors, and irritations that plagued my work with Homer. She seemed to soak up work and responsibility, looking for tasks to do, taking them on. She had little interest in meeting people or cuddling— she even found mealtimes an almost annoying intrusion into her work. But she had an intense interest in any job. Was my infatuation with her yet another obstacle for Homer, another thing to come between us?

Despite my idea that I was getting Rose in part for Homer, she wound up connecting with Orson more. She was completely unfazed by his neediness and intensity, ignoring him or just dashing out of reach. Now poor Homer found himself with two dominant dogs to take his toys, filch his food, and muscle him away from me.

At some point I'd begun to enter the murky area where the boundary between the human's issues and the dog's troubles blur. I became increasingly annoyed with Homer, his avoidance, his lagging, his sniffing at every bush and tree, and, yes, his rejection.

I found myself scolding him, urging him to hurry up on walks, to pay attention. "C'mon, c'mon," I'd hiss in a voice I never used with any of my other dogs. "Let's go, let's get going."

Orson caused vastly more problems—still—but I found his antics endearing, almost appealing. The more of a nightmare he was, the closer we drew. And our training was paying off; he'd grown calmer, saner, more responsive. We were working well together. Rose didn't need any urging to work with me; she seemed to live for it. Homer was different: he was withdrawing, and his withdrawal tested my patience, which probably made him withdraw further.

Many people advised me to stop worrying about Homer. "Look, he's just a dog, and he's living a better life than 99.9 percent of the dogs on the planet. Life doesn't have to be perfect, even for dogs. You do the best you can, and he's fine."

For a number of reasons, that doesn't work for me. Does that philosophy really serve the dog, or is it designed to make the human feel better? My duty went deeper than that, I thought. The day I took on this dog, I accepted responsibility for his care. I hadn't done right by him.

As THE EMOTIONAL INTENSITY BETWEEN PEOPLE AND DOGS continues to grow, this notion has taken hold in many sectors of the dog world: once you acquire a dog, it's yours forever.

To give it to another home or, God forbid, a shelter is a breach of faith, even an act of cold-hearted betrayal. As we've come to see dogs more as members of our families and less as wonderful animals, notions that they're human-like have grown. You'd never give a child away; how could you relinquish a dog?

Yet I often saw and met dogs I believed would be happier elsewhere. Some simply couldn't cope with other pets, or didn't relate to their owners, or didn't have room to run. Some needed to work. Others were violent or aggressive and needed more isolation. Some bit passersby and deliverymen, terrified neighbors, or attacked smaller dogs. In this country alone, more than 400,000 a year bit children seriously enough to require hospital treatment.

Such animals, through no fault of their own, were causing conflict of many kinds. Sometimes their owners got sued. Houses were wrecked, insurance got canceled, police were called. Or the dogs ended up on antidepressants and other powerful medications, or confined by electronic collars. When I suggested that such a dog might simply be happier in a different environment, the answer was almost always the same: "Oh, I could never give her up. She couldn't live without me. I'll never quit on her."

My own sense of canine ethics is different. Our responsibility to these creatures is clear and powerful: we have to speak for them and protect them, since they have no voices. Turning our heads from their problems, binding them to us for life because we can, isn't, to my mind, necessarily loving. It's an abrogation of responsibility. My job is to make my dogs as happy and comfortable as is reasonable and possible. If I can't manage that, then it's my responsibility to help them find better lives. To do otherwise, it seems to me, is the crueler path.

I had messed up in so many ways. There simply are few dogs better than Homer in disposition or breeding. He was beautiful, good-hearted, and bright. He did seem to me less grounded than Orson or Rose, more easily undone. Things they could ignore—claps of thunder, cars backfiring, my losing my temper—rattled Homer, sent him retreating to his crate or scurrying into another room.

Was he happy? I wasn't sure. Was he as happy as he deserved to be? I didn't think so. Was he getting the attention he craved? Did he feel calm and safe? No.

I found it particularly chilling when a psychiatrist friend who has studied human-animal attachment offered an observation based on my laments about Homer: "You sound exactly the way you describe your father talking to you when you were a boy. It's almost as if your father's voice is coming out of your mouth." There could be few more disturbing words for me to hear. But she was right.

You can't live with Orson without shouting once in a while, and I make no apologies for that. He scarcely notices. Rose has been the kind of dog I never want to yell at, one who has benefited from my many previous screwups. But Homer upset me in a particular way, not through spectacular disasters—as when Orson went flying through our lovely leaded-glass window—but from more mundane and everyday annoyances: the way he walked (haltingly), ate (reluctantly), obeyed (intermittently). He didn't seem mine, somehow, and it amazed me to realize that I probably annoyed my father for many of the same reasons. My father and I had been estranged since I was eleven. He was continually frustrated with my sister and me, criticizing her for being overweight and difficult, exhorting me to become more athletic and confident. Impatient and judgmental, he alternately branded me a quitter or a sissy. Although he lived into his eighties, the two of us could never patch up our damaged relationship, overcome the anger we felt.

It was into this minefield—some of the most tortured parts of my past—that poor Homer had wandered. My friend was telling a shattering but obvious truth: somehow Homer had become me, and I my father, a nightmare straight out of attachment theory.

On some level I'd concluded Homer wasn't good enough. He wasn't as adventurous as the other two dogs, nor as resilient. He didn't walk as fast, react as quickly, herd competently.

Poor guy, I thought. No wonder he slept in another room.

Ruminating over how to help him, I heard from a friend in Vermont that the gamekeeper of a forest preserve was looking for a border collie to help with its small flock of resident sheep. I knew the preserve and had often walked there with my dogs; in fact, Homer loved to run there. The gamekeeper had her own house on the grounds. Homer would be an only dog with sheep in his backyard, sheep that merely needed to be moved once or twice a day from one pasture to the other. Beyond the farmstead were thousands of acres of forests and streams. A steady trickle of hikers and tourists would keep any sociable dog happy.

I was going back and forth between New Jersey and Bedlam at this point in early fall, readying the grounds, waiting for and then welcoming our own flock. From New Jersey, I called the gamekeeper for the first of what turned out to be a dozen conversations. She would love to have Homer she said; he was just what she was looking for. She'd keep him by her side all day, every day.

I can only describe the next few days as a sort of dog-related breakdown. The Homer situation had unleashed old demons. I couldn't bear the thought of giving him up but wasn't sure I could justify keeping him. All sorts of ghosts popped up—my father, the frightened kid I had been, the one who himself often felt abandoned.

Lots of people, I knew, would be shocked if I sent him off to another home. That was his appealing face on the cover of my first dog book, *A Dog Year*. He and Orson and I had just spent months traveling the country on a book tour. Yet I couldn't shake the impulse that I needed to do something for him. Sometimes, I thought, you love a dog by letting him go.

I told the gamekeeper I'd drive up the next day to leave Homer with her for perhaps two weeks; then we'd see what happened. She was thrilled. And I could picture him cavorting in the woods, chasing sheep whenever he wanted. He'd be free of my impatience and the bad job I'd done training and protecting him. He'd get to start over with a new human, one-on-one.

But two things derailed this plan. First, Paula came into my study in tears. "You can't give Homer away," she said. "This is too fast. We need to talk more about it. Maybe there's something else we can try. He loves us and we love him."

Paula kept some distance from the canine part of my life. She loved our dogs but left the walking and herding to me. Unless I was out of town, dog care was my thing, not hers. But she cherished Homer.

That same morning, my friend Ray Smith checked in. I'd met Ray and his wife, Joanne, at a reading in Vermont; we'd become instant friends. While I was trekking upstate to look at the farm and make preparations, Ray and Joanne had generously lent me their guest cabin. Dog lovers with their own sheep and a border collie, transplants from a Connecticut suburb, we had lots to talk about.

Ray, a landscape architect, was the kind of friend who dispensed advice rarely, but when he did it counted all the more. I'd e-mailed my plans for Homer and he sensed something disturbed and impulsive about the way I was pursuing it.

"Jon, I normally don't interfere in other people's decisions," he said on the phone. "But I feel I have to tell you that this doesn't feel right to me. I'm afraid you'll regret this if you do it so quickly. You don't even know this person you're bringing Homer to; you haven't even met her. I can picture how you'll feel dropping him off and driving away."

Paula's reaction and Ray's counsel pulled me up short. I called the gamekeeper, with whom I'd now had hours of discussion, to cancel the meeting. I'm sure she thought me quite mad. Actually, she was right. But people I trusted were warning me that I was being precipitous.

A few weeks later, when I called to update the gamekeeper, I learned that she'd quit her job at the preserve and gone elsewhere. My heart nearly dropped through my stomach. I owed Ray Smith a lot; so does Homer.

The next call was to Carolyn, who suggested a tough, daily regimen to repair our relationship. She wanted me to say Homer's name a hundred times a day while offering food. She wanted me—using more food—to work through a series of other grounding exercises that encourage a dog to pay attention, to see his name and commands as positive, and to experience training as a source of good things rather than yelling and disapproval.

If I could make and reinforce eye contact, convey clarity in language, keep our training positive and rewarding, then over time, Homer and I might forge a new partnership.

So every morning for two months—first in New Jersey and then on the farm—I got up before dawn to take Homer outside alone for an hour, working through these exercises. Then I put him inside and trained Rose. Then I took all three dogs for the first—though certainly not the last—walk of the day. It was exhausting. Over time, Orson was getting steadily calmer and Rose enthusiastically obedient. But Homer didn't seem to change much, at least not yet.

One of my strategies for Homer was to start plotting activities for just the two of us. We began to leave Rose and Orson behind several times a day, something I should have done much earlier: at dawn, when we trained; then late morning, when we went out to chase balls and Frisbees; and again in the late afternoon, when I began what I called the school-bus ritual. It was a neat idea, better than I first realized.

Homer loved school buses, mostly because kids came pouring off of them, and he loved kids. He was especially fond of one of our neighbors, Max, a sweet ten-year-old with a shy but easygoing nature. In a funny way, he was much like Homer, which is perhaps why the two connected. Homer adored Max from the first, and vice versa, so I thought it would be nice for him to greet Max at the bus stop.

At 3:30 P.M. the bus pulled up to the corner across from our house and a gaggle of kids came thundering out. Homer waited, and then went into his patented wriggle when Max disembarked; Max beamed and looked for Homer, knelt down to say hello, gave him a hug. Then Max and Homer would walk the half-block to his house.

By the third day, all I had to say was "Let's go see Max" and Homer would go nuts, as happy as if there were sheep outside. The other schoolkids loved Homer, too, and he was nearly drunk with joy from all the attention. The first day or two, he looked nervously around, perhaps waiting for Orson to appear and order him away. But he soon realized that greeting Max's bus was his daily task, his moment, another form of work but without competition from his siblings or scolding and criticism from me. There was no part of this task that Homer could fail at, and it was delightful to see these two guys fall in love.

It occurred to me, after only a few days, that this was the kind of relationship Homer would thrive on, and the kind I couldn't provide.

Max's family was dog-starved. He had a younger sister, Eva. His mother, Sharon, an education specialist, worked at home. His father, Hank, a magazine editor, worked grueling hours in the city but was at home several days during the week. Everybody in the family wanted a dog and talked incessantly about taking one to soccer games and playing with one in the backyard.

In fact, Max asked if Homer could come over and play. So one sunny afternoon, shortly before I was due to head back to Hebron semipermanently, I brought Homer to Max's house. I sat on the back porch with Hank, who sensed that there was more to this encounter than an interspecies playdate, but I didn't tell him what was on my mind.

In a week or two I would head north for the winter for good. I didn't plan on coming back till after our lambs were born; Paula was arranging her schedule so that she could come upstate several times. Whatever was going to happen with Homer had to happen soon or else wait for months.

I wanted, mindful of the Vermont disaster, to be careful this time. I needed to talk to Paula. She had come to see that Homer was struggling in our household but hated the idea of giving him up. And I had to think it through myself. Homer and I had been through a lot; he was like a limb or organ, an integral part of my life.

Sitting on the porch, Hank said only how much they all loved Homer, and what a great dog he was. In the yard in front of me, Max and Homer were lying down face-to-face. Max was throwing a ball over Homer's shoulder; he'd rush to grab the ball, lope back to Max, and slurp his nose.

Homer was having a blast, running in circles, tearing around the yard, smooching Max in between. I'm sure Hank noticed that I was affected by the sight, although I didn't say why. The reason was that I'd rarely seen Homer so uncomplicatedly happy.

The next few days unraveled me. I knew where this was heading, yet it brought up awful pain and anger, much of it having nothing to do with Homer. The experience of being criticized, abandoned, frightened—all feelings I was thinking about subjecting Homer to or already had—resurfaced in me. I couldn't sleep. Not even Paula could quite grasp what was happening to me.

So I called the only person I knew who would completely understand: my sister. "Of course I understand that this is unbearable for you," she said. "You think you're about to send Homer to the hell we grew up in."

Yet as a veteran dog rescuer, she also understood the animal nature of dogs. "He'll be happier. He'll adapt. And he'll be close enough so that you and Paula can watch and make sure." The family I was describing was every dog rescuer's dream, she pointed out: somebody at home almost all the time, everyone eager for a dog, young kids with energy, always somebody to play with and cuddle.

"He's had a great life with you," she told me. "But if he can't get what he wants with you and you can't get what you want with him, it's okay to let him go. You're not doing to him what was done to us. It's different, and it's all right."

An astounding thing, I thought. Finally, we were acting like a brother and sister, each helping the other out, with dogs as the vehicle.

KEEPING CLOSE WATCH ON HOMER OVER THE NEXT FEW DAYS, I could see that Jane was right. Max's whole family lined up to snuggle and play with him. Homer could give these people everything that was expected from a pet and more, and he could get all the affection he needed without having to fight for it. No frustrated owner issuing herding commands, no dominant big brother, no obnoxious puppy.

I asked Hank if he would be willing to have Homer stay there for a few days; if it went well, I said, we could talk about extending the visit further. They'd all love it, he said. I decided to drop Homer off, then take the other two dogs upstate. If things worked out, I would bring Homer up at Christmastime so our family could say its proper farewells. If things didn't, I'd drive down in a few days and take Homer back. We agreed that Paula would come by to check on things, and that Hank or Sharon and I would talk regularly, as long as necessary for us all to feel at ease and reach a mutual decision.

That night Paula and I sat in stone-faced silence and took turns hugging and stroking Homer. I was truly heartsick, going over the choices again and again. Homer would do better as an only dog. He needed a less frenetic life than I lived on Bedlam Farm with the sheep and two other crazy border collies. He needed to be the focus of love and attention. He was powerfully connected to Max, who would probably live at home for most of the rest of Homer's life. Everyone in the family was aching for a dog, and everyone loved Homer. It made enormous sense, yet it felt utterly wrenching.

The next morning, Homer hopped into bed and snuggled with me more affectionately than I could remember. We went for a long walk together before sunrise.

Then I left him in the backyard with Orson and Rose, and took his crate to Max's house down the street, along with a carton of bones, treats, and food. Inside the house, I silently reassembled the crate, lined with his favorite sheepskin and quilt. Then I put Homer on a leash, and Paula and I walked him to what might be his new home. When I handed the leash to Sharon, Homer looked at me nervously; he started to follow me out, then stopped, restrained by the leash. Walking home, I could hear him barking all the way down the block.

That night, on my late-evening walk with Orson and Rose, I saw a dog on a leash coming around the corner. Rose went wild, and Orson began thumping his tail. It was Homer. The sight of somebody else walking my dog, a creature I had loved for several years but had failed, struck deep and hard.

"Is it okay?" yelled Sharon, trying to be sensitive.

"Sure," I said.

Homer came running over to us, tail wagging, excited and confused. "Goodbye, boy," I said, at first walking past him, then turning back to lean down, stroke his head, and kiss him on the nose. He seemed anxious and bewildered, started to follow me, yelped in alarm when Sharon drew him away. His yelps sliced through me like bullets. I turned away and kept walking, feeling as if I'd left a part of myself behind. And of course, I had.

The next morning, we returned to Bedlam.

TWO MONTHS LATER, HOMER CAME UP FOR CHRISTMAS WEEK with Paula and Emma. I didn't think this sort of reunion was something we should do too often. Homer had earned his new life, and returning to ours had to be confusing and difficult for him. Dogs are not like people; they don't miss what they've left behind. They figure out the new rules, check out the food and the folks, and set out to do what they do best—adapt.

The reports from New Jersey had been encouragingly effusive. Everybody loved Homer. Nobody could believe how well-trained he was. Max was in heaven; Homer walked him to the school bus and was waiting for him when he got home. He lay next to Sharon all day as she worked in her home office; he dozed on the couch next to Hank while they watched basketball games. He availed himself of a number of sleeping options—sometimes with Hank and Sharon, sometimes with Max, once in a while with Eva. Max and his friends tossed Frisbees and balls for Homer in the yard, and he was the sensation of Max's soccer team.

Paula saw him from time to time and said he appeared at ease, wagging as he walked along. From the phone calls I could tell he was much loved: for weeks, we'd been discussing his diet, coat, emotional state, bowel movements. Over time, as it became clearer that everybody felt very comfortable about Homer—except me—I'd stopped calling.

When Paula pulled up at Christmas with Homer in the backseat, both Orson and Rose pounced happily on him, and he and I had a joyous reunion. Life quickly grew complex for him, of course. Orson went after his bones, and Rose mercilessly taunted him to play. Within a few hours, he looked beleaguered and wary again.

Over the next few days, though, things sorted themselves out. Rose was more interested in the sheep, Homer was happy to tear through the woods after chipmunks, and Orson generally ignored him. In the early morning, Homer crept up onto our bed as he always had, to bestow a series of quick licks and enjoy a cuddle before retreating—under Orson's glare—onto the dog bed on the floor.

On the last day of his visit, I took him for what I imagined might be his last adventure with sheep, no small event in the life of a border collie. I had no doubt now that he was a happier dog, that I'd made the right decision. Nor did I have any doubt that this sad turn was my responsibility, not due to any fault or shortcoming of his. I may sometimes speak with my father's voice but I will not knowingly make my father's mistakes.

When I opened the gate, Homer tore into the pasture, racing for the ewes. When I called for him to stop, he slowed down. I ran up to be near him, to make sure nobody got hurt this time. But he'd lost a step or two in his cushy suburban lifestyle, and the ewes kept their distance. By the time he caught up with them, he was winded. I came up next to him, put him in a lie-down, and sat scratching his ears while the sheep crunched peacefully on the hillside.

He settled down. "Thanks for everything, boy," I said. "I'm so sorry. You're a wonderful dog. You deserved better."

Homer licked my hand and stared at the sheep. It was probably, I thought, the last time we'd spend together like this, for both our sakes. I was grateful for it. Maybe he was, too. At the end of the week, he drove off with Paula, his head propped on the rear window ledge of her car. He was looking back at me.

It's amazing, this emotional aura that envelops us and our dogs. The pain of Homer's leaving has dulled, but it hasn't vanished. It still feels as if some part of me has gone astray. I worry about him sometimes, especially at night. How do I really know if he is happy? Is he pining for us? Sometimes I think I see him, waiting by the back door to go to the sheep, or sniffing the woodpile for chipmunks.

His is a spectral presence, invoking not only my dog, but the things the dog reminded me of, the demons he unknowingly unleashed. He was with us for three years, and the memories—his adorable puppyhood, his herding of waves and sheep, our travels across the country—don't leave just because he did. They are woven into my neural system, forever part of my life with dogs.

Rose and Orson and I have a bountiful love affair, but I know they are not nearly as good-natured. The neighborhood UPS and Fed-Ex drivers don't love them the same way, and vice versa. Rose is a working girl, through and through, impossible to distract from her mission, the Queen of Bedlam Farm. And Orson, placid and loving though he has become, will always be an idiosyncratic grump. He's the only dog I know who hates defenseless puppies. His only wish is to be within a few feet of me for as long as possible, a wish I've happily granted.

As much as I love these two—and boy, do I—I'll always miss Homer's affectionate heart. How did it come to this, I sometimes wonder. But while I regret much about Homer, I don't regret sending him off to Max and Eva and Sharon and Hank. Things didn't work out as I'd planned, but at least I didn't condemn him to the peripheries of love. Because he couldn't speak, I spoke for him. What I said was: I can't give you what you need, but I can find you somebody who will. In this, I kept faith with him.

One bitter January night, Hank checked in for the first time in a few weeks, thanking me for the hundredth time for bringing Homer into their lives. Grandparents, neighbors, schoolmates—everyone was crazy about him.

"A friend came by and fell in love with Homer," Hank told me. "He told me how lucky we were to have such a sweet, easygoing dog. I can't say enough about Homer. He's such a truly good dog." 🐑

Chapter Eight
COLD MOUNTAIN

I THINK I HADN'T REALLY LIVED A FULL AND MEANINGFUL LIFE until those January mornings when my backyard thermometer registered twenty below zero and the wind chill was far worse—and I had to take a donkey's temperature. Rectally.

To my mind, my time at Bedlam Farm with the dogs was, like the geologic periods of the earth, broken up into distinct eras: preparing the farm, training the dogs, coming to terms with Homer, experiencing a magnificent autumn.

That was the nice part. Then came life on Cold Mountain.

Winter opened early and dramatically with a thirty-inch snowfall the first week of December. By January, it was common to see readings of minus twenty degrees in early morning as I headed out through growing layers of snow and ice to do my barn chores. The cold was relentless, draining, paralyzing. Even a half hour outside left me flushed and exhausted.

My weather service radio channel—which I'd suddenly begun listening to as faithfully as any soap fan glued to a breathless drama—was issuing increasingly urgent warnings about extreme cold and frostbite.

By the third or fourth snowstorm, grizzled locals stopped clucking about Flatlander sissies and started great rolling conversations about the gripping cold that had come upon us like some plague from Canada. Septic systems froze and pipes burst as the frost burrowed deeper and deeper into the ground. Tree limbs cracked and fell. Roads and driveways were coated with ice and slick snow, despite the plow trucks working day and night. Cars ditched and batteries failed and there was an epidemic of fender benders. Furnaces broke down. Toes and fingers hurt. Noses ran. It hurt to breathe sometimes.

In the morning, when I slogged out to visit the animals, the sheep's fleece was ice-crusted. Carol and Fanny's eyelids and nostrils were sometimes frosted over, and I had to carefully brush them off until the sun got higher in the sky. Evenings seemed almost Siberian to me in their bleakness—a black shroud seemed to settle over everything at four P.M. The silence was deep, loud.

As the winter descended into a brutal cycle of cold and storm, my retiring farmer friend Carr dropped by one sub-zero morning to offer some advice. "Be careful out there, young fella," he cautioned. "I've been alone on a farm with animals in a winter like this. It can change a man." I loved the line, mostly because I could practically hear Clint Eastwood saying it. But Carr was right again: it *could* change a man. It altered perspective, changed focus, clarified what was important.

Maybe the severe winter, unusual even in a region accustomed to bad winters, had something to do with Carol getting seriously ill. I discovered her lying in the barn one morning at the height of the Arctic freeze, wheezing piteously, trying to give me her morning bray. It was the first time I'd seen her lying down, especially when I was carrying a bucket of her favorite oats. Donkeys, like dogs, are known best by the people who see them every day. You can sense when something is off, and something was seriously off with Carol.

Dr. Alderink from the Granville veterinary practice arrived a few hours later in her pickup with Tyler, her coon hound, riding shotgun. Ready for anything in her boots, overalls, and knit cap, the vet gave Carol the once over, checking her eyes, taking her temperature, listening to her lungs, examining her droppings.

"Carol, what's wrong with you?" Dr. A. mused, prodding and poking. Since it wasn't immediately clear what the trouble was, she decided to treat the most likely problems, prescribing a series of aggressive treatments for everything from a bacterial infection to sore hooves and the dread wasting disease called foundering. If Carol didn't perk up, she'd try to zero in on a more precise diagnosis. The vet left me with wrappings, syringes, pills, and powders, plus instructions on how to use all of the above. If she had any doubts about my ability to minister to Carol, she didn't let on.

I had plenty. I wanted to run alongside her truck and yell "Wait!" as it scooted out of the driveway. How could someone who months earlier was living mostly in suburban New Jersey possibly change the wrappings on a donkey's hooves? Or take her temperature with a rectal thermometer?

Perhaps Dr. Amanda knew before I did that there was no choice. My farm, my animals; my responsibility. I reviewed Anthony's Three Steps: take your head out of your ass, calm down, pay attention. Though lately I had taken to adding a Fourth Step: If all else fails, call Anthony.

That night, I gave Carol her injections, wrapped her hooves, and took her temperature. She bucked and balked, whinnied and tried to run for it, but I persevered, calmly and with plenty of cookies. Poor Carol. The cold and her illness were bad enough; my amateur treatments would probably make her even more uncomfortable.

Over the next few days, her condition worsened. She was lying down all the time, eating sporadically, wheezing continually. Dr. Amanda came by every day or so, but there wasn't much more to prescribe. All we could do was wait and see.

Anthony also began coming by more often, as he always did when trouble erupted. He summoned his father-in-law, Dean Hanks, and his brother-in-law, Darrow, from Big Green Farm in Salem, one of the largest and best known dairy farms in Washington County; they also took to stopping by.

Nobody said anything, but I knew why they were now regular visitors. First, they'd be a great help in case Carol needed surgery or some intervention and needed to be restrained. These guys were the size of oak trees. Second, if Carol didn't make it, they could help haul her body away. I couldn't bury her on the farm with the ground frozen hard, but they had a bigger working farm where large animals were commonly disposed of.

It was probably five or six days after I began treating her that Carol decided she'd had enough. That evening, she did what she always did when I reached for the thermometer—she tried to bolt. Even cookie bribery couldn't settle her down this time, though. I couldn't manage to close the barn door, either, held open by piles of rock-solid ice.

I brought Rose back to assist, and she lay down in front of Carol—just as the donkey made her break. At least, probably because of the dog, Carol hesitated long enough for me to get my arms around her neck. But though she slowed down, I couldn't completely stop her, and we wound up doing a tap dance up the slope, me holding on with one arm and struggling to put a leather halter on her with the other, all so that I could stick a thermometer up her butt. "It's okay, Carol," I was calling as she dragged me along. "It's for your own good."

Even Anthony's code didn't quite cover this. I was grateful for the darkness, so my neighbors and the Hanks boys couldn't witness this spectacle.

In a few minutes I did manage to stop her; it helped that she was weaker than usual. I took my glove off to open the thermometer case and pull a syringe of medicine from my back pocket.

It must have been then that two of my fingers got frostbitten.

I'd heard the weather predictions and I'd pulled on layer after layer of clothing, but there was no way to manipulate syringes, halters, and medications with gloves (I learned about glove liners only later). The cold was numbing, the wind savage, but they didn't feel all that different than on previous nights. Anyway, I was focused on Carol's medications. After my gloves were off for about ten minutes—much too long—the fingers on my right hand began to ache and burn. But then, so did my nose, my face, damn near everything.

I finished up with Carol, squirted an antibacterial down her throat, took her back to the barn, stuck my throbbing hand into a glove and into my pocket and ran for the house. Inside, I peeled off my outer clothing and saw that the tips of two fingers were a ghostly gray. I filled a pot with warm water, stuck them in.

Although the pain was acute, the discoloration wasn't deep and I could move my fingers, so I wasn't too worried. Anyway, I'd have to wait until morning for the nearest clinic to open. (A new doctor had set up practice in Salem, happily.)

At the clinic, I got some salve and ointments and a lecture on the stupidity of taking gloves off in this kind of weather—though when I explained about my sick donkey, the doctor and nurse stopped chiding and grew more sympathetic.

But I grasped that bare skin can't be exposed in such weather for that long. My fingers would be cold sensitive and in some pain every winter for the rest of my life, and the doctor warned that if I exposed them to the cold that way again, I'd suffer a worse fate.

He also surprised me by suggesting, after an exam, that I might be suffering from hypothermia, too. The fatigue, drowsiness, and other symptoms I'd mentioned indicated a body that wasn't able to keep itself warm. In a way, the diagnosis came as a relief. I was so tired so often, I'd been quietly afraid that something was seriously wrong. For the past two or three weeks, I'd been nodding off by late afternoon. More liquids, more rest, shorter stretches outside, the doc advised.

I hired Anthony to feed the animals for the following week. It seemed so much easier for him: he zipped by early in the morning, Arthur in tow; vaulted over the fence; finished in fifteen minutes what it took me an hour or two to accomplish. The temptation to keep him at it until about May was great, but the feed and vet bills were piling up, and I was committed to caring for the animals myself.

Still, the frostbite was a reminder that I was navigating a strange land, still finding my way. I had learned at my cabin in past years not to take deep winter lightly. But there, bitter cold merely meant bringing in more firewood, taking shorter walks with the dogs. At the farm, my tasks were more demanding, and there was no withdrawing.

So after a week's respite, I resumed trudging out three or four times a day to feed and water the animals and check on the barn. And I kept giving Carol her medications, changing her hoof bandages, taking her temperature.

Outside on winter mornings the smoke curled from every chimney in the hamlet, from the old mill houses down the hill to the white farmhouses off in the distance. There were wispy trails rising from my place, too, thanks to the woodstove I kept going all night to warm the far side of the house. The oil furnace chugged along all day and night as well. The creaky old house held up well, but there were some nights no heating system could keep up.

In the kitchen, I could see my breath. The olive oil and peanut butter froze in the cabinet near the back wall, as did the dishwashing liquid by the sink. At night, struggling to stay awake long enough to read, I sat in the living room swathed in blankets.

RUNNING A FARM CHANGES ONE'S VIEW OF ANIMALS AND, TO some extent, of life. Hours and days are shaped by rituals, the satisfying sense of knowing everyone is well cared for, the need to take action—and never a simple action, somehow—when they're not.

For most of the farmers around me, animals were not pets but commodities, and vet bills could mean the difference between survival and failure. Competing with giant farm conglomerates, these men and women fought to cope with skyrocketing feed and fuel costs, the quixotic and unpredictable nature of animals, the grueling physical work.

In America, the story of the little guy standing up to the big corporation is so painfully familiar nobody really wants to hear it anymore. The little guy always loses, and many of the farmers around Hebron know they are doomed. Their sons and daughters don't want to live such difficult lives, and it seems that every bureaucratic decision and economic shift stacks the deck against them even more. Which is never more on their minds than in a winter like this.

I stopped by the variety store one afternoon when Pete Handley and Stan Bates, two weary dairy farmers from North Hebron, were commiserating there over coffee. They'd been wrestling for weeks with burst pipes, frozen oil lines in tractors and trucks, manure piles that couldn't be shoveled, punishing oil and electric bills. "Every degree down the thermometer is a nail in the coffin," Pete said quietly.

The cold took its toll at Bedlam Farm, too, though the consequences were less dire. Later in January, I noticed one of my ewes wandering off alone—an alarming sign in sheep, who are not given to individual exploration.

I came out one bone-chilling morning and saw her alone in the pasture, wandering in circles, strips of wool hanging from her side. When I went to investigate, I saw that her flesh was ripped and exposed. I'd heard that coyotes, made desperate by the cold and the unyielding ice pack, were getting more aggressive; I'd seen their tracks around the pasture. Perhaps the ewe, sick or weakened by the weather, had wandered off by herself and been attacked.

It was hard to find a large-animal vet available; they were all out tending to distressed animals. I left messages at various offices, describing the ewe's disorientation and her wounds, asking what to do. Her odd behavior was also affecting Rose, who was leaving the flock behind to chase her. I worried that my puppy was getting too aroused, becoming more of a hunter than a herder as she pursued the stricken ewe around the pasture. It was a bad situation for both of them.

The vet who eventually called back in the afternoon sounded harried, even frantic. It would be a day, even two, before he or anybody else in his practice could get to the farm, he said. Horses and cows were suffering from the cold all over the county, and they, worth so much more to their owners, took priority. Meanwhile, the sheep might die from the cold or from infection.

And to be honest, he added, vets and their hypodermics weren't always the most humane way to euthanize a sick sheep. "We might have to stab them six or seven times before we find a vein. It isn't always pretty. Do what you think best."

The forecast was calling for temperatures of minus fifteen or below that night. I gave the ewe a penicillin shot to try to ward off infection and brought her into a stall in the barn, but she refused to eat. This was so unusual that I called a friend, a sheep farmer in nearby Argyle, who was even more blunt than the vet. "If you're asking me what the humane thing is, I would definitely say shoot her. To have a vet do it with a needle is no less stressful and sometimes takes a lot longer. If you do it right, it will be quick and painless."

Doing it right was the issue. I'd gone thirty years since basic training without firing or even holding a gun; now I was contemplating my second execution in a couple of months. I could call Anthony, who would handle it if I asked, yet that bothered me. Did I really want somebody else doing the dirty work? If anybody was going to shoot one of my farm animals, shouldn't it be me? Was it more humane to use a syringe than a bullet? Was it even right to drag a vet out here at the expense of some other animal that needed help and pile further bills on top of what I'd already spent, and was still spending, on Carol?

The cold was horrendous, and the ewe was still refusing food and water. In spring, even in a milder winter, there might be other options. But it was clear that she was suffering. She might even have something contagious that could endanger the rest of the flock, or she could attract predators who would attack the others. I had to respond.

Anthony was matter-of-fact. "I'll be over first thing in the morning," he said when I called with the news. "You have to do what you have to do, what's right for the farm."

Because I did, in fact, know what I had to do, I took Rose and Orson out into the pasture early the next morning to herd the healthy sheep into the training pen. I locked the flock in, along with a bale of hay I'd dragged from the barn on a children's sled. The cold was stinging, and my damaged fingers ached dully. I took the dogs into the house, and came back outside with my rifle.

I went through Anthony's safety checklist, making sure the chamber was empty and the safety was on, pointing the rifle up and away from buildings, property, other animals.

I shooed Fanny into the barn, where she ran behind Carol, still lying listlessly on the straw. Then I put a crook on the ewe's neck and guided her outside, far enough behind the barn for safety. She looked rheumy and weak and her wounds were still oozing. She barely protested when I straddled her back and placed the rifle barrel at the base of her skull. I loaded the clip, slid a round into the chamber, clicked the safety off.

I fired five or six shots in rapid succession. Blood spurted all over my gun, boots, and jeans. The ewe dropped to the snowy ground, twitched for a second, and then lay still. I stood numbly and watched.

Darrow Hanks drove into the driveway a few minutes later; probably Anthony had dispatched him. "What's up?" he said quietly, as if he didn't know.

He took in the scene and, saying nothing else, hopped over the fence. He'd brought a strand of baling wire, with which he tied the ewe's front and rear legs together and lifted her off the ground, where her blood was already beginning to freeze in the snow. He carried the carcass to his pickup and hoisted it into the truck bed.

"I had to shoot her," I mumbled, following slowly. "She was sick and cold, all chewed up, and the donkey is sick, too . . ."

"I know," Darrow said. "I've done it fifty times. It's part of it all." Before he climbed into the truck cab, he turned back to me. "This is what running a farm is like," he said. "It happens. All the time."

I got the message. This wasn't a drama or crisis, but the very nature of raising animals. No tears were going to be shed hereabouts for sick livestock. The farm fantasy was revealing its painful underside. I didn't have the money, or the desire, to hire people to do all the jobs—the happy or the miserable ones—that had to be done. I had to make decisions. I was going to stand or fall on my own two increasingly sore feet.

Not long after Darrow drove off, Anthony himself came roaring up. He seemed surprised that I had done the shooting myself. "I would have helped you," he said, prepared to spare me something he figured I couldn't handle. But because of him, I could.

"I know it's tough, but I'm proud of you," he said.

"It was my sheep," I said.

But I was a bit of a wreck. I didn't bring sheep to the farm to kill them. I had grazed with that sheep a couple of dozen times. I understood death was part of life on a farm, but it still felt lousy. Anthony said nothing, just grabbed a shovel and spread fresh snow over the blood.

THIS WAS THE ESSENCE OF LIFE ON THE FARM—UPROAR AND confusion, continuously, unpredictably. Surprises and setbacks, assaults and challenges weren't the exceptions but the rule. The quicker you accepted that, the sooner you got to steady ground.

Still, the ferocity of winter made daily life a struggle. I was exhausted from tending to Carol, checking on her every few hours. She was hanging in there, but despite the medicines I administered, the wrapped and rewrapped hooves, she still wasn't herself.

I had also fallen several times on the snow and ice, twisting my bad ankle painfully, twice briefly losing consciousness. By now I was hobbling like an ancient man and my chronic bronchitis had erupted with a fury. Paula insisted that I call her every night before going to sleep, so she could be sure I wasn't lying outside, slowly freezing to death beyond anyone's earshot.

If you don't want to deal with it, go live somewhere else, Anthony pointed out in his usual blunt style one night while I was whining on the phone about the cold. Nobody forced you to buy a farm in upstate New York, so take it seriously.

I went to the Salem Agway and bought ski masks to protect my face, insulated nerdy hats with earflaps. I ordered thermal socks online, and liners for my gloves, so that when I took off the outer gloves I'd still have some protection. I put pots of water on the woodstove for moisture. Paula, up for a week's visit in February, brought a tub of heavy-duty moisturizer and I slathered all my extremities with gels and ointments.

I changed my animal-feeding times, so that I ventured out-side an hour or two later in the morning, when the cold was slightly less brutal. And I broke up the chores—tote hay at eight, fill the water tub at ten, put out feed at two. If it was ten below—and it often was—I didn't stay out for more than ten minutes at a stretch. I drank pots of tea and gallons of water. I kept the woodstove roaring day and night.

I refused to yield on the herding lessons, though: each dog, twenty minutes each, one in late morning, the other in the after-noon, every day, no matter what.

Rose seemed unaffected by the cold. She scampered around the pasture as if it were April. But Orson was hobbling as the ice stung his paws and caked up between his toes. Standing out by the training pen, swathed and frozen, was a test of faith for me.

We walked the sheep to the training pen every morning, then worked on directionals—"come bye," and "away to me." Some-times the wind roared so loudly the dogs couldn't hear me. Some-times I couldn't see them even on the other side of the pen, as sleet blurred my glasses. But Rose never wavered in her interest and enthusiasm, and I was determined not to waver in mine.

Keeping faith, like conquering impatience and soothing anger, had become an important goal. To see what the dogs and I could accomplish together, that wasn't negotiable.

THE OTHER ANIMALS HAD THEIR OWN COPING MECHANISMS. Even though the artesian well kept flowing behind the barn, it was quickly surrounded by vast globs of impenetrable ice, so I kept a big tub of water by the barn, stuck an electric de-icer in it, and changed the water daily. Carol and Fanny rarely left the barn these days, so I dumped some hay there for them and closed off one side to protect them from the wind. Carol was hanging on, not worse, not better; at least I could try to spare her the most frigid gales. The sheep climbed to the top of the pasture and huddled together for warmth. They moved less, it seemed, perhaps to conserve energy. I put out extra hay, corn, and feed.

I worried about the sheep. Why wouldn't they seek shelter in the barn? To my farmer neighbors, like Carr, this was more misplaced Flatlander sentimentality. "They don't know it's cold," he said, "and they don't care. They've been living without shelter for thousands of years." They would come into the barn if they needed to, Dr. Alderink agreed. They never did, not once.

Carr could afford to be philosophical. He was about to escape to Florida for a couple of months to share a trailer his daughter had rented for the winter. He'd be playing with his grandkids, sitting out on a lawn chair in the sun, perhaps mulling the knee replacements made necessary by years of milking at all hours. He seemed more resigned to the trip than eager to leave. He confided to me once that he'd never planned to retire—"Farming is a way of life," he said. But, as he put it, his knees and bank account were giving out at about the same time.

Everybody else was still wrestling with the winter. Road crews kept salting and sanding, their trucks grinding and roaring constantly. Plumbers were in high demand. Schools closed. Only Anthony seemed unaffected, shuffling over ice and snow with Ida in one arm, puppy Arthur chugging behind. He hiked, tracked, puttered, snowmobiled. Like a border collie, he hated to be still, and always preferred to be outside, looking for work. Only once or twice did he mutter about the "wicked cold."

The weather affected me differently. Before winter came, writing was my full-time job. Now it seemed on some days a struggle to get any writing done at all; farming had taken over. Sheep needed hay; dogs needed walking and herding practice; donkeys needed medicine. It was relentless. I could only imagine what Carr's much-longer days had been like.

The original snow from early December had hardened like concrete on the ground, buried under several more feet from more recent storms. The National Weather Service announced that December and January had brought the most snow and the longest period of below-freezing temperatures in nearly thirty years.

The outdoors had gone still, songbirds and hawks—even crows—vanishing. The deer and coyotes were growing desperate; I saw tracks everywhere around the barns. When the dogs and I went out at night, they tensed and barked at things I couldn't see or hear. We saw foxes and a few squirrels; otherwise it seemed as if all life had simply disappeared, gone south with Carr.

Everything became progressively harder. Yet I loved the solitude of the farm, the ritual of the chores, the herding with the dogs, the point in the day when we were all spent and the dogs had been out for their final walk, and I could pull off my boots and hole up with a good book until I fell asleep, which never took long. Exhausted by the grueling routine, the dogs were sometimes so tired they didn't notice that I'd gone upstairs to bed. But whenever I woke up—at five or six or seven A.M.—the two of them were in bed alongside me, dozing peacefully on a heavy quilt in a farmhouse at the top of Cold Mountain.

I WAS GRATEFUL FOR THE LOVE AND COMPANIONSHIP OF DOGS. But I never better understood how much I needed humans. Fortunately for me, there were some excellent ones around.

Ray and Joanne Smith met me every Tuesday at the Central House in Salem for steak and a slice of caramel apple pie. We chatted about the cold, their sheep and mine, our working dogs, and the whole strange experience of being refugees from the New York suburbs with new lives we'd come to love.

Even before winter hit, Ray and Joanne later conceded, they'd had doubts about whether I would last here. But they were one of the reasons I had, so far. One or the other of them checked in almost daily. Joanne provided a stream of advice on sheep care, along with names and numbers of everyone from farriers and vets to M.D.s for humans.

In fact, she was the reason I was no longer dodging Nesbitt. Online, she located a 4-H family in Massachusetts who kept Tunis sheep and had a high tolerance for rams—"It's just their nature to get touchy," the father told me sweetly—and who'd come to collect Nesbitt in the family pickup in November. "You better be grateful to Joanne," I hissed as Nesbitt was led out of my pasture and my life. "Otherwise you'd be stew." I resisted the impulse to slug him one last time.

Joanne and Ray had that subtle gift of good friends—they knew when I needed a call, steered me in the right direction when I was doing something dumb, encouraged me when I was struggling. Their calls and our dinners anchored me.

I was beginning to see that some of the real power of dogs, perhaps unappreciated, isn't just in their comforting us when we're alone, but in helping us to be *less* alone. Friends like Ray and Joanne are not common, and I wouldn't have had them in my life if not for our dogs.

Neither would I have had Anthony. Our friendship had solidified during our battles about what kind of ride-along dog to get, and deep winter had brought new reasons to feel grateful for it.

Nevertheless, by mid-January, I was a mess. My fingers ached with frostbite, my knees rebelled at all the trudging and toting, my ankle was in perpetual turmoil from slipping on ice. My back throbbed from hours of dragging firewood into the house and hauling bales of hay and bandaging hooves. My skin was so dry it was flaking off, and bronchitis had me coughing and rasping.

If the winter taught me anything, it was to accept that I was getting older. Yes, it was a brutal winter, taking a toll on everybody. But it would have affected me differently even a few years earlier. There were limits to what I could take now. The morning chores so wearied me that I was falling asleep at the computer at noon. I was popping anti-inflammatory pills like popcorn. My conceit—that I was no "gentleman farmer," that the dogs and I could do this alone—was the epitome of hubris. Yet I couldn't let it go. I am not a brave or courageous person, but I am a willful one. The only way I was going to leave the farm this winter was in a hearse, I told myself. I finish what I start.

One morning, awake at five A.M., I threw on a pair of sweatpants and a jacket and let the dogs out. It was profoundly discouraging to feel so achy and spent even before the sun had risen. The sun was unlikely to show itself that bleak morning, anyway; the valley was shrouded in yet another layer of new snow, topped with a veneer of icy rain.

The thermometer said minus fifteen. I dreaded shoveling and wading through the mess to carry out extra feed and hay. I had to muck out the barn, where the donkeys dumped all night, and put water into the tub by the barn.

When Orson and Rose came rushing back in, snow-covered from charging around the giant drifts that surrounded the house like a Civil War fortress, I made a sudden judgment call. "Sorry guys," I said, "but I'm sleeping in for a while." I turned up the heat and crawled back into bed. It was my lowest point; I was wearing out.

As great working dogs do, mine entered the spirit of the moment, hopping onto the foot of the bed, sleeping quietly alongside me. I think I must have had a fever that morning; I simply crashed. I heard Rose growl a few times, was vaguely aware that Orson had gone downstairs to investigate something, but I paid no attention.

I woke up at eight-thirty in a rush of guilt and alarm. When people ask about the single most powerful feeling in owning a farm, I always say it's the responsibility of caring for so many utterly dependent creatures. If I don't haul feed and hay, they don't eat. If I don't drag the hose out of the basement and across to the barn, they don't drink.

I hustled out of bed and pulled on my thermal socks, long underwear, two layers of shirts, a neck warmer, a hat over a ski mask, gloves and liners, and thermal boots supposed to protect feet at forty below and likely to get a chance to prove it any day.

I must have looked like a country version of the Pillsbury Dough Boy. I could barely climb down the stairs in all those clothes. I was hacking and sneezing and already limping, and I hadn't even left the house.

When I stepped out the back door, I was stunned. Paths had been shoveled everywhere—around the door, around my truck, along the back of the house to the barns and the pasture gates, even to the bird feeders. The hay feeder was filled with hay. The feed trough held corn and feed and the sheep were happily chowing down. The donkeys' oats were in their buckets and Carol and Fanny were crunching away. The water tub was already filled to the brim.

"Lord," I said to the dogs. "This is a miracle." I have never needed a kindness more.

I am a lucky man with a wonderful family who loves his work, but I have not been as fortunate, or perhaps as worthy, when it comes to friendship. I find it hard to talk to strangers. I do not expect help to materialize when I most need it. I don't believe people will extend themselves on my behalf. I'm not good at asking for help, anyway, or at accepting it. But Ray and Joanne had breached that wall, and Anthony just leaped right over it.

Holly told me later that Anthony got up at five that morning to plow driveways for several relatives. "Jon has got to be in trouble, buried in all this," he told her, then headed over to save my life.

The gift was more meaningful than he knew. It was great to walk on the path without falling or twisting my leg, but it was the morale boost that meant the most. There was somebody out there who cared about me enough to do this.

I laughed and whistled. Even the dogs picked up on my mood, tearing up and down the newly dug paths. I thought that even with so much winter still ahead, I'd turned a corner. With a friend like that nearby, I would be all right.

. . .

I WOULDN'T HAVE MISSED A DAY OF THIS WINTER'S EERIE AND demanding beauty, but I also couldn't wait to say I'd gotten through it, although there were times I wasn't so sure I would.

People needed one another in the winter, and they knew it. They seemed to go out of their way to wave to a passing driver, to chat at the market or the gas pump. Nobody could really make it entirely alone, so community seemed to flourish. People kept an eye on their elderly neighbors, shoveled their walks, made sure they were warm, asked if they needed a ride to market.

When I got what was left of my hair trimmed at one of my favorite Washington County places—Janet's Beauty Salon in tiny Shushan—the little shop was usually filled with elderly women sitting under big blue dryers.

One of the women was Miriam, who was ninety-four, mostly deaf and blind, but still went to Grange and town meetings. It took the entire town of Shushan to get Miriam to the beauty parlor, although she didn't know it.

Miriam lived alone in a small house on the edge of town, refusing all offers of help. So when she had her weekly appointment, everyone mobilized discreetly. Somebody stopped traffic on one side of the road when she was ready to cross, and somebody was waiting on the other. Janet held the door open and guided Miriam to her seat.

After her steely hair was done up in waves that were probably very chic in 1948, she crossed the street again. ("Thank you, young man," she told me when I asked if I might accompany her, "but I've been crossing this street longer than you've been alive.") She stopped at Yushak's Market for a cup of coffee and a chat with Dennis or Debbie Yushak, and then somebody walked her home with her groceries for the week. There were probably similar stories to be told in every hamlet nearby.

As Carr predicted, I was not the same at the end of the winter, not even in the middle of it. Even as my appreciation for my dogs grew, so did my sense of human community. Each drop of the thermometer seemed a reminder that people and dogs work best when mixed together. Sometimes, dogs can lead you to the people you need.

While I truly doubt I could have endured winter without my two canine oddballs, I also couldn't have made it without the dozen telephone conversations I had each day with my wife, my sister, friends new and old, and the encouragement and sympathy of this new community. We were in it together, all of us, those with fur and those without.

In early February, I came out of the house as the sun came up to hear Carol's hee-haw. It was nearly thirty degrees, balmy by recent standards, even though another snow-and-ice barrage was due that evening. Carol sounded stronger, and she looked better, too—up on her feet, out of the barn, eating hay in the pasture, Fanny placidly following along.

It didn't quite register that we had saved Carol until a few days later at the variety store. "Good to see your donkey up and around," said one of the townspeople, a woman who looked up at the farm each morning when she got into her car to go to work and loved the sight of the donkeys at the feeder. For a few miserable weeks she hadn't seen them at all as they hunkered in the barn, and of course, like everyone else in town, she'd heard of Carol's illness. Now Carol and Fanny had emerged, like large, fuzzy robins.

"It helped me get through the winter," she said. "Some people would have put her down or let it go."

I allowed myself a little ripple of pride. I had spent many cold hours giving Carol her oats, petting and soothing her, plying her with medications, playing her favorite tunes, bandaging her hooves. Taking her temperature, too. And she had come through it. We had all come through it. 🐑

Chapter Nine
DOG DAYS II

IT TOOK ME A LONG TIME—YEARS OF LIVING WITH DOGS—TO understand how many of the problems that often mark human relationships with these remarkable animals have more to do with the people than the dogs. Only recently have I really grasped that when I complain about something my dog is doing, I'm often speaking about my own behavior.

Training a dog is something of a spiritual experience when done properly, a meshing of the instincts and traits of two very different species trying to live together harmoniously. But the spiritual stuff tends to get subsumed in all the yelling, tugging, even electro-shocking that passes for dog training in much of America.

Dogs are born knowing exactly what they want to do: eat, scratch, roll in disgusting stuff, sniff and squabble with other dogs, roam, sleep, have sex. Little of this is what we want them to do, of course. We ask them to sit, stay, smell pleasant, practice abstinence, and be accommodating.

The manner in which we breach this great divide—a chasm often overlooked in all the happy talk about dogs—defines our relationships with these creatures. We love to share our warm and fuzzy stories, but we sometimes don't want to acknowledge just how alien a mind like Orson's is.

So we scold them, bribe them, at times even beat them, to change them, adapt them to our needs and expectations. Yet they have powerful, stubborn, sometimes immovable instincts of their own.

When there's conflict, people tend to blame the dog. "I want him to sit; why won't he?" "He's defiant," we say. "She's so independent." We never say, "I don't know how to train him" or "I lose my temper" or "I say too many confusing things."

If it's true that having a better dog requires that we be better humans—and I believe it—the daily drama of Orson and the donkey droppings reminded me of how far he had come, and how far I have to go.

Orson herding sheep is a spectacular sight. He can herd trucks, buses, and kids on skateboards with Discovery Channel grace. But he herds sheep by charging full speed into the fray, wreaking havoc. He is an excitable kind of dog; any voice command results in his spinning, barking, and racing pell-mell across the pasture. The first time I entered him in a herding trial, beginner's division, he knocked a judge down and the sheep leaped over the fence and ran for their lives.

Things are calmer now, but not by as much as I'd hoped. I thought that by spring, after months of practice, Orson might begin grasping the fundamental principle of herding—that the idea is to go around, not through, the flock and bring the sheep to me, or to wherever I tell him.

I understand that this is an ideal, a goal; it may happen and it may not, and I will love him just as much either way. I also understand that for this to happen, the creature who has to change is the one without the fur.

One February day, Orson rushed up to the pasture gate, barking and spinning as always. When I unlatched it, the donkeys prudently headed for the barn.

I always said the same thing at this point: "Let's go get the sheep."

Rose would have raced out to wherever the sheep were to begin circling and collecting them.

But Orson, marching as usual to the beat of his own odd drummer, invariably raced to the apple tree fifty yards away where the donkeys like to take their dumps and began scarfing down chunks of donkey poop. This was just as disgusting as it sounds.

Every day I told myself I would pay no attention to this behavior. Every day I ended up screaming at him to leave it, drop it, or come *now*.

"Forget about it," Carolyn had advised me back when we first began herding in Pennsylvania and the attraction was sheep poop. "It's perfectly normal, it won't hurt him, and the sooner you shut up about it, the sooner he'll stop doing it." So I had no excuses. I knew from the first that this was a behavior that had to be ignored to be eliminated.

Orson is a genius at attracting my attention; it's his true sport. He doesn't do tricks, and his sheepherding is, to say the least, spotty. But he never tires of seeking my attention and rarely fails to get it, nor does he care much about the consequences.

He barks when the crowd applauds at readings. He muscles other dogs aside if they come within ear-scratching distance. He insists on staying within a twenty-foot radius of me, even if it means leaving sheep behind or letting them run off.

I understand, and have for years, that the proper way to train a dog is to make commands simple, clear, and positive. Perhaps the most common mistake owners make is that they only pay attention when their dogs are misbehaving. Thus the dog learns that to get his human to talk to or look at him, he has to do whatever provokes a reaction. The proper response, however, is to avoid reinforcing unwanted behaviors by ignoring them, to notice and praise behaviors that *are* wanted.

I also know that it's quite common for dogs—especially predatory ones like border collies—to eat other animals' droppings. They were bred to spend days out on the moors with their charges, not to enjoy organic food from clean bowls. To lap at a mud puddle or scarf up calorie-rich poop is actually sensible. But because we see dogs as quasi-human, we react as we would if human members of our family were doing it. Yelling at dogs to stop just makes them anxious—thus more likely to eat the stuff—and calls attention to the behavior.

Almost any experienced dog trainer on Earth would offer the same advice: ignore it and it will go away. Don't scold when your dog's screwing up; praise him when he isn't. I get this idea; I embrace it fully. I try to incorporate it into my training.

Yet I doubt there's been a day in my relationship with Orson when I haven't grumbled, muttered, or yelled at him, even as my love for him has grown.

For example: because he doesn't want to be out of my sight, when we go for walks, he trots fifteen feet ahead, then turns around to wait. If I stop walking, he sits down. This bugs me, not because it matters, but because Orson isn't living up to my expectations of a happy dog. I want him off running and romping and looking joyous, not clinging neurotically to me. So I snarl—"Get away!"—and urge him to run, go, be free. I know better, but sometimes the more we love the dog, the more we mess up.

Similarly, in the three years that we've been around sheep, there's hardly been a time when we enter the pasture that I haven't made a mental note to be quiet when he eats sheep poop. I can count the times I've managed to do it.

At the farm, this issue escalated. Orson had developed a taste for donkey dung.

Why did I care?

I found the sight repulsive. I found it infuriating, believing (wrongly) that he was challenging my authority. It impeded our herding lessons since while he snacked, the sheep were heading rapidly up the hill. He was a sheepdog. I'd gone to great trouble to put him together with sheep. Why would he rather eat poop?

It was also embarrassing. I'd been training this dog for nearly four years. Shouldn't this issue be resolved?

It hadn't been, not because there was something wrong with him, but because there were things wrong with me. Orson couldn't reason all this out the way I supposedly could. His instincts guided him to an action; but my intellect should prevail over my reflexes. It hadn't.

There were, of course, certain practical issues. Trainers can talk all they want about ignoring the dog while he gobbles this stuff, but they're not around when the dog later vomits in your truck or has diarrhea on the living-room carpet. Dog lovers know that what comes in goes out, often in explosive fashion. I didn't care how natural the behavior was. I didn't like it; I didn't want him to do it.

Yet he truly couldn't help it.

So knowing all this, why couldn't I stop? Why couldn't I reinforce him for something else, like *not* eating poop? Why did he get my goat every time, despite my Churchillian resolve? Every day I failed, until this February day in the middle of the winter from hell. It was a freezing morning. We were slogging through the still-deep snow, augmented by a few fresh inches from a squall overnight. I had decided that morning to calm Orson down by saying nothing for most of our lesson.

Because of the new snow, most of the sheep and donkey

droppings were covered. But up by the apple tree, there was a fresh pile. As we entered the pasture, Orson veered off and made a beeline for it.

I stopped, closed my eyes, took a deep breath. This was going to be the day I made some progress.

As Orson veered right, straight toward the pile, I headed left, straight toward the sheep. I didn't turn to see what he was doing, just quickened my steps. Moving steadily, silently toward the sheep, I muttered a little mantra: "Keep walking, say nothing. Keep walking, say nothing." I felt something shift within me. Like an alcoholic walking away from booze, I felt a higher power at work, and it was an exhilarating sensation. Maybe I could change.

As I neared the sheep in the training pen, I tossed a few handfuls of corn over the fence and yelled, "Hey, sheep! Yo sheep!" I heard paws thundering behind me and Orson came racing past, circling the pen and barking.

We finished our lesson, then turned and left the pasture. Keep walking. Say nothing. Keep walking. Say nothing. All the way to the gate and out.

Victory! I had done it. I dropped to my knees and shouted for joy. Orson came rushing over, alarmed, and I gave him a giant bear hug. How strange he must have thought me, praising him effusively for what he hadn't done.

After years of trying, including more than four months at the farm, I was finally able to look the other way.

I did the same thing the next day.

The day after, I forgot and yelled at Orson. But then the next time, I got back on track.

It was a small thing, but it felt great; I was proud of us both. I was allowing Orson to change his behavior naturally, without tension or shouting. I was getting some reinforcement, too. Day by day, the intervals between my heading for the sheep and his appearing at my side grew shorter.

On the seventh or eighth day, he loped right past the pile and headed for the sheep. I raised my arms to the sky and danced a small jig. When Orson came running over, exuberant but confused, I showered him with hugs and treats. "Thank you, thank you," I told him. "You have helped me to be a slightly better human than I was last week." Forgetting for a second where it had so recently been, I kissed his nose.

I can't say that he has never eaten droppings since, or that I have never reflexively yelled at him to stop. I have. But these outbursts are becoming rarer, as his interest in fecal matter diminishes. We're having fun.

Who knows? If we herd sheep for another decade or so, I might make it: I might become a patient man. So much for Freud. Give me a good dog any day.

I HAVE KEPT MY WORD. WHEN I CAME TO THE FARM, I PROMISED myself each dog would have a daily herding lesson, no matter what. And we didn't miss a day, not in rain nor snow, et cetera, et cetera.

After the sheep and donkeys were fed and watered and the barn mucked out, and before I began to write, I had a cup of morning coffee and some toast and fruit. I ate breakfast standing by the kitchen window, watching and studying my sheep. If I didn't yet love them, at least I could try to understand them.

After a second cup of coffee, I put on my earmuffs, ski mask, knit cap, hooded jacket, et cetera et cetera (and that was only the top layer), and tossed some beef jerky into Orson's crate; he happily trotted inside. Rose then ran to the mudroom, where I kept my now-repulsive rubber boots. If I began putting them on, she barked and headed for the back door. By now, Rose and I were starting to act in rhythm.

I'd watched Carolyn Wilki train dozens of herding dogs in Pennsylvania, read many books, and e-mailed some trainers I liked and trusted. Still, it was risky to put a high-powered working dog like Rose in the hands of an impatient, gimpy, and easily frustrated novice. If it didn't work, I'd have harmed another dog—hardly the reason I came to Bedlam Farm.

Take the long view, an Irish trainer e-mailed me. Let Rose find her own comfort level. Discourage freelance chasing around, but give her enough freedom so that she can build her confidence and hone her instincts. Keep lessons short and focused. Have a goal in mind, and if she achieves it, cut your losses and get out. Don't talk too much: you don't want her looking at you all the time; she's supposed to be watching the sheep.

That added up to a lot of things to keep in my head during lessons. But I clung mostly to what Wink, my favorite trainer-advisor, had said: "Trust her. You trust the dog to herd the sheep; the dog trusts you to tell her what you need. Respect her. Let her show you how it's done. Support her when she needs it, correct her when you must, but they're her sheep and it's her pasture.

"One day you will find that the two of you are working together, and that will be a beautiful day," he predicted. Yes, it would. But it still seemed quite a way off.

Though she was less than a year old, Rose already had a commanding authority around sheep. She also had the speed to move around them quickly and head them off without getting nasty.

Still, the Homer experience made me gun-shy. I had messed up one dog I loved, to the point that I had to give him to somebody else. I didn't want that to happen to Rose. We were lucky enough to have more than forty acres and our own sheep; now we had to live up to this happy opportunity.

Some border collie owners are among the dog world's most rigid snobs. A number of them had already made it clear that they thought it reckless, even irresponsible, to train a puppy without a professional herding trainer.

Maybe so. But such trainers have loads of dos and don'ts, often contradicting what other trainers insist on: Never praise the dog, always praise the dog. Always use a stick, never use a stick. Always reinforce with food, never reinforce with food. It gets my back up, makes me tense—and then I pass the tension on to the dogs.

This time, the only voice I wanted to hear in my head was my own. I understood my biggest dangers—my big mouth, my short temper, my bad leg (which makes it hard to move quickly), my difficulties in trusting a dog.

As it happened, trust was never an issue with Rose. My hand-feeding, rigorously positive training, and liberal use of beef and liver treats had gotten us off on the right foot from the very start. Now all the indicators for successful herding were good: her head swiveled when she heard her name; she made eye contact; our training sessions were short, fun, and focused. On those occasional days when my voice got sharp or I lost patience, she could shrug it off.

Besides, the context was so different up here. We weren't driving an hour to someone else's farm, just walking out the back door. As a result, Rose didn't go crazy whenever she saw sheep; they were simply always around.

She had already bailed me out so many times—warding off Nesbitt, keeping the sheep at bay while I delivered feed, rounding up escaped donkeys and ewes. I was coming to understand that she really *was* the teacher and I the pupil. Getting her to lie down, come quickly, back off when I said "That'll do"—all of that would come in time. We didn't have to learn it all at once.

Meanwhile, whenever she moved to the right, I'd say, "Good come bye!" When she went left, I'd praise her for going "away to me." I praised her all the time, in fact. That awful censorious voice rarely came out of my mouth.

In general, I kept in mind Stanley Coren's great all-purpose training maxim: Never give a dog anything for free. To get into the pasture, Rose had to lie down and stay. To move closer to the sheep, she had to lie down again. To stay with the sheep, she had to remain calm and focused. Her confidence grew with her experience. Yet it was also true, I had to admit, that some things she simply seemed to know without my ever teaching her. These instincts ran deep in her bloodlines. If I could shut up, she would figure it out.

We got into a routine. Inside the pasture gate, I'd walk toward the small training pen and see what happened. Over several weeks, I noticed that by the time I reached the pen—and I tried not to look back at Rose or at the sheep—flock and dog were close behind. When I finally did look, it wasn't a pretty sight: Rose was steering the sheep all over the pasture. But inexorably, she brought them to me. I gave this behavior a name— "take the sheep to the pen"—and the sheep and dog began to follow a trail they'd worn down through the snow. The process almost took care of itself after a while.

Some trainers wouldn't like this, I knew. They liked sheep moving in straight lines; they preferred traditional verbal commands. But Rose was doing what I needed her to do.

Some of my own attachment issues, I was coming to realize, had to do with respect. People want their dogs to respect and obey them. I'd argue that it's equally important that I respect my dogs.

I respected Orson tremendously for his big heart, despite his grievous past. He had every right to be nasty and unforgiving; instead he'd responded to me with great affection. I respected his intensity, his intelligence and his devotion.

I respected Rose for her energy and professionalism. She was a working dog through and through, a different creature from Orson or Homer. She wasn't especially interested in being my intimate, my confidante. She kept tabs on me, popping up every hour or two to lick my hand as I wrote or talked on the phone or prepared meals. Then she'd wander off to move her toys around, chew a bone, monitor the sheep through the window.

Orson was always next to me. He curled up beside me on the sofa when I watched TV, slept with his head on my shoulder at night.

If Orson was my soulmate, Rose was the farm manager, my partner. Each took care of a vital part of me. Orson supported me in the most elemental, emotional way; Rose was already making it possible for me to stay on the farm, caring for my animals through a punishing winter. I believe they sensed my respect and returned the favor.

As had happened with my Labs, Julius and Stanley, I felt I was forging an almost mystical relationship. Together we were beginning to find that lovely state of harmony and comfort that our two species can sometimes achieve. I was a lucky man.

ORSON WAS PROGRESSING, YET IT WAS HARD TO IMAGINE HIM ever herding the way Rose already did. Still, the working dog is nothing if not ingenious about finding work. One night I got a telephone call from a farmer in North Hebron with a problem: he had a half-dozen cows that had been living in his back fields for years, rebuffing every attempt to bring them into the barn. They'd virtually become wild animals. Now, about to start clearing his property for a new outbuilding, he needed to get them into the barn. He had heard from his friend Carr that I had two working dogs. Was that true?

I said it was.

"What do you do?" he asked.

"I'm a writer."

"Oh." He was disappointed.

"But the dogs are really quite useful," I added.

"Oh, good," he said, audibly brightening. Could I bring them over?

A half hour later, I pulled off Route 31 and down a side road alongside a huge farm. Reg was sitting on a giant tractor, waiting for me. I could never let Rose loose on cattle; she could get kicked to death. But nothing made Orson happier than when a goose tried to peck at him, or a cow or sheep tried to kick. He danced, weaved, and nipped; if he wasn't much of a shepherd, he was a master at domination.

So we walked into Reg's back field. Perhaps a quarter-mile away I saw a knot of cows staring warily down at us. I told Reg to open the barn door, then walked toward them with Orson. "Get ready," I said, a command that always put him on red alert. He spun, then crouched. I pointed to the cows. "Go get 'em," I yelled, slapping my leg.

He took off like a fighter jet, straight through the meadow and into the woods behind the cows. His outruns, iffy around sheep, were magnificent around everything else. He came roaring in behind the cows, who bunched together protectively. One of them turned to go nose-to-nose with Orson—a mistake. Orson got in her face, yapping, and nipped at her nose. She bellowed, turned, and ran. The others followed, Orson in pursuit, barking and circling as the little herd hustled through the meadow and into the barn.

It had taken perhaps ten minutes. Reg was impressed. He closed the barn door, then chugged his tractor over and handed me a crumpled ten-dollar-bill. I intuitively knew I ought to take it.

"Good job," he said. "That's a good dog you have there. Anytime you want work, call me." We headed home, feeling satisfied.

Soon the word spread. People thought a man who wrote about dogs was worse than useless, but they grasped the power of the working dog.

A woman in Salem had a "shy" sheep who was also wary of the barn. When we pulled up in the truck, Orson merely stuck his head out the open window; the sheep trotted into the barn before I could even open the door to let Orson out.

A border collie in Rupert kept getting butted by an obstreperous ewe. Orson and Rose and I showed up. The ewe rushed out to challenge us, and Orson nipped while Rose took her backside. Shocked, the ewe retreated to the back of the flock and behaved, now "dog-broke" for good. Orson's fame spread further, through sheepherding circles, and we "dog-broke" sheep in Hebron, Granville, and Cambridge. Just a few sessions, and the sight of any working dog would get such sheep to move. It was great work for Orson: no blood, no biting, no real training. Just his raw craziness could tame rams and convince ewes that obeying dogs was the wiser choice. Intimidating livestock was his calling.

If we were dealing with a frightened dog, I'd have the owner leash the dog and walk behind us. The dogs couldn't tell whether they or Orson were moving the sheep, but they usually concluded that they deserved the credit, so their confidence grew with each visit. Meanwhile, if this could be said of a dog, Orson seemed to be having a blast. We kept our standard fee at ten bucks, but also accepted pies or muffins.

There are no trial ribbons for helping traumatized border collies or prizes for dog-breaking sheep. But I had a champion on my hands, no doubt. Every few weeks, I got a call that began, "Are you the dog guy?"

Yes, I'd say, I'm the dog guy. And, as I proudly announced to Paula, after a few months Orson and I had earned eighty dollars, several pies, and three dozen free-range eggs.

As for Rose: Wink was prescient. During a thaw, when the temperatures briefly turned upward and some of the snow was melting, I saw the sheep clustered by a gate in the highest corner of the pasture. Rose and I clambered uphill to see what they were so interested in.

There were a few clumps of grass and weeds appearing just beyond the fence at the very top of the hill. Perhaps the sun was warmer there, the patch sheltered somewhat from the wind. In any case, something green was visible for the first time in months, and the sheep wanted at it.

I had never taken the sheep off my fenced property. If anything went wrong—sheep running off, Rose getting overwhelmed, stray dogs appearing—I'd have no way to restrain my herd, and little likelihood of getting it back intact.

Still, I kept picturing the old print I had hanging in my office: a shepherd walking a path in the deep woods, his small flock behind him and a happy border collie behind the flock. I had dreamed of living that scene. I thought it might be years away—but maybe not. All I had to do was open the gate.

It was gorgeous at the top of the pasture. The day was cold but the sun felt good, and the view was mesmerizing. I took a deep breath and unlatched the gate.

The sheep rushed out, Rose right behind them. I instantly feared I'd made a stupid mistake. The sheep went skittering all over and Rose, excited by this new adventure, was confused, chasing one and then another.

"C'mon, Rosie," I exhorted. "Let's round 'em up and take a walk." She turned to me, head tilting as it does when she seems to be trying to figure something out. Then she sprang into action, circling the ewes into a tight cluster. I led the way, a walking stick in my right hand. Faith, I said to myself. Have faith. If I keep going, the sheep and the dog will end up behind me, just like they usually do.

Which is just what happened, Rose playing the role she'd been rehearsing for all her young life. Had Orson been there, the sheep would likely be diving into the woods. But they stayed pretty calm around Rose. When they stopped to graze, she stopped. When one wandered too far from the group, she nudged it back into place. When I moved, she moved, and then they moved. She began "wearing," walking a curving path back and forth behind the sheep to push them unobtrusively forward, though that was a technique I still hadn't taught her.

It was a triumphal procession. I was the man in the print, the shepherd, and she was my herder. For much of an hour, we walked through my neighbor Adam's land and my own, stopping now and then so that the sheep could munch at patches of green that might not reappear for months—we hadn't seen the last snowfall, I was sure.

Everything about the setting was lovely and soothing—the view, the sweet, sharp air, the quiet of the woods, the sight of a dog who makes you understand why there are domesticated dogs in the first place.

I regretted that Orson couldn't join us, but I also accepted that he probably never would. Dogs pay the price for the awful things people sometimes do to them. There was part of him, I knew, that would never operate the way border collies were meant to function. Still, he had his other work, which he loved, and I couldn't imagine there were many dogs living a better life.

After a while, as the sun started to weaken and my leg to throb, Rose and I walked the flock back over the crest of the hill and down into our own pasture. I'd hardly said a word the whole time, but we both seemed to have read the same script, a sweet moment in the life of any dog and owner working together.

Not bad, I thought. Score one for this terrific little dog, and another for the balding middle-aged Jersey guy with his odd entourage.

On the first really warm day of spring, I decided, Rose and I were going to walk those sheep right down the road in front of my house, down Route 30, and right up to the doorstep of the Bedlam's Corner Variety Store. 🐾

Chapter Ten

FAMILY CIRCLE

BOTH OF US WERE LAUGHING, THE TALL, MIDDLE-AGED WOMAN with the picture of a Newfoundland puppy on her sweatshirt and I. Despite the fact that we were freezing, standing at the edge of an ice-covered pond outside a small town southeast of Buffalo on a raw, blustery day, we were happy.

Neither of us could believe that we were there together. We had only distant memories of being together at all, even though this was my sister. And we were about to score some huge points in her new neighborhood.

Rose was in her classic border collie crouch—nose almost to the ground, right paw lifted, head tilted, eyes focused intently, awaiting my command.

"There are sheep hiding out there," I said quietly, gesturing to the thickly wooded hillside in front of us. "The sheep we saw last night. And we are going to get them."

At the mention of "sheep," Rose knew more or less what we were there for. A working girl knows when there's a job to do.

It was late February. I'd had more laden moments in my life, but not many.

Two weeks earlier, after many discussions with me, my sister and her tribe of Newfoundlands had moved from her home in a working-class Boston suburb to a five-acre tract with a ranch house above this pond.

In Massachusetts, Jane and her big, gentle dogs—all rescues of one kind or another—had been confined by convention and local ordinances to a small fenced yard with daily treks to a nearby park. Here, in this bitter winter, they were joyously in their natural element. The healthier ones were romping through their much larger fenced yard; those with various ailments had a quiet environment in the finished basement.

Finally, and at great cost, Jane had found a loving and peaceful family, and like some wise, powerful elder, she'd led them into the wilderness where they all—including her—could live undisturbed.

Jane seemed as happy as the dogs. Even though I hadn't seen her in many years, I couldn't remember seeing so calm a look on her face.

We'd been talking about a visit, but intended to wait until later in the spring, when the weather was more agreeable and I was finished with lambing. Her new place was a long drive from mine.

But things had speeded up, taken a strange turn, the fates intervening with a clear message. Jane's brand-new neighbors were up in arms over some wild sheep living on the edge of the pond.

Abandoned by a couple that had divorced, they had originally numbered five, and had been living in the woods for several years. Now there were only two left. They fled from dogs, people, snowmobiles. Nobody could catch them, or had even gotten near them. Some neighbors occasionally threw down some hay, but mostly the sheep lived off brush and weeds. Now the wretched creatures were starving in this unusually bitter winter, ravaging people's shrubs and "ornamentals."

A number of border collies had been worn out trying unsuccessfully to herd them out of their hiding place. In fact, one of Jane's neighbors had called a nearby border collie owner a week earlier to ask for help. The sheep, growing increasingly desperate for food, had begun chewing the bark off trees. The owner had refused, saying it was too dangerous a mission. This ticked me off, as Jane knew it would. There are some appeals you just don't turn down if you have border collies. How often does somebody ask you and your dogs to save some sheep? Isn't that more or less the reason for a sheepdog's existence?

Still, the woman had a point. These sheep were not "dog-broke"; they'd never been around working dogs. They were likely to flee when a dog approached, just as if they were confronting a coyote or another predator. Trained dogs, in turn, get easily unhinged when sheep behave so unpredictably. Instead of herding, the exercise becomes an unruly, sometimes bloody chase. Nine-month-old Rose wasn't large or experienced; she was used to moving fairly compliant sheep who'd been around border collies all their lives. I wasn't sure she'd developed the presence to deal with these rampaging wild creatures.

It would be a test of all our hard work together, more important to me than any trial ribbon.

Besides, rounding up wild sheep was a pretext; this visit had many dimensions. How apt, though, that a dog was the spark.

When Jane heard about the recalcitrant border collie owner, she told her neighbor, "My brother Jon won't like that. I bet he'll come up here with his dogs when he hears about this." Jane knew me. Brothers and sisters don't need to talk all the time to understand one another. And I loved the idea that perhaps for the first time in our lives, she was asking her brother for help.

Of course she was right. I called Anthony and asked him to watch over the farm and its inhabitants for a day or two.

Even though Orson was keen to join the posse, I decided to put him in a kennel. He thinks Newfoundlands are sheep and would probably go ballistic at the sight of them, and I didn't even want to picture what runaway wild sheep would do to his arousable nature.

This was no small step. I could never have left Orson in our first few years. But I'd worked hard to get us both to this point. I've always believed that quality kennels are among the safest places to leave dogs; you know they'll be fed, safe, and right where you last saw them when you return.

It was time, past time. Sometimes I wonder if I liked Orson's dependence, seeing it as a sign of his devotion. It's hard to teach a creature you love to move away from you. But in many ways, it's the essence of love. What if something happened to me? Shouldn't he know that other people could love him, too?

The folks at the Borador Kennel in Salem knew his story well. Dog lovers all, they would adopt him, visiting him throughout the day, stroking and cooing and offering treats. For an attention junkie, this wasn't half bad. I also enlisted Derrick, the twelve-year-old son of one of the technicians, to come visit Orson in the evening after the staff went home.

So I dropped Orson off with little fuss, and Rose and I headed west, bound for a great adventure for us both.

I HAD NOT SEEN JANE IN A GOOD TEN YEARS, MAYBE LONGER. Until a few months earlier, I'd resigned myself to the likelihood that I'd never see her again. I hadn't seen or talked with my older brother in years, either. Jane—the person in my family to whom I was the closest and, in many ways, the one I'd loved most— seemed lost to me.

Now, on a gray winter day in a far-off corner of New York

State, closer to Canada than to the lives either of us had known before, we were like refugees reunited in a foreign land.

A lot seemed to be riding on this, much more than the welfare of a couple of sheep, and I was afraid that we might both be disappointed. After all that had happened, I had no reason to believe my connection with Jane could survive as more than a phone friendship.

We were nearly strangers now, however close we'd been in our early years. She'd been very ill for a long time. She had only seen my daughter once or twice, years ago. She'd virtually abandoned her own two children; one daughter had come to live with Paula and me for a while and the other had gone to live with her father. Neither talked to her much now. I knew how bad she felt about our family and hers, how hard she had struggled to recover. But so much damage had been done, to her and by her.

It was hard to forget those awful years, or to believe they were truly over. It would be extraordinary even to talk with her face-to-face. Paula and I have been married for more than three decades, and I can't imagine being closer to another human. Yet Jane knew me as no one else in the world could. The same crucible had shaped us; she understood, literally, where I came from. To lose my family was a catastrophe. To get even a piece of it back was a miracle.

I'd arrived the previous afternoon after a long drive, with Rose navigating. As we cruised along, I was surprised at how rural and remote a region my sister had chosen. She'd never lived outside an urban area. In our telephone conversations—increasingly frequent, now daily—I'd tried to warn her of the particular challenges of life upstate. Boston winters are rugged, but she had stores and services and movie theaters close by, dog-rescue friends to commiserate with. My sister still seemed fragile to me, and at my urging, she'd seen a doctor, just before moving, for some medication for her anxiety and depression. It had helped.

But I knew what nasty winters in unfamiliar, rural areas could be like. This was a brave undertaking. It wouldn't be an easy transition for her, and she had a lot less support than I did.

She had little money to spare. After being laid off six months earlier from her programming job, she was living off savings and real estate proceeds until she found new work.

She knew nobody upstate apart from an e-mail friend in the dog-rescue movement who lived nearby. One daughter was in California, the other back in Massachusetts. There was no community around to keep her company or help her out. She had eye and leg injuries from an accident—I was surprised to learn she'd had a related knee replacement a few years ago—and now felt considerable anxiety about driving.

Plus she had about two thousand pounds of dog to take care of, some with heart, dietary, or orthopedic problems that required ramps, special food, vet visits. A fervent believer in raw natural diets for her dogs, she fed them only chopped-up turkey or chicken parts. I hated to think how much time she'd spend in her minivan (without four-wheel drive), making the rounds of vets and butchers.

Yet Jane felt strongly, as I did, that change was necessary and that time was growing short. She needed to shed her past and move forward. Twelve-step recovery programs had saved her, but she wanted the next phase of her life to be different, more meaningful.

It was surreal how similar we'd become. All those impulses, apart from the addictions, were issues and themes I had experienced, even written about. But it was also daunting how different we were. In some ways, she seemed much more damaged than I; in other ways, more peaceful, less angry. Neither of us needed a shrink to explain the powerful pull drawing us toward quieter, more peaceful surroundings with our canine companions.

A mile or two from her house, I put the directions down and pulled over. I needed to catch my breath a bit, settle down, adjust my expectations. What if this visit didn't go well? What if we just didn't like each other after all this time? Rose, puzzled at the stop, moved in to lick my face. Perhaps she sensed my anxiety, or wanted to urge me to get moving. She was not good at being idle.

I had great memories of times with my sister when we were young children—the long yaks at bedtime, the funny stories we exchanged, an aborted attempt to run away to our grandmother's house. That happy period was short, though. Mostly, we huddled together against the storm that was my family.

Would I be greeting a ghostly survivor with whom I could never reconnect in any of the old ways? Or a close-to-home version of a dog person like Laurie, somebody who had turned her physical space and emotional self over to dogs so completely that she shut out human beings?

Cranking the truck, I continued down the road to Jane's. It was time to know.

The night before, she'd told me on the phone that she wasn't going to make "a big deal" out of the visit. "I see you as another dog friend," she said.

"I'm not another dog friend," I said. "I'm your brother. It's different."

She apologized quickly. Even after all this time, we could still read each other. She was simply taking that view to keep from getting too wrought, putting too much weight on a quick visit. I understood.

But I didn't want another dog friend; I wanted my sister back. I wanted to be the kind of brother she deserved, and to have the sense of family that neither of us had had as kids. We didn't have another decade or two to feel estranged.

The sheep-chase gave the visit a wild, dog-related dimension. It was bizarre, but also safer; it took the pressure off.

I saw the white mailbox she'd described and pulled in, down a long driveway. A white ranch house sat on the top of a rise, with woods on one side, an open field leading to a pond on the other. I had called Jane on my cell to tell her I was close—I'd gotten lost twice on the endless drive—and she told me she'd be outside the house, waiting.

But at the end of this driveway, a strange woman was standing on a porch. She seemed elderly, perhaps in her late sixties or early seventies, with a worn, weary, almost ravaged face and dyed red hair. I had pulled down the wrong drive.

"Do you know where Jane lives?" I asked, leaning out the truck window. "She just moved in last week. I'm her brother."

The woman looked puzzled, then smiled faintly. "It's me," she said. "It's me, Jane."

I WAS SPEECHLESS, SUFFOCATING, ALMOST GASPING FOR AIR. I got out of the truck, Rose bounding out behind me. Jane came down the steps and we had a long hug. Then we pulled back, both anxious not to make "too big a deal" out of something that was a staggeringly big deal.

In my head I'd carried a picture of my sister from another era. Time and afflictions had aged her. The hard years—she'd had precious few easy ones—were etched in her face. Did I look as old to her?

Fortunately the shock and discomfort of the moment was quickly supplanted by the charge of enormous, friendly, slobbering Newfoundlands, barking, wagging, and encircling the normally assertive but now stunned Rose, who looked at me, then retreated under the truck.

Rose is never stymied for long or by much, but this time she was rattled. These huge creatures bearing down on her—which might have looked like sheep but weren't—were a new experience. She studied the situation, emerged from her hideout, and tried all her herding moves—nipping at noses and heels, circling around. The Newfies seemed amazed at this hyper little creature, their heads swiveling as she barked and charged. She got bewildered but genial responses until, finally, in the amazingly adaptable way of dogs, everybody started sniffing around the yard. Rose seemed to grasp that these were dogs, not livestock, and started stealing their toys. Jane and I watched for a while, amused by this clash of cultures, relieved not to have to say much.

"How did we get from there to here?" she wondered. Even before I walked into her new house, we were joking about this odd location for the Family Circle. This was an organization of our extended family in Rhode Island and Massachusetts that had met regularly for years at different relatives' homes, an organization she and I had carefully avoided. We walked into her backyard—it had a gorgeous, sweeping view of the Adirondacks. Suddenly, Rose froze, and in the dimming daylight I saw two sheep sitting on a hillside perhaps a quarter-mile away. Rose was already giving eye and creeping along the ground. "We'll take care of them tomorrow," I told her. She didn't move from her crouch.

"Was it the dogs that got us together?" I asked Jane.

"I don't know," she said, truthfully. "Maybe. Probably."

That was a bittersweet reality. It was great that dogs were responsible for this, sad we hadn't managed it ourselves.

Surveying the scene, heading back for a tour of the house, I told Jane I didn't think it likely that we could corral these sheep. They looked restless and emaciated despite thick wool that had surely gone unshorn for years. They were probably suffering from worms and parasites as well as malnutrition.

Rose had never seen such creatures, even though she herded sheep every day. I thought she was too young, the sheep too fearful, the woods too deep to accomplish this task. Jane shrugged. Either way, she said, my arrival had already raised her stock in the neighborhood.

We all filed inside. It was hard for even a border collie to get wrought up around these sofa-like Newfies; they simply aren't excitable. They all sat down to stare at the visitors, which led Rose to settle down with a bone while Jane and I sat down to deal with each other. She was sweet, easy, a bit vulnerable, much as I'd remembered her.

The house was spartan, the carpets cheap and worn, the walls bare. Almost all the furniture was shoved into two rooms, the living room and the basement. There were bowls and buckets—Newfies love water—everywhere, and the floors were littered with bones and toys.

The place suited her. It was modern, with two propane stoves and a sunlit "California room," and potentially comfortable. But it reminded me of a dog motel suite, temporary and impersonal, more than a home, partly because Jane had only been there a few days, partly because she didn't seem to have much interest in or talent for domestic life. She told me she hadn't had a visitor in years.

As it got dark, we sat in the living room and she made me a cup of tea. This talk had been a long time coming, and there was so much water under the bridge to deal with that we both sensed we might drown if we tried. We took it slow and easy. She talked about each of her dogs, and got a huge kick out of Rose, who immediately set about organizing the Newfies, moving one here, the other there. They didn't exactly comply, but they didn't object to her efforts, either.

We proceeded as if we got together all the time, as if this were normal. We didn't stray far from dog talk. After a bit, the shock and dismay of not recognizing her began to wear off. I said I was excited about our looming encounter with the wild sheep.

"I see why you like border collies," Jane told me. "You and

Rose are both obsessive about work." This was true. Though I doubted we could round up those sheep, we were going to give it a hell of a try. I kept peering out the window at the landscape across the pond.

After a while, I brought my bags in. Jane's guest quarters consisted of a bare room with little heat or light and a threadbare carpet. The sofa bed was a nightmare, with a pronounced tilt and murderous springs. I knew there wouldn't be much sleep that night. I also realized that this was the first night I'd ever spent in any place my sister lived. She would be getting dinner ready, she said—another first.

Jane's ranch house had been purchased and set up with her dogs very much in mind. Two of her Newfoundlands couldn't walk up stairs—one had debilitating heart diseases, the other had serious hip problems—so they stayed in the basement, which was furnished with sofas, a carpet, and a propane stove. Just the day before, she told me, she had taken in still another Newfie, a puppy named Simon, who suffered from dwarfism, which left him with short, basset hound legs. He was, of course, the perfect dog for Jane—cute, sweet, in desperate need. Simon, strange-looking but playful, had attached himself to Rose, and the two of them were rolling around on the floor while the other dogs sat placidly watching.

I'd offered to take my sister out to dinner but she said, with some pride, that she'd already prepared a meal.

I sat down at her small Formica table and she brought out some salad greens, rolls, and a pan of microwaved macaroni and cheese. I could see Jane wasn't used to guests. She couldn't quite coordinate the food and drinks in sequence. She had spoons, but no knives or forks, plates but no napkins. She hadn't bought anything to drink, so we had tap water. Dessert was ice cream. It felt strange. Our own family dinners had been elaborate and delicious, but always difficult; this one was quiet and peaceful. Rose curled up against one of the enormous Newfies, and my sister smiled down at her dogs—those who could climb the stairs—all sitting quietly around her. We were surrounded by dogs, in fact, and had to thread our way through them to clear the dishes.

For the first time, we talked about our parents a bit, and some shared childhood memories. Then she described her dogs again, one by one.

"I came here for them," she said. She had all kinds of plans for them: expanded fencing, ramps for the ailing ones, dog doors so they could go in and out independently, treks to nearby state parks. She was extraordinarily gentle with and attentive to them.

After dinner—it was about eight P.M.—she announced that we had to go downstairs and visit the basement-bound Newfies. I made what I hoped was the appropriate fuss over them. Cold-weather dogs, they were delighted by the snow and bitter temperatures. She'd had to buy multiple air conditioners to keep them comfortable during Boston summers, Jane said; here, she might not need them.

I went outside to walk Rose and to clear my head and calm down. When I returned, Jane was settling into what was clearly her evening routine. In a room off the family room, she unearthed some turkey carcasses from an enormous freezer, and chopped them apart with a small hatchet, putting the parts in a bucket on the floor.

The dogs stared at the pungent bucket for fifteen minutes or so as Jane worked. Then each got a turkey leg or thigh, plopped down on the living room carpet and began crunching away.

"I know," Jane said, following my gaze. "But this house is for them. They're why I came. Why shouldn't they eat on the carpet?"

This long trek to an alien place, a completely different way of life, far from friends, family, a half-century of experience and memories—it made more sense now. She wasn't leaving a home, she was creating a home conceived for her dogs. It was a peaceful retreat for the last years of her life; I had no doubt that she intended to die here.

Our conversations were low-key, nonemotional, just as she had wanted, and always interspersed with her comments about, observations of, and discussions with her dogs. "Susie, what? Are you hungry? Simon, do you want to go out? Phyllis, what are you saying?" Often, she burst out laughing at something the dogs were doing, some expression on their faces. She loved Rose, and was careful to include her in the running commentary and to make sure she was comfortable and plied with bones. She immediately grasped the depth of love I had for my own dogs, and I found it oddly comforting that nothing had to be said.

When I took the dogs outside for their final walk of the night, they put on a show under the back-door floodlight. Rose would zoom in, grab one of the Newfie's toys, rush to a safe distance and crouch down, daring the big guys to come after her. Several of them tried, charging a few feet, then watching bemusedly as Rose tore out of range again. I looked up and saw my sister's face in the window, beaming at the sight of me, of our dogs playing together.

Could I possibly imagine a more unlikely likely sight, I wondered, feeling much of the same pleasure.

After a while, the Newfies wore out, something that typically happens to Rose's playmates. I opened the door and they filed into the basement one by one, with Rose left outside, staring at me expectantly. I threw her a ball for another ten or fifteen minutes. When I came in, Jane was again surrounded by all her dogs, old and young, healthy and sick. She talked to each one about their play session, distributing pats and hugs, accepting their licks. I began to see the working nature of these dogs, too. They had enveloped my sister in a loving, furry, protective cocoon, where she was insulated from some of life's rough edges, disappointments, and pain.

Life never gave her that, but they did.

These were profoundly gentle creatures. There would be no sudden moves, no squabbling, no intrusions. They were the temperamental opposites of the people who had raised us, this house the opposite of the one we grew up in. There was no nagging, fighting, or cruelty in Jane's new house, and very few rules except that dogs could go anywhere they wanted, eat wherever they wanted, and always—always—claim the affection and attention of their owner.

I was spent and said goodnight. It was a long time until morning. I think we both felt awkward. Jane really didn't have much experience with hospitality, and I was still struggling with the surreal nature of the visit.

The guest room was cold and stark and dusty, and when I climbed onto the sofa bed, one half collapsed to the floor. I couldn't level it, so I ended up swaddling myself in blankets and my coat, lying with my head elevated at the foot of the bed and my feet on the floor.

I didn't sleep a wink, but I doubt I could have anyway. Rose curled up and slept against me, great comfort through a strange, uncomfortable night.

In the morning, I got up early and scoured the kitchen cabinets for cereal or bread or coffee, but there was no breakfast. So I took Rose out for an early walk, and we circled the pond to a spot where we could clearly observe our quarry—a ram and a ewe perched on a hill, vast woods behind them. At the first close-up sight of us, they could easily take off deep into those woods, and we'd shortly be on our way home.

One of the neighbors, whose gardens the sheep had decimated for several years, had prepared a wire pen, if we could move the sheep to her property. It was only about two hundred yards from their customary spot. But Rose expected sheep to behave a certain way, and this pair was unlikely to oblige. That pen might as well have been in Ohio.

· · ·

AT EIGHT, JANE AND I AND ROSE DROVE AROUND THE POND to the small rise where we'd seen the sheep. I could see where they'd chewed the bark off trees. I also saw sheep droppings, but not sheep.

I parked, let Rose out, then climbed out myself, overoptimistically carrying a rope halter a neighbor had provided. Jane, whose knee still troubled her, stood alongside the car. I scrambled up the slope and sent Rose out to my left. "Get the sheep, girl," I yelled, her usual command. Rose sniffed and scanned, then took off. I glimpsed the animals moving in the woods, then turning and running. So much for that.

I couldn't see or hear Rose, but after a few minutes, she came exploding out of the woods, barking at me Lassie-style ("C'mon, Timmy, this way!"), then turning back into the trees. I followed. A short walk ahead, Rose had the ewe and the ram cornered between some downed trees and a length of old stone fence. She was crouched in front of them, barking and lunging every time they tried to flee.

Both sheep were in pitiful condition, their wool filthy and matted, their faces too thin. My own Tunis ewes looked fat and sassy by contrast.

When I crashed up through the underbrush, the sheep broke out of their trap, vaulting the crumbling fence and dashing off in different directions. The ram turned and butted Rose, bouncing her about ten feet. But when she got up and charged, going for his nose, he backed off, turned, and ran.

So Rose swiveled and took off after the ewe, who was heading for pond. The two battled for nearly half an hour, the ewe trying one path, then another, Rose always in front of her, charging, barking, nipping. The ewe was tiring—as was I—but Rose seemed as unstoppable as the Energizer Bunny.

Finally, the ewe broke out of the woods and headed across the ice-covered pond. Rose wasn't about to give up now; she followed the ewe onto the ice and the two slipped and slid around each other. Rose couldn't get a firm purchase, so she coasted around the ewe on her butt—the strangest outrun I'd ever seen a border collie make. The scene went on and on, Rose and the ewe running, falling, skidding, the ewe panting but frantic, Rose tireless and focused. My sister and a growing number of neighbors—some popping out of their houses with video cameras—were cheering her on. Even as Rose slid past the scrambling ewe, she nipped at her, managing to keep herself between the ewe and the far side of the pond.

I was afraid of falling on or through the ice, so I ran up and down along the bank, shouting praise and encouragement to my puppy. At that moment, I knew that no matter what else happened that day, Rose would get her prey. She would not be deterred.

Finally, the ewe gave up, shuffled back across the pond and into the brush. The neighbors were whooping and applauding for Rose. But we still didn't have the ewe.

Panicked, she plowed into a snowdrift and stopped momentarily, a bit stunned. I lunged for her and slipped the halter over her neck.

The poor ewe, terrified, bucked and charged and tried to escape. When she went down, gasping, I'd loosen the halter to make sure she could breathe. Up close, I saw how her eyes were sunk deep into their sockets; how, beneath her unshorn coat, she was skin and bones. When she recovered a bit, she leaped to her feet and began battling all over again, with me pulling on her head and Rose nipping at her behind.

The epic struggle lasted another half hour before we finally dragged her, still protesting, into the neighbor's corral, complete with a heap of hay. By now, I was so drained I wasn't sure we had strength left for the ram, who was bigger and surely more aggressive. My sister, despite her bad knee, had been following along. She was amazed, she said, at my stamina, as I went scrambling up hills and dragging livestock around. I was amazed myself.

We walked from the corral back to where we'd begun, and Rose took the issue out of my hands. She roared off into the woods, reappearing five minutes later with an impatient where-the-hell-*are*-you look, then charging back into the trees. Here we went again. The ram was at least a third larger than his companion, and far more ornery. When he butted Rose right in the head, the crack was terrifying and sent her flying. This, of course, was why rational border collie owners didn't want to risk their dogs.

I screamed obscenities at the ram and charged him, waving my shepherd's crook. He plowed into my leg, knocking me down. I picked up my stick and whacked him across the nose, and he backed up, startled. Terrified for Rose, I turned to look for her. A black-and-white blur came hurling past me and attached itself to the fleeing ram's behind.

The Second Battle of Jane's Pond was on, far bloodier and nastier than the first. Rose, seemingly unfazed by her head-butting, was furious. She launched one of her boxing-ring rope-a-dopes, bewildering the enraged ram with her fancy footwork, darting, nipping, barking, and growling. The ram, turning this way and that, growing dizzy and disoriented, broke through the woods and into a neighbor's yard, startling the chickens and ducks penned in coops. A goof. Now he was hemmed in by the coops and the house. Rose and I came flying down the hillside, me half-sliding on my butt, Rose leaping from stump to snow-drift.

The ram charged again, but I got a halter on him. Unlike the ewe, however, the halter barely slowed him down. He dragged me along through a cluster of trash cans, a patch of garden, a pile of firewood. He was pulling me as if I were a twig, but he was gradually losing strength, struggling and reeling a bit. I was bleeding from my nose, and my leg was killing me, but I hung on for dear life. Rose was staying in his face, keeping the pressure on.

This struggle was more prolonged. For ill-nourished creatures, these sheep had astonishing strength and energy. It took another hour before we could steer him—wheezing, snorting, gasping—toward the corral, and finally inside. It was such an effort that only days later did I think to ask Jane what would become of the animals. A local farmer would take them, she said.

Closing the gate to the pen, I collapsed, and Rose rushed into my arms, happy and proud. She knew she had done something swell, and so did the people applauding her from all over the pond.

We took our plaudits, but it was late in the morning. I was exhausted and I faced a long drive. I also wanted to spring Orson from the kennel before it closed for the night.

So we drove back to Jane's. "This was wonderful," she said. "Thank you."

It was wonderful for me, too, I said.

She apologized for not having food or coffee to offer me before I headed home.

"I have to get used to this guest thing," she said. "I hope you'll come back, anyway." I said I would, and meant it. We would not, I swore, lose each other again.

ALL THE WAY HOME, ROSE RODE SHOTGUN, AND ALL THE WAY I praised her for her companionship, her steadfastness, her courage, and her herding skill.

Driving down the New York State Thruway, I asked whatever higher power had brought Jane this far to help her find comfort and happiness. I loved her very much, this strange red-haired woman with her big sweet dogs and her freezer stuffed with poultry.

I felt depleted, though, and not just from our protracted sheep roundup. My lost sister, now found, had found herself a loving place, but a place for dogs, about dogs, and dependent on dogs.

I couldn't decide whether or not it was a good thing to live like that. I missed Paula every day; I missed having lunch with Emma and arguing about movies. For me, dog love, wonderful as it was, wasn't enough.

But what about my sister? Would she be all right? Should I have done more for her, and should I do more now? I wondered if it was okay for her to end up this way—living out her life with and for a herd of loving, sick, and needy Newfoundlands.

And here's what I decided: Yes, it was okay, and I needed to accept it. Dogs had done what humans couldn't: they'd brought Jane and me together again. They'd taken me to that pond and those sheep, a fittingly weird kickoff to our new relationship.

Jane had done the best she could. She hadn't wound up in a destructive relationship, in awful health, on pills or alcohol. She was hurting no one, meant no one harm, had devoted herself to making these sweet and soulful creatures happy.

I also realized, driving back to what I now instinctively called home, that my own center of gravity had shifted. New Jersey was where Paula was, which made it important. But home was where my farm was, where Jacob and Anthony and my other friends and neighbors were, where Carol and Fanny would be at the hay feeder, braying happily when I pulled into the driveway. Where the sheep would look up in their detached, appraising way to see if I emerged from the truck carrying a bucket. Where Orson and I would climb the hill to see the sunrise.

BACK AT THE FARM, I SPOKE WITH MY SISTER EVERY DAY. IT WAS still awkward at times; conversations never went on long without circling back to her dogs. She wanted to know about me, my life and my work, but there were limits. My reports were invariably interrupted by observations about her Newfies.

At first, I found this sad, sometimes irritating. I'm exhausted, I would tell her after sleepless nights during lambing season. Get some rest, she would reply, and then: It's Charity's first birthday!

But over time, I came to terms with it.

I usually call her around sundown now, when I can look out my tall living-room window at the barn and the shadows lengthening behind the barn. I always feel grateful, lucky to be surrounded by such beauty, and lucky to be able to talk with my sister again.

Part of me still feels I only have a part of my sister back, that I share her with some Newfoundlands. But so what?

For some people, dogs and other animals are the only beings they can trust. Dogs show them it's okay to love again, no matter the trauma or mistreatment they have suffered. Sometimes, dogs lead the way back. But even when they don't, it isn't my place to make judgments about these people's choices. Jane was happy and at peace. Her home was an oasis of calm and affection. If dogs had brought that about, then good for them. 🐾

Chapter Eleven

LAMBING SEASON

AT ABOUT FOUR A.M. ON MARCH 3, ROSE AND I STOOD A BIT uncertainly, looking up at the small paddock behind the barn. Ewe number 57—that was the number on her tag, and except for the shaggy Paula and old Minnie, I'd given the sheep no other names—was in labor. She was stomping the ground, circling, panting. Lambing season was officially under way.

I'd never developed much love for these sheep, but I'd worked hard to take the best possible care of them. It was a bit presumptuous, probably. Lots of people could train dogs better than I could; sheep farmers knew vastly more about sheep and lambing; anyone who'd lived here a few years knew more about winter.

But plain old determination is underrated; it can take you far. It had brought me through five strange and challenging months to this very disquieting night. I was now responsible for multiple ruminant lives, and my goal was to have uniformly healthy, well-cared-for lambs; I didn't want to lose a single one.

It was beautiful but cold, twenty-two below and windy, according to my all-weather radio channel. Shepherds don't like icy gusts when lambs are born. I found myself staring into the paddock every few minutes, eager to get mother and baby into the safety of the barn as quickly as possible after the birth.

Apart from our one agitated ewe, the paddock was eerily quiet. Rose and the flock were rarely as calm together as they were tonight. The ewes we usually shuttled around were lying down, untroubled and still. Rose wasn't harassing them, and they seemed curiously unbothered by her. All the creatures in the paddock—me, Rose, the sheep—had wordlessly agreed to suspend our normal behavior.

Lambing purists probably would have been horrified, and maybe border collie snobs, too, but I'd decided Rose should be present for every birth. I couldn't trust Orson around tiny lambs—he'd be thinking *snacks*—but with Rose, I had a chance to experiment. I wanted her to see the lambs join our little encampment, rather than simply encounter them one morning in the pasture. I wanted her to be comfortable around them and to see them as creatures under her care. Her job description was about to change radically; so was mine.

I'd brought a high-powered flashlight outside with me, along with a sling that my friend Joanne Smith had given me for toting newborns, a set of surgical gloves, scissors, a bottle of iodine, a tube of lubricant, and a towel. Plus—to keep the lamb midwife going—a granola bar and a mug of tea.

The ewe was moaning and tossing her head. I saw the fluid sac emerge, then burst. The birth should follow in a couple of hours. I was shivering with cold, but mesmerized by her struggle.

After a while, she lay down on her side, groaned and pushed, her tail up. I didn't want to get too close, but Rose crept up, sniffed the ewe's face, gave her a quick lick, and then came back to me. The ewe, who normally moved away from Rose on sight, didn't budge.

Rose had never seen lambing before; I wondered which old border collie instinct was being awakened. I, on the other hand, had seen several lambs born while helping Carolyn during previous lambing seasons in Pennsylvania. But those weren't my sheep. This was different.

Rose seemed hypnotized, sitting perfectly still, taking in this strange behavior. We kept watch for nearly two hours, pacing a bit to try to keep warm. I didn't want to miss the first birth, but as dawn approached, I was growing numb with cold.

Remembering my frostbite and the doctor's hypothermia warnings, I decided to put on additional layers of clothing. I took Rose inside the house, fed her and Orson, and made myself a pot of coffee. This was something Orson really couldn't be part of, so after breakfast I gave him a pat and tucked him safely away.

I tried to warm my hands. Then, in my Michelin Man outfit of multiple layers of clothing and long underwear, I headed back out with Rose.

Life at the farm had become a series of scheduled shocks: I knew certain challenges were approaching, but when they arrived—sheep, donkeys, winter, lambs—bedlam followed anyway. There's a difference between conceptualizing something and living it.

Amanda Alderink and Kirk Ayling from the Granville vet service had each delivered lectures on lamb care during their unnervingly frequent visits to care for Carol and the flock. They explained how to spot trouble during labor, how the fetus should be positioned, how to reach in and pull it out if necessary, how to trim the wool around the udders so that the babies could reach them, how to keep the mothers and lambs strong.

I joked weakly that I'd probably just phone one of them instead, but the vets reminded me that I'd be the one out there in the pasture in the dark (invariably) and that sometimes birth moved fast and got ugly.

So Amanda and Kirk both spoke slowly and repeated their instructions several times, perhaps noticing the look of growing alarm on my face. Besides listening to the vets' lectures, I'd also trawled websites, ordered pamphlets and books, and talked to a half-dozen sheep farmers. Joanne Smith, who'd been through this several times and whose advice was rock solid, warned me that I was in for a rougher ride than I imagined.

On one level, I was certainly ready. I had ordered supplements called "sheep's first milk" and "milk replacement," plus vitamins and penicillin, worming medication, tubes, and syringes; I'd collected basins, buckets, and towels. Joanne's sling would allow me to carry a newborn while slowly walking backward, to lead a new mother into the barn.

I'd bought implements I'd never heard of before, notably a pig castrator to dock the lambs' tails (for sanitary, not aesthetic, reasons), taggers, and ear tags to identify the lambs and ewes. I had molasses ready to mix with warm water to recharge famished mothers after delivery. My kitchen looked like a hospital triage station, covered with bottles and nipples, medications and needles. Inside the creaky old barn, we'd rigged up a series of lights and lamps and enclosures.

Anthony had installed a green swinging gate to divide the space and keep the donkeys apart, enhanced the electrical power to the barn, and built plywood pens with sliding wooden entrances. He checked in several times a day, usually leaving a message that said, in its entirety, "Yo! You alive?" Joanne and Ray had lent me a more elegant enamel lambing pen.

The new electrical outlets allowed for giant tubs of heated water, so that the exhausted moms wouldn't face frozen buckets, and heat lamps to keep newborns warm during their critical first few hours. There were bales of straw for bedding and hay for food tucked everywhere.

But if I felt ready on a practical level, I was in every other way unprepared. Lambing seemed an enormous undertaking. I was already wearied by the long winter and the simple but endless chores of farm life. Now everything was about to get more complex; even sleeping in a warm bed for more than a few hours at a stretch seemed hard to manage. The specter of dead ewes or dying lambs haunted me. All sorts of things could happen out there, with nobody to come to your rescue at two A.M. Besides, I didn't really want to call a vet every time there was trouble, tempting though that was. I wanted to handle lambing season myself, if I could.

This post-midnight visit to the pasture, now a nightly routine, wasn't about having a mystical experience; it was necessary. When I'd set up Bedlam Farm, I imagined I would grow restless and bored after five or six months, anxious to spend more time back in New Jersey or begin working on another project. So I'd decided to breed the sheep right away, ensuring births in early March. Not grasping the implications, or imagining the severity of the winter, I had brought Nesbitt in early to do his stuff. As it turned out, I was never either restless or bored, not for a second. The winter had been difficult, but exhilarating. I had expected to move on, but now could hardly imagine life away. Nevertheless, I was lambing at this time of the year, which meant that the complexity and dangers had increased dramatically.

Lambs, like other mammals, are born slippery and wet, covered in fluids. And my flock was lambing in one of the most brutal winters in recent history. A newborn could freeze to the ground in minutes.

Those first moments are crucial in many ways. The mother not only tries to make her baby warm and dry by licking it (gaining some important nutrients for herself in the process), but that's how she understands the lamb is hers—she bonds with it by its smell and its sound. After a couple of days in a pen, lambs and ewes will not forget that they belong together. Outside the barn, that can make the difference between warmth and freezing, protectiveness and rejection, nourishment and starvation, a grisly encounter with a predator or a safe spot in the herd. A lot of things can do in a tiny lamb.

My geography didn't help. In the cold and dark, with ewes milling around a fairly large sloping pasture, a newborn could easily get separated from its mother. After just a few minutes apart, she was likely to reject her lamb, who would then either starve or require risky and less healthy bottle feeding. Ewes, I was told, varied wildly as to mothering. Some were attentive and diligent, others flighty and quick to abandon their offspring.

So there were all sorts of reasons I needed to be on hand tonight: to make sure the birth went smoothly, to intervene if necessary, to keep the ewe and lamb together, to get the lamb into a sling as quickly as possible. Then, walking backward with the lamb in my arms, slowly so that the ewe wouldn't lose her lamb's scent, I'd bring them both into the barn, into a pen and under a heat lamp. It would be no small feat, especially in subzero temperatures.

Many farmers lamb in barns, but my hardy Tunis sheep had never developed a taste for barns. In fact, they'd bust through doors trying to get out. Even when the wind chill reached minus fifty one January night, the ewes sat huddled together at the top of the hill, exposed to the cold and the wind. I'd put grain and hay in the barn to tempt them down, but they showed little interest. Besides, even my spacious old barn didn't have enough space for more than a few ewes in labor. There was really no other way: they had to be, and wanted to be, outside, so I had to be with them.

Carr and some of my other neighbors ridiculed my worries about these lambs: "Let nature take its course." "They'll take care of themselves." "They've been doing this for hundreds of years." "You might lose a few, but that's nature's way." It wasn't my way. I had strong feelings about keeping faith with creatures under my care. If lambs died under circumstances I could have prevented, it was on my head, not nature's.

BACK IN THE PADDOCK, ROSE STIFFENED, THEN TORE UP THE slope and picked something up off the ground. I recognized it: the afterbirth, part of it on the ground, some still smeared on the ewe, who was licking a tiny brown lamb. Our first. I wanted to rush over for a closer look, but I held Rose back in a lie-down and waited for ten anxious minutes.

When I thought the baby was mostly dry, I released Rose, who trotted over and gently sniffed the wobbly little creature. The mother got nervous, and I was about to take Rose out of the paddock, but remembering my ideas about trusting this dog, I let her stay. She sat fifteen feet away, so still I almost forgot she was there.

I was excited. Lambs are intrinsically cute, and this one—I named it Jane—was adorable. But I was more surprised and impressed by the mother. I'd sometimes written off my sheep as a bunch of crowd-following grazers, but this mom was impressive, keeping a wary eye on me and on Rose, alert for any danger. She made an affectionate clucking sound I hadn't heard before as she methodically licked every inch of Jane.

I approached slowly, carefully picked up the shivering lamb, and placed her in the sling. She was still slippery, and it was difficult to position her hooves properly, even harder to get her to hold still. But I held her in front of her mama and began walking backward down the muddy slope. I had to leave the flashlight behind, so I was feeling my way in the moonlight.

The ewe followed me down the slope, around some trees, alongside the artesian well. It took a while for our little procession to reach safety. Whenever the ewe wandered or strayed—

she lost track of her lamb several times—I had to clamber back up and hold the sling in front of her nose. When we finally got to the barn, I set the lamb in a stall, slipped off the sling, slid down the gate, and turned on the heat lamp.

I gave the pair a clump of hay (called a "leaf") and a bucket of fresh water, which the ewe drank hungrily, alternating gulps between lamb-cleaning. I got my special scissors, held the lamb up—the mother circled in alarm—and snipped the umbilical cord, then sprayed the spot with disinfectant. Rose had slipped in quietly to watch; the ewe didn't seem to mind.

Jane had tightly curled fleece in a warm cinnamon color that would fade to cream with age, and a white blaze on her head. She had a high-pitched bleat that, to her mother, would always distinguish her from the others. And she quickly found a teat and began nursing, her tail wiggling frantically—a sign that milk was being consumed.

This wasn't so bad.

Rose and I were both transfixed—but also weary. We left the pair in the barn and went inside to rest up for the next round.

I CHECKED THE PADDOCK SEVERAL TIMES A DAY, BUT THE weather was so cold—nights still in the single digits and wind chills below zero, even in mid-March—that I set my alarm clock to ring every two or three hours during the night as well. I kept my jeans and jacket and boots by the bed so I could yank them on fast and dash out on patrol with Rose and a flashlight. I soon came to understand the concept of sleep deprivation as torture. In the daytime I became useless—irritable, exhausted, grimy. After the first few nights I simply slept in my clothes, like a fireman; all I had to do was pull on my boots.

The next birth was more complicated. I came into the paddock early one morning—weren't any of these ewes going to deliver in daylight?—and noticed a ewe near the fence, obviously in labor. She stomped and groaned until 5:30, but this time, I wasn't about to miss the moment of birth. I saw her water break, bursting from the dangling sac, followed by a gooey brown mass that slid to the ground, coughed, and started to move. I saw that membranes covered the lamb's mouth and, using my plastic surgical gloves, wiped them away. The lamb gurgled, baahed, and struggled to its feet; the mother began licking.

That was when I messed up. I went into the house to fetch my birthing supplies. It took no more than ten minutes—my fingers were so numb, I held them above the toaster oven to try to regain some feeling—before we returned to the paddock.

I climbed the hill, waited a few more minutes for the ewe to finish her licking, then maneuvered the baby into the sling. This was a diligent mother, but she seemed to lose her bearings easily. We went back and forth on the hill for what seemed forever, though it probably was no more than fifteen minutes. I called for help from Rose, who circled behind the ewe to get her moving. That focused her on the lamb, and the four of us found our way quickly into the barn and into the second stall. In the other one, Jane and her mom were thriving.

After cutting the cord and making sure the new pair had hay and water and heat, I went back into the paddock for a final look around before going back to bed. I was cold and sore— lambing was hard on my leg—and it was a long climb up to bed.

My heart lurched. Another lamb, clearly newborn, since it was tiny and wet, was bleating at a ewe that didn't seem to mind or chase it away, but wasn't being attentive, either. She wasn't licking the baby, which made me suspicious. I shined my flashlight around and saw no traces of afterbirth. When I walked closer, the ewe simply moved away. For a new mother, she was awfully diffident.

Then it struck me: this was a twin. When I'd gone into the house for supplies, the ewe had given birth to another lamb.

When I came back to the paddock and carried her firstborn away, she'd followed me, and we'd left this baby behind. Or perhaps it had simply wandered off, beyond the mother's attention. I could see no other ewe in labor. This had to be a twin, and it was cold and alone, and therefore in trouble.

I was running out of time. I wrapped the lamb in a towel and with my other hand grabbed a handful of the afterbirth still on the ground; sometimes if you smeared it on the lamb the mother would connect with it. I rushed to the barn, sliding, falling once but keeping the lamb and afterbirth up out of the muck. Freezing, covered in mud and other stuff, I rushed into the barn and put the lamb into the pen. I took the first twin out so that the ewe would concentrate on this new one.

But she immediately butted the baby right into the pen wall, then charged at him again. Maybe if we tried Joanne's fancy blue lambing pen: it had a separate compartment where newborns could go to be safe. I put both babies inside, then the ewe; she kept butting the second twin with great force whenever she could. The baby looked miserable, battered; he retreated into a corner just out of reach and lay down, shivering, while the other lamb crawled out and began nursing.

I tried smearing afterbirth on twin number two, pulling first one lamb and then the other out of the pen, so that the second baby could nurse and ignite the connection. Nothing helped. For two hours the ewe rejected her baby, until I realized this wasn't going to work.

I named the poor guy Arthur and left him in his safe corner. I went into the kitchen, got out my lamb survival supplies, and called the vet while mixing up some milk replacement in a baby bottle. When I came back into the barn Arthur had given up on his mom and was huddled forlornly. He loved the bottle instantly.

I pulled out the lawn chair I'd bought the day before at the Salem Hardware Store, realizing I'd never survive standing for hours every night. I put a towel in my lap and sat down with Arthur and the bottle. He drank greedily.

It is impossible, I suspect, for anyone who loves animals not to bond with a newborn lamb that's curled up against you, drawing sustenance from the bottle you're giving him. I could feel Arthur's heart thumping as he gulped. I told him how sorry I was that I'd screwed up his first hours and promised to take care of him.

In the morning Dr. Amanda came from Granville—we'd gotten to know each other well by now—and said the mother and twins were doing fine. Arthur was thin, but if he was taking the bottle, he might make it. He would have a rough time when he was released into the flock; the other mothers would butt and kick him. He would survive, if he could, by grabbing the occasional passing nipple and learning to eat grass and grain early. Without real mother's milk, he might never be as robust and disease-resistant as the others, but he had a decent shot.

"Arthur thinks you are his mom," the vet told me. And, true, he baahed furiously at the sight of me. But the lamb was nothing like a puppy, able to drowse in his human's presence. He was all instinct and drive, all about food, battling relentlessly for every drop of milk. It was curious to see the instincts nature gave these creatures to help them survive.

Every three or four hours Rose and I came out into the barn and I sat down in the chair with Arthur while he scarfed down half a bottle. I usually also brought a cup or two of oats for Carol and Fanny, who were getting fewer snacks and less attention than normal but accepted lambing season with their usual equanimity. Those cold nights in the pasture were considerably warmer for the presence of Carol or Fanny, who stood alongside me, nudging my pocket for cookies or presenting their heads for scratching. They took in the lambing drama the way they took in everything, with their soulful eyes and calm manners.

The morning after Arthur's birth, the sheep named Paula was

standing matter-of-factly in the pasture at five A.M. with a big brown bruiser of a newborn ram alongside her. She'd handled the whole business efficiently in the few hours since I'd last checked. Her lamb, twice the size of the others, ran right up to me and Rose. I named him Brutus. Paula, like her namesake, was a great mom, attentive and affectionate.

I wished my own Paula were here, but she'd been traveling for work and wasn't scheduled to arrive for another week. Meanwhile the house was a shambles, dirty dishes piling up in the sink, syringes and bottles all over the kitchen and pantry, dust and caked dirt and sprigs of hay all over the floor. I'd had no time for laundry or shopping and was wolfing down frozen dinners, stale bread, and an occasional apple or slice of cheese. The lambs were eating more nutritiously than I was.

By the second day of nursing, Arthur and I had bonded. He was a fighter; his determination was appealing. I kept him near his mother in case she had a change of heart, and he had grown adept at darting into her pen, trying to grab a drink, then retreating into his safe corner. He looked miserable whenever the ewe butted him, and watched silently as his sister nursed. But I thought he was gaining weight.

Tired as I was, I looked forward to pulling the lawn chair out, sitting with the lamb on my lap, donkeys hovering nearby and Rose sniffing around. A few times I brought Orson out on a leash to inspect the new arrivals. I didn't especially like the way he eyed the lambs, particularly defenseless Arthur, but it was neat to have him be part of the season.

Rose was growing more comfortable by the day with our expanding cadre of lambs, but a new problem had arisen. The same ewes she'd been happily pushing around for months had suddenly become monsters, hissing, kicking, and butting whenever she came near. Rose was shocked, yelping in surprise and retreating. Conventional herding-dog wisdom dictated that she shouldn't be there at all, but she was my partner in all things sheep. I watched in fascination as she sat next to me and studied these newly aggressive creatures as they ate and nursed.

I had no doubt she would approach the matter with the same resolve and ingenuity that she brought to the rest of her work, but for now, she was stymied. That was fine; it wouldn't hurt for her to respect her charges a bit more.

On the third night, I saw Arthur weaken a bit. He was cold, shivering; he didn't baah when I entered the barn. At a shepherd friend's suggestion, I'd tried smearing the afterbirth from another ewe on him and tried to slip him in with her as a fake twin. That didn't work. I tried him with Paula and her brute in the lambing pen; she rammed him full force against the plywood wall. So I put him back with his mom, cursing her indifference and my own carelessness.

The next day, I came outside at six A.M. with Arthur's morning bottle. He was subdued, but gamely took two or three gulps of milk. Then, as I held him, I actually felt his heart stop. His head tilted off to one side. I'd lost him.

I could hear my neighbors' voices: "It's part of it." And they were right: if you were going to have lambs, whatever your resolve, you were going to lose some. It was as intrinsic to the experience as cooing over them as they gamboled about.

But I was surprised and sad. If I'd been thinking more clearly, I might have been able to connect Arthur and his mother sooner, given him more of a chance. I admired his spirit, but I'd helped doom him. Anthony, who had no time for Boomer guilt, came by in the afternoon to take his small body away; the ground was still too hard for a burial, and the possibility of coyotes being drawn down from the woods would have imperiled the rest of the flock.

I had changed somewhat in my relationship to animals, I realized. Even my piddling effort at farming had forced me into actions and decisions I wouldn't have thought myself capable of—shooting a feral cat, killing a ewe, messing around with sheep placentas in the middle of a freezing night. Life and death seemed close.

The welfare of the farm and the herd came first; any individual creatures were subordinate to that. I'd been pulling for Arthur, but he wasn't a companion in the sense that Rose or Orson were. He was something different, somewhere between a pet and a wild animal. His loss meant that I'd already, through my own dumb mistake, failed in my goal of keeping all my ewes and lambs alive. But I didn't have the time or inclination to make too much of it. There were too many other lambs arriving, too many other demands.

The next few weeks were high-voltage bedlam: cold, wet, late snow, sleeplessness, fatigue, long labors. The thrashes and moans of a laboring ewe could now wake me—like any parent—from a sound sleep. I got used to popping out of bed, into my boots, and scrambling out to the paddock.

Mostly, I then stood by for hours with my coffee, stomping my numbed feet, watching while the ewes pawed and struggled, waiting for the lamb (or two; we had multiple multiples) to emerge.

The slimy blobs slid to the ground, then suddenly moved and stood, fighting from the first for milk. Good moms started a meticulous and careful licking, nuzzling their babies, helping them find the teats. Bad moms seemed schizzy from the beginning, losing focus, getting their babies confused with others, sometimes running back and forth.

After they'd bonded, I carried the babies into the barn, the ewes following me, Rose following them. I'd cut the umbilical cord, spray iodine on the wound, give an oral vitamin supplement and a shot of Bo-Se vitamin booster. After forty-eight hours, I'd tag the baby, then remove most of its tail with the pig castrator, a distasteful but necessary process.

For the first four or five days, I managed to keep careful records, noting the time of birth, sex, tag numbers, and the ewes' maternal skills. But my ballpoint pens kept freezing; my fingers stopped working; and after a few too many late-night labors, my system fell apart. Paula (the human one), who has as much passion for order as I have a gift for bedlam, said she'd help sort it all out when she came up.

Though all the births involved hours of sleeplessness, most of them were fairly routine, especially after the first few, and most of the moms diligent. When labors grew too long or rough, I put on my surgical gloves, applied the lube, reached in, and pulled the lamb out, careful to make sure that the hooves and head emerged together. Something that would have been unthinkable just a few months ago was now just another day in Bedlam.

Each time I midwifed, my confidence grew. I knew by now what a birth sac felt like; I could grope around to feel the hooves and head and position them properly while the ewe pushed and I pulled. I vaguely remembered our own nurse-midwife telling my wife to do much the same thing when Emma was born. I came to appreciate women even more. "Push, push!" I found myself urging the ewes.

One lamb's head got stuck in the birth canal, and it took me nearly an hour to maneuver it out. I was sure the lamb would be dead, but it sprang to life right after it hit the ground. By now the lambing pens were full, and I had to cram a mother and baby into a barn corner with a pile of straw or kick a comfortable mom and baby out into the cruel world a bit early.

I found this cycle—birth, nesting, nurturing, reentering the life of the herd—fascinating, even reassuring, but also relentless. Even when we hit a lull, I had little time left after moving heat lamps, mucking out used pens, replacing frozen buckets of water, providing fresh hay to exhausted mothers. The pile of used gloves, syringes, and stained towels mounted. The rest of the world receded; writing became a distant memory; so did casual phone calls, opened mail, cooking, and routine chores. I talked to Paula and Emma in hurried snatches.

Nature, I came to see, didn't really "take its course" all that reliably; she needed backup from me, vets, and various other helpers.

My farmer neighbors stopped by, joking at my anxiety, scratching their heads at all the heated tubs and Joanne's beautiful enamel pen. They thought I was crazy, but I was also proud to have their grudging respect.

"I'll say one thing for you," said Carr, returned from Florida a couple of weeks earlier than he should have, when he came by one morning to find me injecting vitamins into a lamb's shoulder. "You keep your animals well." It was one of the nicest compliments I'd ever heard, and from one of the toughest sources.

Two of the ewes had vaginal prolapses, a serious, life-threatening and evidently very uncomfortable condition that required one of the vets to insert and attach a plastic retainer. Nobody liked this procedure—not Amanda or Kirk, certainly not the unhappy ewe, and not me, the writer of checks.

One of the ewes with a prolapse was one of the few I felt any attachment to. This was Minnie, Carolyn's oldest ewe and one of the first sheep my dogs and I had ever worked with. Minnie was such a herding veteran that if I yelled "come bye," she'd head in the right direction even if the dog didn't. And she was one of the very few ewes who seemed to appreciate human contact and sometimes came up to me for nose scratching and a handful of corn.

I had seen her go into labor in the middle of the night, but no baby came out; after six or seven hours, I called the vet. Dr. Amanda had to insert a retainer. I worried about Minnie, even so; she didn't smell quite right and seemed intensely uncomfortable. Rose—following the invisible signals of the animal world—ignored her. Perhaps she sensed that Minnie was sick and was responding with some sort of border collie Geneva Convention.

Nesbitt, bless his nasty soul, had done his job well. After two tumultuous weeks, I had nineteen lambs from fourteen ewes. And then there was Minnie, still expecting.

She was wide as a barn, her udders hanging nearly to the ground. She would be the last to give birth, and everyone—me, farmers, vets—thought the fetus was likely to die within her, if it hadn't already. One vet suggested a cesarean section, something I was reluctant to put her, and all of us, through. Various neighbors offered to put her out of her misery, Hebron-style. I decided to wait it out.

I put her in a barn stall and kept tabs on her, bringing her hay and water. She was trying hard, unable to settle down; she was also old, in bad shape, and smelling worse by the day. We couldn't let this go on indefinitely.

The night before had been an all-nighter. A ewe gave birth to twins and, not wanting to repeat the mistake I'd made with Arthur, I'd hovered over her for every minute of her labor and birth, then picked both lambs up carefully, walking them backward into their pens.

The surviving lambs, tagged and docked, were already frolicking with one another, hopping on and off hay bales, and nursing—*and* managing to dart through tiny gaps between and under fences. Unlike their elders, they had lively personalities, and they seemed to grow bigger and more confident by the day. I wanted no further losses due to my stupidity.

By the end of the week I was wrecked, and quite willing to leave things to nature, as everyone advised. But I couldn't go to bed without checking on Minnie one more time, so I left Orson sleeping by the woodstove, called Rose, grabbed my lambing bucket and gloves, and slogged out to the barn. Winter was in its final days but was going out hard. The back-door thermometer said fifteen degrees, downright tropical, but there was a sharp wind, bad conditions for newborns if we had any more. I was expecting a stillbirth.

Entering the barn, I could see that something was wrong. The wooden gate to Minnie's stall had been split in two, evidently after some intense thrashing. In front of it, Minnie lay on her back, feet in the air, swollen udders hanging to one side. She was lifeless, cold and stiff.

"Goodbye, girl," I said as Rose sniffed at her body. "You were a sweetie." It seemed unfair that one of the few ewes I knew and liked had gone this way. But to be honest, I was too tired to feel very much. In the way even a small farm demands, I had already moved into the gritty, practical phase: How far can I drag Minnie's heavy body? Where should I take it? It would be hours before I could call Anthony to move her to his father-in-law's farm, with its dead-animal pile.

Kirk Ayling, the vet who'd stopped by to see Minnie just that morning, had told me that if anything looked wrong, I should put on gloves. "Go in there and pull anything you can feel out," he instructed. This is part of it, I thought for the umpteenth time. If you want to have a farm with sheep and donkeys, you're going to put your hands in some previously unimaginable places. So I did.

The cavity was warm and filled with fluids, some of which—smelling foul and infected—came gushing out. I felt a sac, which I grabbed and pushed back, trying to align the head and hooves as I'd been told. I pulled gently but firmly for several minutes until a gelatinous blob came out, looking nothing like a lamb. It plopped, motionless, to the barn floor. The odor made me gag.

As I turned to grab a towel and wipe my hands, the blob suddenly moved and coughed. A brown lamb with a white forelock was shaking itself off, struggling to its feet, searching for its mother. I was stunned. If the baby were alive, I wondered, could Minnie really be dead?

This was a case for Anthony's Three Steps.

I grabbed the lifeless Minnie and rolled her over, pushing her to her rigid feet. Upright, she shook her head and began searching anxiously for her lamb. Too startled to kick into gear—cut cord, apply iodine, switch on heat lamp—I noticed after a few moments that I'd been staring and muttering, "Oh my God. Oh my *God,*" for too long. Because it *was* a bit Godlike, watching that lamb clamber to its feet, alive because of me. Minnie was licking her tiny offspring frantically, trying to clean it and warm it up. The baby, a female, could barely walk but was fighting to get to her mother's teat.

Could it possibly survive? Would Minnie? I made sure the lamb was breathing and getting cleaned off, rushed into the house, washed my hands, put out an SOS to the Granville vet.

I was elated to think that if my foolishness had cost the life of one early lamb, my experience might have saved another. I was also afraid, as I waited to hear Kirk's truck in the driveway, that mother and perhaps baby were too sick to survive.

Kirk would probably have been amazed to know just how happy I was to see him. He was as shocked at Minnie's resurrection and delivery as I was. "On the way over, I was thinking about a C-section," he said, "wondering if you'd go for that to try and save the baby."

Then, oddly, we looked at each other and, without any prompting, said the same thing at the same time: "Where is the afterbirth?"

If there was no placenta, it had to still be inside. "There must be another lamb," said Kirk. I asked him to try to pull it out, but he smiled and shook his head. "No, you do it," he said. Reluctantly, fearing I might harm the remaining twin, I gloved up and reached in. I wasn't sure what I was feeling, so Kirk felt around and positioned the fetus. I pulled and pulled and out came a ram, Leo, to join the female I decided to call Gert.

Kirk and I spent a half hour settling Minnie down, cleaning her up and tending to her twins. Then we shook hands and I thanked him for his encouragement. "That was awesome," I said, and it was.

I could hardly believe that people like these large-animal vets existed any longer in contemporary, liability-obsessed American society. On call almost all the time, they rushed from farm to farm over long distances in dreadful weather, often working with people who had little money for animal health care. They pulled colts out of horses and calves out of cows, got bitten by pigs and kicked by donkeys. They worked in open spaces, mud, and manure. They made educated guesses, improvised, innovated; they made do with what they had. They were amazing.

I felt pretty amazed myself. A ewe I had given up for dead was alive and nursing two small but healthy twins. Kirk said Minnie had developed a vaginal infection—hence the odor—and gave me penicillin and syringes. She'd need shots twice a day.

Still, my lambing season was over, or so I thought. The next day I would dismantle the other pens, put away the heat lamps, muck out the barn, and try to return to my real work—writing. I felt tired, exhilarated, and vaguely triumphant. I had lost a lamb but brought many healthy ones into the world.

One lamb, Murphy, had been shipped off to Anthony's because its mother seemed to have no milk. Murphy was thriving on bottled sheep's milk, but having him join two large dogs and a toddler proved a strain on an already clamorous household, so Murphy moved on to a shepherd and spinner friend, Sheila. A couple of volunteers, including Jacob, had helped with barn chores and hay hauling. Even with two prolapses, we'd gotten through, with the help of some good friends and a couple of great dogs.

MY RELIEF WAS, OF COURSE, PREMATURE. THE ENSUING WEEKS just brought a different kind of chaos.

Lambing season, it seems, is not over when the last of the lambs are born. Apart from all the medical care and maintenance, a whole new set of crises can erupt.

A third ewe had a prolapse, requiring another vet visit, more stitching, another bill.

Minnie's twins didn't gain weight the way their peers did. Maybe her milk was insufficient or poor quality; in any case, I had to resume bottle feeding. Leo attached himself to me, while Gert hung out with the donkeys. Visitors found this cute, but it was poor animal husbandry, dangerous to the lambs. The only protection sheep have is the impression of bulk they make when they flock together; otherwise they are defenseless. Predators look for sheep wandering off alone, as Gert and Leo had taken to doing. Border collies really don't like to see sheep traveling solo, away from the herd, either. It made Rose and Orson crazy to see individual lambs roaming around.

Rose already had her problems with this reconfigured bunch. The lambs were too small and inexperienced to respond to her herding attempts, and the once-docile ewes were still morphing into rampaging beasts when she approached their young. Her pasture became a battleground. Several times, as she was charged, kicked, or butted, Rose yelped and ran behind me, frightened and confused.

In one way, my gamble had paid off: Rose, having attended all their births, was very tender toward the lambs, even as their mothers continued to chase her across the paddock.

But she struggled with the problem of how to work with this complex mix. Sometimes she tried herding Fanny rather than take on the ewes. The lambs didn't understand what Rose wanted them to do, and the mothers stuck with their offspring, so herding became virtually impossible, especially for a young dog who was still learning.

Rose tried all her moves, but she got run off time after time. Resilient and determined, she was also failing for the first time; I saw some signs of stress and hesitation.

Perhaps it was time to recognize our limits and pull back. The problem was, I'd never needed her more. I'd already found lambs outside the pasture several times; they could slither between fenceposts and under gates. Meanwhile vets were roaring in and out of the driveway several times a week and would soon want to castrate the young rams. The farrier would arrive shortly for hoof maintenance, followed in a couple of weeks by the shearer, ready to relieve the ewes of their shaggy, matted fleece. I also had to administer various medications. I needed to move this unruly mob around.

So I turned to my secret weapon. Orson had been around sheep for years, and if he was too excitable to herd in the approved way, I had nevertheless been working with him every single day throughout the winter. I'd set up our training sessions so that he could not fail, locking the sheep in the small training pen and simply sending him around its perimeter one way or the other, using the "come bye" and "away to me" commands. Usually, he spun himself around a few times, then tore toward the pen, raced around the fence with his beautiful lope, and came roaring back to me for a treat. The sheep, nervously watching as he galloped past with that wild gleam in his eyes, were probably grateful for the fence.

It wasn't herding, exactly, but we'd worked hard on it. Now, I owed Rose a break while the lambs grew up. Why not see whether Orson could dog-break my suddenly unruly herd? We had done that for farmers in New York and Vermont, for ten dollars or a couple of pies. Why not do it for ourselves?

On a blustery afternoon, holding my breath, I walked into the pasture with my complex and excitable soulmate. The sight of all the lambs hopping around surprised Orson; he stopped and stared. But he didn't stop for long.

The ewes who'd rushed up to challenge Rose had grown bolder of late. But the first ewe who challenged Orson got a nip in the butt, followed by a tug at her shaggy fleece that pulled her over onto her side. This only had to happen once. The ewe was unhurt but rattled, and after that, at the mere sight of Orson, the ewes all bleated urgently and nosed their lambs toward the training pen and swiftly inside.

Orson wasn't subtle—no inspiring interplay between human and dog, no graceful minuet between dog and sheep—but he did the job. When the vets came or I needed to administer shots, I just opened the pasture gate and let Orson in. In seconds, no matter where they'd been, the whole flock was either inside the pen or huddled in the barn, whichever was closest.

This deference, I quickly discovered, also helped Rose. Orson was teaching the sheep and lambs to respect a dog; Rose, challenging the ewes calmly but firmly, was the dog who needed their respect. I noticed the butting and charging becoming less frequent, Rose growing more confident. I praised Orson relentlessly. If he couldn't yet herd like a true border collie, he could help the process along.

AFTER ANOTHER WEEK OF NASTY WEATHER THAT SENT ME scampering out to the barn with heat lamps and hay at night, the winter at long last softened its grip on the farm.

On March 20, the day after the last lamb was born, Paula showed up, joking about her exquisite timing. She'd be here for a week, during her semester break, and I've rarely been happier to see anybody. Like me, Paula has never been particularly skilled in the domestic arts; unlike me, she is superbly well organized. In a day or so, the house looked like humans occupied it. I was eating home-cooked (or, at least, defrosted) meals, wore clothes that had been washed and dried. She prepared a Paula-like census of all the ewes and lambs, listing every relevant detail from birth date to quality of mothering. She trekked out to the barn to brush and feed Carol and Fanny, a bit neglected of late. She even helped hold a stricken ewe when Dr. Amanda had to correct another prolapse.

Paula's very presence cheered me up and helped me believe in the possibility of spring. It was a joy to see her settle into the roomy old farmhouse between chores, camping in front of the woodstove, transcribing her taped interviews and editing her students' papers.

By midweek, spring did in fact arrive. The temperature rose into the fifties and I felt comfortable outside for the first time in months. My frostbitten fingers stopped aching; the ice pack around the house and barns was receding; the mud began to dry. Paula reintroduced the notion, after my weeks of wolfing down bread on the way out to the barn, of the civilized breakfast. She cleared the syringes and lambing supplies from the kitchen table.

It was a pleasure to spend a little time chatting over our coffee, looking out the kitchen window at the ewes and lambs moseying through the pasture, framed by a donkey or two.

As March rushed by and Paula returned to New Jersey and her work, things began to quiet. I got to sleep through the night. The lambing crises became less frequent.

I did, to my real sorrow, lose Minnie and her twins. Weakened by age and infection, pregnancy and delivery, she stopped eating. I tried to tempt her with grain, but she seemed to have lost interest. I was sad but not shocked to find her dead in the barn one morning, and this time, I couldn't revive her. Gert and Leo, never very hardy despite my supplemental bottles, didn't survive her for long. It was a grim warning against feeling Godlike.

So our census dropped to thirteen ewes, and seventeen lambs (including the absent but healthy Murphy, who was settling in nicely at Sheila's place down the road).

But moms and babies were beginning to nibble at the early grass; bales of hay were no longer disappearing at the winter's frantic rate. Birdsong returned to the trees around the house. I allowed myself a little pride. I'd had help—from Anthony, the vets, the friends advising me and cheering me on, my sister, and Paula. But true to my original covenant, I'd done most of the work myself. Coping with my strange new responsibilities, I'd learned what I had to learn, done what I had to do.

I could hardly believe how much I suddenly knew about placentas, prolapses, milk and teats, tails and tags, and animals' instinctual struggle to survive.

And to help others survive. I saw some great moms when I walked through the pasture now. The donkeys, always accepting and generous, didn't seem to mind sharing their barn. No dog could have worked harder than Rose or been of greater assistance to a beleaguered human. As for my brooding Orson, as always an emotional pillar, the great instincts of his breed had risen to the occasion when the need arose.

I had assembled a peaceable kingdom, and how I loved caring for it. It touched the deepest parts of me, whole and broken. If there is a link between our dogs and our humanity, there is also a link between our humanity and the care we provide to creatures that depend on us.

Early on, I'd planned to get rid of half my sheep after lambing season. I'd keep a small flock for herding, sell the rest to local farmers. But I was having second thoughts. It would be tough for me to separate these lambs from their mothers and their birthplace.

I could just hear my neighbors snort. *Farm animals aren't pets,* they'd growl. *No point in feeding one more sheep than you need. Just money down the drain.*

But when you've pulled a lamb out of its mother, when you've carried it into the barn, you have a different point of view. At least, I did. ☜

Chapter Twelve

DOG DAYS III

AT THE START OF APRIL THE NIGHTS WERE ONCE AGAIN COLD enough to encrust the water tubs with ice and cover the pasture with frost. I had to haul out the de-icers and stick them back in the water. With a pitchfork, I stirred the hay to bring the dry stuff up for the animals.

At least the spring sun was strong, unlike its winter predecessor. It quickly spread over the meadow and the barns, warming the still-brown grass, drying things out. The soaked ground gave off a continuous sighing, sucking sound as if cold were bubbling up from far below. The roads were still blanketed with sand and salt and bore scars from the Highway Department's relentless day-and-night plowing.

The donkeys and sheep loved to catch those first morning rays. They were sun worshipers. It was pleasant to look out the window and see them lying down, half-dozing, at ease in the sunlight. For me, these moments were the saving grace of sheep.

Seeing how much Carol loved the spring, I was beginning to understand how rough the winter had been for her. Next fall, Anthony has a plan to build her a heated shed in the barn, maybe with the same lamps that warmed the lambs. He also means to build a south-facing shed for the sheep, so that even if they don't want to come in from the cold, they can stay dry and out of the wind.

The dogs, freer to follow their usual pursuits now that the lambs were rapidly getting bigger, seemed fond of the longer days and yielding earth, too.

ROSE WAS NOT THE SAME DOG WHO HAD ARRIVED IN OCTOBER. She was a young lady now, responsible, mature. I was filled with admiration and respect for her diligence and work ethic.

Her energy remained breathtaking, and her sense of responsibility had only grown. By dawn, she was already scooting from window to window upstairs to scope things out in the pasture. Rose reminded me of those NFL coaches you see pacing the sidelines at football games, their clipboards full of charts and plays, earphones picking up invisible chatter, always thinking, scheming, reacting. Rose was preparing her herding plays long before we went out to the sheep.

I believed Rose had a secret plan for the farm, a detailed map in her head that showed exactly where all her ewes and lambs and humans ought to be. Though I was nominally the herder, I wasn't privy to the map. Herding trainers all said you needed a plan, but it seemed to me that I didn't, as long as Rose had such a good one. My job was mostly to latch and unlatch gates and tell her where I'd like the sheep to go that day. The rest was up to her.

There were moments with Rose when I felt like a ticket-holder at my own show, lucky to be there, in awe of what I was seeing, but incapable of completely understanding the nuances of the production. Some herders talked about the importance of leadership, of directing and guiding the dog. I wish. Most of the time I did what Rose suggested, and it worked out fine.

Her day now began around seven A.M., as she and Orson and I took our first walk. Our walks were getting more exciting. In deep winter, there was little to smell, no holes to dig, nothing to chase. Now chipmunks, field mice, rabbits, and deer, to name a few, had reemerged to keep the dogs occupied as they dashed here and there in an effort to organize things. Border collies are heroic in their ambition, but doomed to fail. They simply cannot position every moving thing in the world where they want it to be.

After our walk, we came back to the farmhouse for breakfast, the first of many daily phone yaks with Paula, and a cup of coffee to help jump-start me for the morning chores. They were easier than in winter, but not easy.

Orson stayed behind for this round. Eager for the beef jerky he knew was coming, he was usually already waiting in his crate.

Rose had the drill down, too. By now, she knew the boots I used for herding, the sweatshirt I wore to ward off the morning chill as we headed for the barn, the pocketknife I carried to cut open the hay bales. Deploying any of these items had her sitting by the back door in a flash, staring at me impatiently.

She was my partner in anything relating to sheep, donkeys, barns, and pastures. Orson's turf was the rest of my life. It was a good division; both seemed happy with their work.

Outside, Rose and I went first to the former pig barn, the small, askew outbuilding where I stored the feed. Big bucket of feed and corn for the sheep, until there was enough grass growing for them. Smaller bucket of oats for Carol and Fanny. Rose, the centurion, scoured the barn for any signs of mice or the two barn cats still living there.

I sometimes glimpsed them skittering around the barns at night when I came out for my final check; otherwise, they remained invisible. Unlike the one that attacked Rose, these two made no trouble and were welcome. I occasionally left a can of tuna fish open on a ledge in the pig barn; it was always empty in the morning.

I carried the feed buckets outside, unlatched the barnyard gate. I put Rose in a stay; she waited, stiff and alert, until I told her, "Go get the sheep."

It was a statement of how far we'd come that I no longer paid much attention as she tore up the hill to wherever the ewes and lambs had gathered. Without fail, Rose and the sheep were heading down the hill within minutes. When they reached the trough and started crunching, Rose positioned herself between the sheep and the barn and lay down, on guard.

For weeks during the winter, chaos erupted after the sheep finished their feed and then headed for the donkeys' oats. Almost daily, a sheep would plow into my legs and topple me. It was hard enough to stay upright on the icy slope, impossible with sheep crashing around. Fanny and Carol were too gentle to fight the marauders off and always backed away while I cursed. Rose didn't like it.

So she began sitting between the sheep trough and the donkeys' feed buckets, and now woe to the sheep who even looked our way. I went about my chores while she kept order.

Each day, I walked around to the main barn's back door, slid it open, and hauled out two bales of hay. Rose hopped up the step and into the big drafty barn and chased out the napping pigeons.

I dragged the hay to the feeder, Rose patrolling ahead to keep the sheep from rushing at me and the hay; then I cut the baling twine, which I wrapped around a fencepost, and shook the bales into the feeder. (Farmers all have cascades of baling twine around their fenceposts. I've adopted the custom without ever figuring out why.) The sheep came up and started crunching. Rose never bothered them while they were eating; she sat regally off to the side, carefully observing everybody's movements, including mine.

This was usually when Rose and I had our first herding session of the day. When I moved toward the sheep and said, "Let's go," she sprang into action and circled the herd, gathering them together, nudging wanderers and slow movers along. Silently, I picked someplace to walk—the training pen, the paddock, the path over the hill—and set out. The sheep followed me, she followed them, keeping the flock together. Rose has a tendency to circle around to the front, slowing their progress, so I sometimes held out my hand and yelled "Back" to steer her to the rear of the flock.

I'd never had a dog like Rose before, nor a relationship like this. It was a strange thing to say, for someone who believed in not blurring the differences between dogs and humans, but I couldn't help thinking of Paula when I watched Rose on the job. Like my wife, Rose was a working girl, focused and businesslike, picky about the people she liked, supportive even when skeptical, devoid of guile. And I couldn't exist without her.

Rose had been a gamble in lots of ways. Orson and I were firmly attached when she'd arrived, much of our work with each other well under way, so there was little risk to him. But Carolyn had warned that a new puppy could have serious consequences for Homer. His anxiety, avoidant behavior, and herding problems might never be resolved if an energetic new puppy entered the picture. And as it happened, they weren't.

A new puppy is always an adventure. I loved adventures. Still, I'd never imagined Rose would be the dog she was. For one thing, she and Orson were crazy about each other from the first. He tried all of his domineering, possessive tricks, and she just blew him off.

Nothing stymied or bothered Rose for very long, and, as my

ewes were learning, nothing intimidated her for long, either. After a few months, Orson had given up trying to push her around. In fact, I was astonished to see Rose tease Orson into playing tug-of-war one spring morning. Each grabbed one end of a rope toy and they raced off together in ever widening circles around the house. Rose had opened up even this intense creature.

I admitted, as I watched them romp, to feeling a bit triumphant. Orson had grown almost Lablike in his sweetness and obedience; Rose had thrived on our home schooling; I had survived the winter. But anybody who loves dogs knows that life with them is filled with unpredictability.

ONE DAY EARLY IN APRIL I WAS TAKING THE DOGS FOR THEIR final evening walk, a routine and simple affair. Usually I stood by the back door, and gazed up at the sky while the dogs rushed up the hill, did their business, and came in for the night.

We'd followed this routine for months without any kind of trouble, without my even paying much attention. Rose ran around more than Orson, but she never left my sight or sound. And her recall was terrific; from her first day, I never said "Come" without tossing a treat on the ground; now all I had to do was yell, "Rosie, come!" and she would tear down the path or through the woods toward me. She never strayed far, anyway; border collies like to keep an eye on the humans who bring them to sheep.

On this cool night, just a few days before my first longish visit home in months—I planned to stay four or five days—I opened the door, strolled alongside the house, and shined my torch out into the pasture to see the sheep's reflecting eyes. They were way up on the hill, their lambs huddled near them.

Orson drifted back to the door. No Rose. I called her once, twice. Nothing.

After months of walking, herding, lambing, cuddling, I knew this dog. She'd never run off or failed to come within a few moments of being called.

I waited for five or ten minutes, my desire to do something growing along with my anxiety. I walked outside, yelled, pointed the high-powered flashlight everywhere I could see. I took Orson out and we trekked through the brush and woods and up the dark hill. I blew the whistle I sometimes used during herding training and called her name.

I told myself she'd be back any second. When I called Paula, just to let her know I might be outside for a while, I said Rose was probably chasing some woodchuck into its hole. I didn't want to take this seriously. But as the minutes ticked by, my lame effort to stave off terror faltered. I started to think about the coyotes and bobcats and even—rumor had it—a mountain lion that prowled these woods.

I'd heard more than one horror story about a dog attacked by coyotes in a backyard, about dogs who ran off and got trapped in the nested strands of barbed wire left all over the woods from long-abandoned farms. Sadly, their bodies were usually found much later. The thought of Rose cornered by some animal or trapped in a ditch or wire chewed at me.

I ran up and down the dark road shouting, flashing my light and blowing the whistle.

I thought of calling someone for help. Anthony would have roared over with Arthur and the nuclear lights mounted on his Toyota pickup. But I clung to the notion she would pop out of the woods any second.

I could already hear the Country Bullshit: "Aw, hell, what a nervous Flatlander you are! Dogs around here run off all the time. She'll be back."

Country wisdom is often right, and a healthy counterpoint to Flatlander anxieties. But for all the dogs that come back, there are plenty that don't, hit by cars on those dark dirt roads, killed by predators, lost in the vast woods. As I often told my neighbors, just because somebody is anxious doesn't mean his fears are always groundless.

Rose was a small, intense, and impulsive creature, whose confidence sometimes outweighed her common sense. She also had ferocious predatory instincts, boundless energy, and insatiable curiosity—all potentially dangerous qualities.

After two hours of walking up and down and shouting, I was wiped out and hoarse. Orson and I got into the farm truck and chugged up the road. He was peering ahead through the windshield; I was blowing the whistle, hitting the horn, shouting, "Rose! Rosie!" out the window. About a half-mile along, I thought I heard some barking.

I turned the truck to shine the headlights up the hill and didn't notice the deep drainage ditch to my left. In ten seconds the truck slid smoothly off of the road, tilted at an angle, and sank up to its fenders in thick mud—probably the only thing that kept it from rolling all the way over. Pushing the door open with some difficulty, I crawled out and saw I was mired in muck over the tires.

Orson and I began the long slog back down the dark road. I saw one or two lights down driveways, but it was getting late, not a good time to be knocking on strangers' doors. As I walked down the hill I kept calling out for Rose, my heart sinking.

Clearly, something was wrong. You could hear a call for miles in this valley and she had always responded instantly. Something had hurt or trapped her.

I couldn't shake off my visions of her struggling in barbed wire or running for her life.

Rose was still a puppy; she weighed only thirty-three pounds. She was used to pushing around our bovine sheep, who sometimes butted or resisted her but rarely gave her any serious trouble. She would have no chance against a pack of coyotes or a bobcat. But if she was all right, why hadn't she come, why didn't she respond to the whistle that always brought her flying back to me? Why hadn't I been more vigilant? Why didn't I call her five minutes earlier?

I nearly forgot I'd ditched my truck, I was so frantic.

I got home, spattered with mud, hobbling on my bad leg, and got my Ford Explorer out of the other barn. I hadn't wanted to bother my neighbor Adam. But he was direct and action-oriented, at home in these environs. A hunter and snowmobiler, he'd know back roads and paths. And his truck, a huge Dodge, was equipped for everything from plowing snow to hauling wrecks. I needed him. Rose needed him.

I called Adam's cell phone and left a message, trying not to sound overdramatic. Then I drove up the steep driveway to his house, on top of the hill above mine, and knocked on his door. No truck and no answer. He must have been away. It was so late by now that I felt there was little point in calling Anthony or anyone else.

Besides, what could anybody see or hear on this dank night that I couldn't? Orson seemed frantic, whining and sniffing in circles, but if he didn't pick up any scent, how could I? I would keep walking and shouting through the night, then call for help in a few more hours, when it grew light.

But I was losing hope. Even if Rose had chased an animal, she shouldn't have been gone for three hours. She would have made her way back by now.

Suddenly my driveway lit up. Adam pulled in, his truck roaring—the Hebron Marine Corps. "Get in," he said, as always a man of few words. I left Orson in the house and we headed off. It was shocking, when his headlights picked up my truck, to see it tilted over nearly on its side. Adam hitched a nylon towline to my rear bumper, which miraculously stayed attached to the body as he pulled the truck out. It took maybe five minutes. Then we both drove back down the road.

If only finding Rose could be so simple. After this long winter, after all she'd done for me and with me, she was lost.

Which wasn't like being lost in New Jersey, where somebody would be sure to spot her and call the police or a shelter or me. She was wearing a bright red collar with my cell-phone number written large, plus several tags engraved with every number I had. But who would notice her out in the dark? She could be out there for days, bleeding from an injury or starving to death.

My house was lit up like an ocean liner, all the floodlights and porch lights blazing. As my resuscitated truck brought me back down the hill, I saw a nearly motionless dark creature by the garden in front of the house. At first I thought it was a skunk or raccoon. But as we got closer, I saw, with a flood of relief, that it was Rose, lying eerily still. She was shaking and panting, even though it was cool and dark, her tongue hanging. She looked spent.

I jumped out of the truck and called to her and she came flying into my arms, licking my face and neck. But she was trembling. I brought her inside, and she rushed into the kitchen and gulped down half a bowl of water, then lay down beside me. I massaged her back, held her, talked to her. "It's okay, girl, it's okay. You're okay now." But something bad had happened. She ran into her crate, then out, then in again, and finally settled down and dropped into sleep. I called Paula, then sat down on the floor and hugged Orson for many minutes.

When I finally staggered off to bed, Rose roused herself, came upstairs and curled up on the pillow next to me. When I fell asleep, she was still shaking.

I didn't sleep much. In the morning, Rose still lying beside me, I saw a little blood on the bed cover. I couldn't find any deep wounds, but we hastened over to Mary Menard, our vet in Salem. Some scabs, a few small puncture wounds, Mary said, examining the still-quiet Rose; nothing major. Most of the blood, she thought, was not Rose's.

She did appear exhausted, though, Mary said. Sometimes such trembling occurred when a dog's blood sugar has dropped.

Running for hours might explain why she was so exhausted; I'd never seen Rose so subdued. It appeared Rose had been running for a long time from something that had frightened her a lot, and from which she'd had to fight her way free.

Her confidence and ebullient energy were absent for a while. She stuck to my side as if taped there. Her confidence and constant motion were such integral parts of her that this seemed a different dog. It took Rose several more hours of sleep—and an unusual amount of time in her crate—to recover.

Rose was a sweet dog, but her usual priorities were clear: If you didn't have fleece, you were just taking up space that could be put to better use. But for the next couple of days she would impulsively rush over to me, lick me frantically, then curl up at my feet. Maybe the experience had left both of us even more appreciative of the other.

But sleep and sheep were powerful restoratives. I took her out with me for animal chores the next morning, and she shot through the open gate, ready for battle with any rebellious ewe.

I loved the resiliency of these creatures, how they hewed so faithfully to the routines and rhythms of their lives, adapting to change, trauma, and confusion. Things regularly happened to them—fights, accidents, late-night mysteries—that would level me for weeks. Fortunately for us, dogs don't hold grudges or dwell on bad memories.

The sheep were her work and focus, her grounding. I would probably never know what happened to Rose that long night. If you love dogs, loss and risk are never all that far away.

I kicked it around a hundred times in my mind, wondering if I had been neglectful or mistaken, had forgotten to take some obvious precaution. One friend insisted that Rose should only be walked on a leash from now on. Another suggested a radio receiver attached to her collar. Our culture, built on alarm and liability, likes to guard against all possible dangers.

But I came to a different conclusion. Rose was such a spectacular animal in part because she had been allowed to live the life she'd been bred for, roaming the farm, a working dog. My faith in her was the cornerstone of our work together, and she reciprocated by obeying and watching out for me.

In fact, when I thought about my time with Rose on the mountain, I figured there were two things I'd actually done right.

One was positive-reinforcement training. Rose was the first dog I'd trained entirely positively (okay, being human and being me, I'd lost it more than once, but not too often). She was the first dog I ever had who grew up with virtually no experience of being shouted at, subjected to the jangle of a thrown chain, menaced, or reprimanded. What she did came from affection, encouragement, and reward, not coercion, bullying, or "showing her who's boss."

I created situations where she couldn't fail. When she lay down, I said, "Good lie down!" When I held up a treat and she sat to look at it, I praised her for sitting. I'd worked relentlessly on rewarding and praising her for making eye contact. It was the antithesis of much that had happened to Orson, before me and even with me, and it worked. Rose was the keenest, most responsive and easy-to-train dog I ever had. Our relationship was almost entirely without conflict. I will never train a dog any other way.

The second idea that lodged in my mind came from my Irish border collie trainer Wink. "Trust the dog," he would say to me, on the phone or in e-mail, day after day. It was his mantra. "She knows how to herd sheep. Respect what she knows and trust her. If you give her the chance to solve problems and succeed, she will." So I had trusted Rose and it had paid off in so many ways, even as I understood and accepted that it involved some risk. I had rigorously street-trained Rose and did daily run-throughs of all the basic commands, but her life came with no guarantees.

I can't be sure that a ewe or ram won't catch her from the wrong angle and injure her, or that she won't rip a ligament or muscle as she tears across a field, or that she won't follow her great, intense instincts and tear off one day—or night—to the wrong place after the wrong thing.

I will watch her and train her and love her—more every day— but I won't ask her to live a life that undercuts the very instincts and traits that give her (and me) so much joy and satisfaction. Within reason and boundaries, she will be a working dog.

SOON AFTER, I DROVE HOME TO NEW JERSEY—FOR THE FIRST time since a two-day New Year's Eve visit—to be with Paula. I missed my wife. I needed to see my house, visit with my daughter, do some business. And I needed to see my former dog's sweet face. I understood Homer wasn't my dog any longer. But I had to see for myself that his new home was working out.

I had gotten some neighborhood reports that he'd been seen walking about with his new family, and was getting a bit plump. When I called, concerned, Sharon and Hank said they were aware of his weight gain and had already taken steps to change his diet and crank up his exercise. Otherwise, they said, everything was swell and the love affair continued unabated.

As it happened, I'd barely arrived and was unloading in the driveway when Sharon brought Homer over. He came skittering around the front of the truck, waggling furiously, squealing with glee, slurping all over my face. I was very happy to see him. The two of us rolled around on the ground, wrestling, exchanging hugs. He had gained some weight but not as much as I had feared.

The reunion packed more punch than I expected. It hurt. I could tell myself that I was feeling easier about him, and in most respects I was, but a piece of me will always live with Homer, and vice versa.

I brought him into the yard to visit everyone. He rushed up to greet Paula, and before she could plant a kiss on the top of his head, Orson was on him, backing him into a corner of the fence. When I called Orson off, Rose, wanting to play, dashed up with a rope toy. Homer hesitated, and Rose grabbed him by the tail and began pulling him around. Homer flashed me that old nervous "save me" look.

Sharon, watching the tussle from outside the gate, had just been telling me how crazy she was about Homer, how much Hank and the kids adored him. He got everybody up in the morning with licks and barks, walked each kid to the school-bus stop, and went along to soccer games. My former dog, herding partner, and book-tour companion was living a different kind of life than I could give him.

It seemed clear that he was fulfilling his particular canine destiny. Where Rose was largely uninterested in humans, Homer loved them. Orson eyed strangers warily, barking and circling them; Homer greeted every stranger as if this were his long-lost cousin. Being with people was his work, every bit as meaningful as herding or tracking or anything else. And he was meant to be an only dog, to get the attention he needed and deserved without having to fight for it.

"Let's go home, Homer," Sharon said as Homer edged toward the gate. He was more than ready and raced across the street with her, rushing down the block toward his new house and family.

I maintained visitation rights, though. A couple of weeks later, I came back to New Jersey for a medical appointment, leaving Orson and Rose kenneled upstate. I'd acquired an infection, and I needed to rest and be with Paula and see some doctors.

Almost the first thing I did when I got back was to ask Sharon and Hank if I could take Homer for a stroll. They agreed, graciously and enthusiastically. Homer had bonded strongly with his new family; nobody was feeling insecure about it.

I couldn't recall the last time I'd been alone with Homer—probably at Christmas, when we'd gone herding together.

Homer was happy to see me, as always, squealing and wriggling. I thought I saw a look of expectation in his eyes: Are we going to herd sheep? To the park to chase geese? Or to the ocean to chase waves? For all our frustrations, we'd had many good times, and I believed both of us remembered them.

And we no longer had anything at stake, none of the tensions that can sometimes arise between dogs and owners. Homer seemed tickled to head out with me, and I was happy to have him. We had several walks over the next few days, around the neighborhood, down to the high school field, past familiar landmarks. Alone together, without my perpetual scolding, his remarkable sweetness emerged. Dropping him off one day, I turned around and saw him staring plaintively through the storm door at me. I know better than to try to guess what a dog is thinking, but it seemed to me that we felt some mutual regret.

He was clearly happy in his new home, as I was with my remaining two dogs. But if my relationship with Orson and Rose reflected a capacity to grow, relocating Homer was a potent—and painful—reminder of my failures. Fortunately, I'd realized that in time to rectify it.

On the street one afternoon, a neighbor and dog lover who'd known us for several years hesitantly asked if he could pose a personal question.

"Sure," I said, guessing what it would be.

"I saw how much you and Homer loved each other. I know what a great dog he is. Tell me, how could you bear to give away a sweet dog like that?"

I smiled and shrugged and said nothing much. But I thought, How could I not?

SOMETIMES I THINK THAT SOON AFTER ORSON ENTERED MY life that night at Newark Airport, he developed a confidential strategy for dealing with the curious stranger he suddenly found himself keeping company with. His past troubles may have prevented him from herding sheep the way border collies are supposed to, but that doesn't mean he isn't a working dog. I believe his work became: me. He was as focused on me as Rose is on sheep.

Sometimes while I sat reading in the living room, he hopped up onto a rocking recliner chair, rested his head on one arm, and, rocking slightly, watched me for hours.

This guy is a mess, he must have thought when he landed in New Jersey, and perhaps still did. Few friends, no hobbies, rarely gets outside except to walk those slowpoke Labradors. Not writing about the stuff he ought to be writing about. Not living where he ought to be living. Not in touch with anyone from his family.

One by one, these realities changed. I could imagine him checking them off on a list only he could see. If working with him had improved me in some ways, simply living with him had profoundly altered my life, for the better. I often wondered what else he had in store for me.

On an April morning back at Bedlam after one of our Jersey visits, Rose and I fed the sheep and donkeys and mucked out the barn. Then it was time for the daily herding lesson with Orson.

Our lessons were now conducted mostly in silence. Not only did I not yell at him about donkey leavings, I didn't speak to him much at all. My voice was arousing and distracting for him, I'd decided; his own herding instincts would either emerge and develop, or not.

I put aside my own agenda. He was the herding dog, and he would either keep going at it or let it go—his choice. Orson liked the new drill. And it was generating more rapid and dramatic change than years of my previous training, so much more vocal and more stressful.

I opened the pasture gate and the two of us walked inside. Orson rushed past two steaming piles of donkey dung and, glancing over his shoulder at me, took off for the sheep at the top of the slope.

While I watched, startled—this was usually the point where he spun around like a pinwheel, barked and panted, rushed back toward me, or all of the above—he loped gracefully up to the fence, curved alongside it, and came up behind the ewes and lambs. As always when Orson appeared, they started rapidly down the hill, straight for me. As always, his authority and presence were impressive. What a herding dog he could have been, and might yet be.

I held up my hand—the "stay" command—and to my further surprise, Orson actually stopped. The sheep rushed toward the barn. I ran up to my dog and dropped to my knees to greet him, his signal to rush up and lick me. We walked out of the pasture together.

Then, on impulse, I turned back and brought him back in. He broke into that beautiful but seldom-seen outrun, gliding once more around the sheep, who turned and ran in my direction. I unlatched the gate, checking first for traffic up and down the road.

The sheep hustled across the road and into the greening meadow below, Orson cantering behind them. I closed my eyes and said nothing. If I were a religious man, I would have prayed.

When I looked, I couldn't see sheep or dog. But when I walked across the road, there they were behind the small barn, the sheep grazing, Orson sitting behind them, looking particularly pleased with himself, as if to say, "See? You thought I couldn't do this?"

A couple of the neighbors drove by and honked, then slowed so their kids could see the dog and sheep and lambs. "Beautiful dog," yelled one of the mothers.

Yes, I thought, he is. After ten minutes or so, I walked back across the road, yelled, "Get me sheep," and stood back as ewes, lambs, and dog came flying back into the pasture.

A herding trial judge would have knocked off points for all sorts of things—Orson ran too fast, got too close, didn't respond quickly enough to some commands. But it was the most beautiful sheepherding I had ever seen.

ON A WARM SUNDAY AFTERNOON, IT SEEMED THAT HALF THE hamlet had driven up with their kids to see the new lambs, watch the dogs at work, bring carrots and apples for the donkeys, who were delighted to have their fuzzy noses scratched in return. At one point, there were five or six pickups in the driveway and more than a dozen people milling about. At my more solitary mountain cabin, this influx would have driven me mad. Here, I was pleased that my creatures were giving people so much pleasure—and to no one more than me.

We'd had so many visitors by now that we'd developed our own drill. Orson, whose interest in sheep never extended much beyond working with me, moved from one dog lover to another, working the crowd, wolfing down biscuits, offering kisses and receiving hugs and scratches.

Meanwhile, Rose, showing her usual marginal interest in things that were not sheep, put on a show, moving the herd into the training pen, up the hill, down into the paddock and back. Orson loved all the cooing and cries of admiration; Rose hardly seemed to notice.

When she grew tired and I called her off, she would lie off to the side, staring at the sheep until I released her. If somebody came over to pet her, she'd be polite, give a wag, but it was clear where her loyalties lay.

It was fascinating to see these two border collies evolve in such different ways. Orson vastly preferred cuddling and food to the rigors of herding; Rose only wanted to work.

At first, there was much oohing and aahing at Rose's herding. But Orson was always the bigger hit. What a beautiful dog, people said. What a sweetie. What a character. Now and then, I'd come over and mock-scold him—"You biscuit slut! What about the sheep?" He'd bound toward the flock, circle once, receive his hosannas, then go back to the laps and treats.

Seeing him so happy and at ease reminded me of the look on my sister's face when she saw Rose playing with her Newfies. I knew how she felt. It was a pure, visceral sense of love and joy.

More than Rose, this dog reflected the pleasures and crises, twists and turns, nooks and crannies of a life—my life. He mirrored my pain, my confusion, but also my determination to keep moving, changing, improving. He not only reflected those things, he made many of them possible. To joy I added gratitude.

What I told Orson as the last pickup exited the driveway and the last kid waved goodbye was just what I'd said when a trailer full of sheep had pulled up months before.

I leaned down and hugged him. "Look what you've done," I said. 🐑

PEACEABLE KINGDOM

EASTER SUNDAY 2004 WAS COOL AND SUNNY. THE FORECAST called for rain, but the bad weather didn't materialize, and we woke up to sunlight streaming through the blinds and a nicer day than I'd expected.

Green grass and leaves were making their first appearances, but the winter was still fresh and had left the farm and the valley with a wasted look, brown and spent. Though spring was here, it was hesitant.

I'd planned to take the sheep on a hike to the top of my hill to munch and mow my neighbor Adam's lawn, but looking out over the valley, I had a different idea.

Sitting on the porch with Orson and Rose, watching the parking lot of the Presbyterian church down in the hamlet fill up with worshipers, I remembered my dog-eared and largely forgotten copy of Saint Augustine's *City of God*. Six months earlier I was still mesmerized by the book and the idea. Now I wasn't even sure where it was.

That early glow had been rudely obliterated by the first thirty-inch snowfall weeks before winter's official onset, then kept at bay by feral cats, hypothermia and frostbite, the reemergence in my life of the complete stranger who was my sister, countless treks in and out of the pasture to haul hay and water, herding lessons in sub-zero temperatures, round-the-clock midwifery duties, and one gravely ill donkey.

My journey, it turned out, hadn't been to a heavenly city but to someplace quite different. My days had not been bright, peaceful, or pastoral. I had not entered a place of calm and spirituality after all, but a place of literal Bedlam, a state of my own unnerving creation.

Bedlam, as it happened, was a much more accurate reflection of my inner being. At least I had my dogs as spirits, prophets, guides, fellow citizens, and companions. Thinking back on my mood that October day, I wondered if Augustine had had a dog, and if so, why he never mentioned it.

Just five days before Easter, a final blast of snow and howling winds had engulfed the farm. Bits of the barn had blown all over the place, and another lamb had died. I took this last nasty snarl personally, as a forceful reminder of what had been and what would, in just a few short months, come again. I was already ordering hay and firewood for the coming winter. I was getting a breather, not a pardon. But it was a welcome breather.

Although I am not a religious man, I was conscious of Easter, in part because of the two lovely church spires that pop up through the trees below the farm. Also, in part, because in this overwhelmingly Christian community, normal life and commerce had halted to celebrate the holiday.

I thought of the Easter story, of the power and promise of the Resurrection, the spiritual roots of my donkeys, the faithfulness of my neighbors, driving into the church parking lot early to make sure they got a seat at the packed Easter morning service.

In this world of dirt roads, blue jeans, and muddied pickups, it was fun to sit up on my perch and look down at the bonnets and ribbons, the flowers and finery.

Gazing at the stream of families in their go-to-church best, anticipating the hymns of the choir soon to ride the sharp spring breezes up the hill to the farm, I decided to join the celebration. Bedlam Farm should contribute to this Easter scene.

I was feeling a bit blue that morning. Returned from my short visit to New Jersey, I was sorry to find myself back in the tug and the pull—missing the farm, worrying about my animals, needing to be with my wife and closer to my daughter in the city, unable to have all of it all the time.

Things had gone too far that winter. As my friend Carr had predicted, the experience had changed me. I could shuttle back and forth, but not in the same way as before. Too big a chunk of me was here, with these barns and pastures and animals, and that chunk had taken root.

Back in the suburbs, the tension and traffic, the din of leaf blowers and garbage trucks were no longer so easy to bear. I needed the quiet of West Hebron. I missed the leisurely, circular chats that characterize the best Country Bullshit. I missed drivers waving to me from their cars and trucks as they passed on the road. I missed the hee-haws that echoed from the barn practically the minute my feet hit the bedroom floor in the morning, and the urgent cries of ewes and lambs locating one another.

Jersey's soccer uniforms, the vans and SUVs whizzing kids from lesson to lesson felt strange. There was certainly nothing wrong with it, but it was not my world any longer. I had found—built, really—a new one.

I felt invisible in New Jersey, irrelevant. People could pass on the sidewalk and not smile or say hello. Here, although we were different, my new friends were wise and empathetic. Farmers go through much, understand a lot.

At "home," apart from time with Paula, which I cherished, I really didn't know what to do with myself. On the farm, I never knew how to get to all the chores that awaited me each day.

Although she handled it with her usual enthusiasm and eagerness, New Jersey was also hard on Rose. The reigning Queen of Bedlam Farm, she'd grown accustomed to roaming and herding sheep until she dropped; back there, confined and leashed, she really had nowhere she could safely (or legally) run free, and try as I might, no work to do.

A favorite neighborhood park, I was horrified to learn, had been covered in expensive artificial turf at the urging of the soccer and lacrosse parents—worshipers of the new suburban religion—and sealed off by a ten-foot fence more suited to a minimum-security prison than a neighborhood.

Yet in New Jersey, the company of my wife, the garbage pickup that replaced drives to the county dump, the Thai restaurants and multiplex movies were a pleasure.

That was the thing about the tug and the pull; it tugged and it pulled. After so intense a connection with this place and its people, I felt split in half again. I wasn't a gentleman farmer, nor a real one, yet I'd never felt more comfortable or engaged—or at home—than slogging up that icy hill with Rose and a bale of hay in the brutal cold.

While many things had changed, many hadn't. Paula had just accepted a teaching position at Columbia University's Graduate School of Journalism in New York. She loved teaching and was great at it, so I was happy for her. But between that and the stories she'd still be reporting and writing, she wasn't moving anywhere anytime soon. She loved the dogs, but they weren't as integral to her life as they were to mine; while she appreciated Orson's gathering calm and Rose's herding exploits, she did not consider them the triumphal, landscape-altering miracles that I did.

For all the drama and punch of the winter, I felt on that Easter morning that in certain ways I'd ended up closer to where I'd begun than I expected.

Where did I belong, anyway? Perhaps I dreaded the honest answer: no place, really. Was I one of those people, I wondered, who's addicted to change for its own sake and drifts from experience to experience? Or had I rooted and landed this time? I wouldn't know for a while.

So sitting up on my hill with my dogs, I sniffed a bit of the Easter fever that had swept the town, and understood some of its power: a transition from one season to another, the notion of resurrection and redemption.

I settled Orson with his beef jerky and left him dozing serenely in his crate. I was happy about this, and it was no small thing. Orson had for years hated being left behind. In his early days he'd tunneled under fences and jumped through windows in protest. But years of training and pounds of treats—plus a significant increase in understanding, patience, and anger management on my part—had soothed him.

Me, too. Learning what really makes a dog like him tick had forced me to grasp more about what made *me* tick. I often didn't like what I saw in me, but I was determined to do right by him. Which meant, as Carolyn had suggested, that I had to be better. Orson, like all my dogs, was a measure, a barometer, a mirror of me.

Before we came to the farm, Orson would surely have run to the door and tried desperately to squeeze out if I tried to leave without him. Now I simply said "Crate" and he rushed off happily and without complaint for a snack and some quiet time. Quiet time is good for border collies.

It wasn't so much that Orson was a different dog as that the real dog had finally emerged: a profoundly loving, happy, playful, and, most important, calm creature.

Only the two of us could possibly know how much work had

gone into this new reality. I couldn't honestly compare our relationship to any religious milestone, but I did feel on that lovely morning that this dog had been reborn. And so had a part of me. By the measures I'd set, I was calmer, less angry, better able to deal with frustration. Somehow, Orson and Homer and Rose had led me back to my sister, too. Out of a painful shambles, a part of my family had reemerged.

Perhaps Orson was still not calm enough for this Easter walk, but he was getting there. Next year, I vowed, I'd take the same walk with him.

This Easter jaunt was tailor-made for Rose, though, my partner in all things sheep-related, my fellow adventurer and farm manager.

I put on my rubber boots, wordlessly. Rose, who knows the location and sound of every farm boot in the house, appeared out of nowhere, her nose at the back door. We went out toward the barn, but instead of entering the pasture by the main gate, I walked over to the side, to a gate we hadn't used all winter. She stopped and looked at me curiously.

"C'mon, Rose" I said. "We're taking the sheep for an Easter walk."

One of the things I love most about border collies—who certainly aren't for everyone—is their enthusiasm, their appetite for fresh tasks. The lurking danger of middle age, for me, is old-fartism, that mental rusting that leads you to cherish stasis and squawk about change. If you have a brace of border collies, that's unlikely to be your state of mind; your dogs simply won't allow it. The official motto of the breed ought to be: Move along or perish.

At the mention of sheep, of course, I had Rose's full attention—eyes wide, head cocked. She didn't know what I had in mind but was ready for whatever I might propose.

I opened the side gate and Rose ran inside, looked around for the sheep, then charged up the hill as usual. I called her back.

"No," I said cheerfully. "We're going somewhere else. We're taking an Easter walk." She sat down and waited. I pointed to the sheep and then across the road. "We'll take them into the meadow and down along the creek," I said, explaining my plan slowly, as if I were talking to a small child or slow adult. "And we'll wind up right across from the church parking lot."

Rose didn't care about my explanation, of course. She dashed up the hillside and pushed the sheep down toward me. They didn't seem to care, either. Rose was happy as long as she was moving sheep around; the sheep were delighted as long as the place to which she was moving them offered food.

I greeted the ewes in my customary way. "Good morning, ladies," I said. "Hope you're up for an adventure. We're going to visit some pilgrims." We weren't headed for a City of God, but we'd drop by one of His houses.

Without further elaboration, I turned toward the road and told her to bring the sheep. She had no trouble grasping that part: behind me on the run came the thirteen surviving ewes and their offspring—the Winter of 2004 Brigade.

They were a healthy, plump, high-spirited, and raggedy troop—the ewes' matted coats in urgent need of shearing, lambs hopping all over the place, nervous moms stopping and starting. There were almost twice the number that had arrived in Wilbur Price's trailer.

Carol and Fanny, whom I'd lured into a separate pasture with some oats, hee-hawed reproachfully as our curious little band set out. Like the dogs, they always wanted to come along, and sometimes did. But we were navigating alien turf that day and donkeys, unlike sheep, have wills of their own. If they took it into their heads to go south, Rose wouldn't be able to do much about it.

We'd never taken the sheep on this route. By now Rose had regained the upper hand with the rebellious ewe-moms, so I had no doubt about her ability to propel the flock toward the church, but with all the lambs it would be tougher than usual. After taking them across the road, she'd have to move them along a narrow trail edged by brush and woods, then alongside a muddy swollen creek before we all emerged into a clearing about fifty yards from the church parking lot.

"Next time, girls," I yelled to the donkeys, and set off.

The herd paused a bit in confusion when we got out of the gate, and I had to send Rose back a few times for some stragglers—a few lambs didn't want to go, causing their mothers to hold back. But in a couple of minutes I was standing by the road, watching for cars, and Rose had brought the herky-jerky crew up behind me. I was carrying my shepherd's crook for the occasion, which seemed fitting for Easter Sunday. "Let's go, girl," I yelled, and off we went.

The sheep were excited by the fresh spring grass in front of them, and they spread out and started grazing. I sat down on a rock and Rose sat alongside me, keeping a close eye on her charges, veering out to gather strays. She was fond of Brutus, Paula's big brown lamb, and he returned her affections. She dashed over to nuzzle him, then lay down by my side. The sun felt good on my long-chilled bones. Saint Augustine's city seemed closer once more.

After the sheep ate a bit, I got up and our procession resumed. Rose kept to the back, circling around from time to time to lick my hand or check out the front of the herd.

Some of the ewes balked at the narrow path through the woods—no grass!—but Rose pushed them along from the rear. Our Easter parade wound its way along, the burbling water on one side, trees and brush on the other.

In a few minutes we emerged across the creek from the church parking lot. The sheep spread out and started crunching on grass.

Churchgoers pulling into the lot were amazed to get out of their cars and see a man, a dog, and thirty or so sheep and lambs just across the creek. The kids especially shrieked and rushed over. I was sorry I hadn't brought the donkeys, who would have given the walk an even more timely sheen. About a dozen cars emptied out, their occupants clustering on their side of the creek to wave, cheer, and wish us all a Happy Easter.

Everybody loved watching Rose work, including me, the proud papa and the shepherd in this Easter rite. Rose seemed to enjoy herself, too; she preened for the crowd, puffing out her chest. Soon, the kids across the bank were cheering her on by name—"Go, Rose!"—as she wheeled and circled.

Then the audience had to leave; the kids wanted to stay and watch, but their parents hustled them inside the church for services. It was time to head back to the farm.

There was little dallying. In a few minutes we were back inside our own gates and I was showering Rose with praise. The sheep walked to the top of the paddock, spread out, and lay down with their babies to take in the sun and get some rest.

We settled on the porch's wicker settee, Orson's head in my lap, Rose against my left hip. Soon they were both asleep, a rare sight in daylight. I felt blessed.

THAT AFTERNOON, THE TEMPERATURE ROSE WELL INTO THE fifties, according to the thermometer behind the barn. I was drinking up the quiet; because of the holiday, there was none of the usual Sunday traffic, friends dropping by, folks who wanted to see the dogs work or visit the donkeys.

We'd all have lunch together, I decided—our own version of Easter dinner. I brought both dogs out by the hay feeder behind the barn, set up my folding lawn chair, tossed some treats their way. They struggled with the idea that their task was to do nothing, but they were willing to try to relax.

I'd brought a bucket of special low-fat milled oats for Carol and Fanny, which I poured into a bucket a few feet away. Soon the donkeys were crunching contentedly. I'd also brought out a bucket of corn and sheep feed and tossed it into the feeder. The ewes, a bit slowed down after birthing and nursing, and the lambs, playful and oblivious to danger, began inching their way down to their feeder.

"Stay, guys," I told the dogs. "We're off the clock. This is a holiday."

Where was a painter when I needed one? In a few minutes, I was at the center of a strange but lovely scene, sitting in my tacky lawn chair, Yankees cap tilted back so that my face could catch the sun, eating my tuna-fish sandwich and apple. Rose, off to my left, was staring intently, but calmly, at her sheep and lambs. Orson was asleep at my feet, taking the rays. Carol and Fanny nibbled at their oats, and every few minutes, one or another would come over and rest her head briefly on my shoulder.

The ewes, who would risk nearly as much for corn as they did for their babies, had come slowly down to the feeder and were also eating with gusto, then nosing around for fresh grass.

We were, in fact, a peaceable kingdom. The natural antipathy between a dog and her herd was still there—there was nothing truly peaceable in Rose's gaze at the sheep—but the adversarial relationship had been suspended for a bit. And I was as calm as I ever get.

I was also proud of everybody, including myself. We had worked hard for this moment, earned it; our lunch had a triumphal feeling. We had come through the move, the winter, and the lambing largely intact. For newcomers, we'd suffered relatively few losses.

The ewes had risen above their obsession with food to do a fine job of mothering. All they needed was shearing and hoof trimming. Almost all the lambs were fat and happy and healthy.

Carol had overcome her illness and was appreciating the spring. Fanny was as loyal and loving as any dog. Rose had risen to the challenge thrust on her somewhat prematurely and saved my hide. Orson was blossoming into a dog who wanted to work but was also learning how to be still.

I hadn't done so badly myself.

I composed, in my head, an after-lunch speech to the assembled company, praising the ewes for their fortitude, thanking the donkeys for their faithful affection. I nearly raised my water bottle in a salute to Rose and Orson, and I reserved a few kudos for humans, too: Anthony, Ray and Joanne, Paula. Myself.

I didn't give the speech, of course. Talking at length to animals is a no-no when you spend the winter alone with them. Just one of those ground rules, like no more than one scotch on a dark and stormy night.

OVER THE NEXT COUPLE OF WEEKS, THE GRASS GREW TALLER and greener; I stopped feeding the ewes hay and grain as the pastures grew lush. In late April, a shearer came to denude the flock and I sold its fleece to a local spinner—my first revenue from the farm, I bragged to Paula, though it amounted to $3.50 and a dozen eggs.

It was time for one of my biggest decisions about the sheep: who would go and who would stay. Some friends urged me to keep them all; I had sufficient pasture for a flock of thirty. And after all, we'd been through a lot together. Carolyn was willing to let me keep them. But Anthony and my other Hebron neighbors brooked no sentimentality. These were livestock, livelihood.

I felt in the middle of these camps. These sheep weren't pets. If I were going to call my place a farm, I had to make sensible choices in the interest of the flock. For herding purposes, fifteen sheep was plenty. With thirty, the trough and the training pen would get crowded and it would be difficult to steer them all into the barn for vet visits and shearing. I'd have to order twice as much hay, after I'd already invested a daunting fortune in barns, fencing, and feed.

Besides, I felt increasingly conscious of the trials of the farmers around me. How could I justify keeping twice as many animals as I needed, eating hay and costing money? A true farmer struggling to make ends meet who heard about that wouldn't like it.

Yet I felt more attached to the ewes after lambing. How much more intimately involved with animals could you get?

I'd land in the middle, I decided. Some sheep had to go, but I would keep a slightly expanded flock.

A number of people had called, offering to buy sheep—people with herding dogs who wanted dog-broke sheep, several butchers seeking mutton or lamb, locals who wanted pets for their kids. I said no to them all.

Instead, I called Bob Wood, a farmer over in Pawlet, and we struck a deal: he'd add some of my sheep to his own flock and transport the others to market in Rutland, and we'd split the proceeds.

Dr. Alderink came by to review the herd with me. She pointed out the ewes that looked most vital and those that appeared weaker. I consulted my notes so I could weed out the poor mothers, those who'd abandoned their lambs or been careless with them. The devoted black-faced ewe with twins? A keeper. The one who'd stranded Murphy with inadequate milk? She had to go. I planned for ewes and lambs to either go or stay together. Though they were no longer nursing, the lambs were still likely to stay close by their mothers; I didn't want to separate them.

On a rainy Sunday night, Bob Wood drove over with a wooden box in his truck bed. Rose and I gathered the herd and pushed them into the barn, where Bob and I grappled to load my designated sheep into the truck. The scene was chaotic, ewes and lambs bellowing and scattering every which way, Bob and I lunging and grunting and cursing.

It took a good ninety minutes, and when he finally left—full of praise for Rose, and leaving me a bottle of his own maple syrup as a gift—I suddenly saw the black-faced ewe racing around, looking for her babies. Somehow I had put her twins on Bob's truck by mistake.

I knew better than to call him and try to reshuffle the flock. So I left the barnyard.

"It was hard," I told Anthony. He and Holly had invited me for dinner. He rolled his eyes. But all night, I couldn't sleep, listening to the ewe bleating for her twins. "I'm so sorry, girl," I told her next morning when Rose and I took the sheep to the meadow across the street. She ate hungrily, but paused frequently to look around forlornly and complain.

For two days, as the ewe baahed fruitlessly, I cursed my carelessness. She settled down on the third day, consoled somewhat by the bits of carrot I slipped her when the others weren't watching. In fact, she became my favorite, the one who'd put her nose in my hand for a scratch. Still, I'd done her wrong.

But I had twenty healthy sheep, my herd for the foreseeable future. They were all responsive to Rose (though she still favored Brutus), and she seemed easy and confident with this number.

They would have a good summer. The artesian well was running, providing a constant supply of fresh, clean water. I had plenty of pasture. The vet had given them all their shots, their hooves had been trimmed and their fleece shorn. Barring some unforeseen obstacle, they could munch their way clear to the first frost.

Already I was thinking ahead to future pleasures and ventures. A Lab breeder in Pawlet I'd visited a couple of times raises some of the most beautiful dogs I've ever seen, and she was expecting a litter. Annie, who works at Gardenworks, down the road, asked me the other day if I wanted two young goats. And my friend Sheila wondered whether I might consider giving a home to her gimpy rooster, affable but lame and getting on in years. I identified with him.

I didn't need any of these new additions, Paula pointed out. She was right, but that had never stopped me before.

.   .   .

I'D COME TO THE FARM IN PART TO EXPLORE THE IDEA THAT our own humanity was linked to our love of animals.

Was Carolyn right in the question she posed, what seems like a very long time ago? Can working with a dog really make you a good human?

Probably not.

Can it make you a better one? Yes.

Do you sometimes need to be better to have the dog you really want? Absolutely.

Shrinks, friends, spouse, editors have all worked on me over the years to be more patient, less impulsive, less angry, and more focused. My own rage and confusion at the state of bedlam in which I grew up has plagued me all my life, an unwelcome and unwanted legacy.

Dog love is a powerful, perhaps underappreciated force in the life of someone like me. If dogs are a measure of my humanity, the legacy of my winter at Bedlam Farm is that I did do better.

If Orson is herding well, then I must be growing less angry and more patient. If Rose has developed her amazing skills without interference from me and my big mouth, then I have learned something about patience and trust.

If I could muster the strength to give Homer to another family, then perhaps I am grasping the real meaning of love.

I often wonder—if we humans did a better job of taking care of one another, would we still love dogs so much? I doubt we'll ever know.

BEDLAM, AN IDEA WOVEN THROUGH THIS EXPERIENCE, SUGgests our struggle to survive in a bewildering, sometimes cruel, and chaotic world. It reflects our human ability to mistreat one another, but also to improve. This is a fundamental difference between people and dogs: they adapt, but we can change.

The story of the Bethlehem asylum, my farm's unlikely godmother, still captivates and sometimes haunts me. It was a story about so much more than a place. Bedlam was a nightmare in the seventeenth century, its inmates brutally confined, horribly abused, restrained, humiliated, mistreated.

Over time—centuries—conditions there improved, along with human learning and compassion. The idea of paying for the privilege of throwing rocks and tomatoes at hospitalized mental patients horrifies us now, but just a few hundred years ago it was deemed no different from going to the theater.

I have more than once felt the fuzzy line between normalcy and other people's notions of insanity. People have told me my whole life that I'm crazy, and I used to think they must know something.

Now I believe that no one can really judge—or know— what's in another's mind. It's impossible to locate the boundary between what most people think is rational and what isn't. It made no sense of any sort, for instance, to spend so much money to buy a farm in a remote corner of upstate New York and gather donkeys and sheep and dogs there. No one I knew thought it sensible. Yet it's turned out to be one of the best, most meaningful experiences of my life. For someone in late middle age, I've come to believe, such change can be vital in keeping one's eyes open to the world.

Even Bedlam, originally a metaphor for inhumanity, eventually became a model of enlightened medical care, a metaphor for progress instead of cruelty.

I've been learning a lot about the world's first crazy house. In the spring, Tag Heister, a researcher at the University of Kentucky's Department of Psychiatry (and a fellow dog lover), sent me a 1989 book—*The Discovery of the Art of the Insane* by John M. MacGregor. It included an eighteenth-century etching by Paul Sandby; the cartoon, which is housed in the British Museum, is titled "The Author Run Mad."

The image shows a barefoot artist (said to be modeled on William Hogarth) clad in a rakish feather hat, a book open at his feet, a chain attached to one ankle. He's working on a drawing—a story sketched on a wall.

The etching is funny, yet not funny. It gives me the chills. Looking at it, I sense how easily I could have been that author.

He is in a cell in Bedlam, a primitive thatched bed behind him. On the rear walls are elaborate religious drawings, including several animals (one looks like a dog). He's holding either a long paintbrush or a pointer. Judging from the satisfied expression on his face, he is working on a good story, oblivious to his surroundings. The book seems more important to him than the fact that he's being held in a notorious lunatic asylum, the object of ridicule and public humiliation.

I think of the young boy who came across me in the meadow one afternoon while I was out grazing the sheep. He was bicycling on a track through the woods and nearly plowed into us. He stopped, took in this large and rumpled man with his battered Yankees cap, dirtied jeans, and walking stick.

"You the dog guy?" he asked.

I nodded, and he seemed relieved to bicycle off down the hill, too polite to throw tomatoes.

My imagination reaches out across time to this mad author thrown into Bedlam. I couldn't shake the feeling I not only understood what he was doing but was at work on a contemporary version of it in a world which, for all its flaws, has improved. It still punishes individuality sometimes, but now allows the mad to wander freely and acquire farms and dogs and sheep.

I imagine him pleased with this progress, the Bedlam author from hundreds of years ago, a rotund man in his outlandish hat and flowing cloak. Apparently unaware that he's in a crazy house, indifferent to others' view of him, he is not in a beautiful place, but he's making something that's beautiful to him, constructing his own reality.

It seems relevant to me.

I, too, sometimes think I'm in a crazy house, and others must think me crazy, at times, to be here. I also happily do my work amid almost indescribable chaos, and no matter what's happening outside, I'm always happy and engaged to be telling my story.

But there this mad author and I diverge somewhat. My Bedlam is different.

I am not mad here, but clear and calm.

I am not transformed, but allowed to be wholly myself.

I am isolated, but have never felt more connected to people.

I am not imprisoned, but free.

I am not cut off from my family and my roots, but am brought back to them.

I am not living alone with dogs, but permitting my dogs to lead me somewhere I need to go, and it has been a great trip. We have more distance to travel together, I'm sure, before we are through.

Acknowledgments

Thanks to Paula Span and Emma Span for so many things, including rushing to my rescue when I needed them. Blood is, in fact, thicker than anything.

Thanks to Richard Abate and Bruce Tracy. Particular thanks to Brian McLendon for his friendship and unwavering advocacy. And to Julie Kurland for her support of my work.

Thanks to Anthony Armstrong, his wife, Holly, and daughter, Ida, and the Hanks clan, especially Dean and Darrow.

Thanks to Jane Richter.

Ray and Joanne Smith have been dear friends and fellow pilgrims on the road to paradise. Vickie Maxwell, Don Coldwell, Louise Jones, and Nancy Fortier have been great help; so has Jacob Worthington, a valued friend and aide. Thanks to his mother Barbara and to Mary Zeller, and also to my neighbors Adam Matthews, Christopher Wirkki, and Jeremy and Andrea Harrington. And to the Reverend Bill Hoffman and the choir and congregation of the West Hebron United Presbyterian Church.

I will always be grateful to Deanne Veselka for bringing Orson, Homer, and Rose into my life. Thanks also to Pam Leslie and Heather Waite.

I appreciate Meg and Rob Southerland and Becky MacLachlan, role models in so many ways. My gratitude also to Pat Freund, Sheila Blais and Nancy Masson, John Sweenor, Nancy and Jamie Higby, Jim and Maryann Boyter. And to Ralph and Jesse Corey, Patty and Tom Calabrese, Ginny Tremblay, and Loren Tucker for making Bedlam Farm mine.

I am indebted to Dr. Debra Katz and Tagalie Heister of the University of Kentucky for their perspectives on human-animal attachment and for invaluable research help.

Deep thanks to Alice and Harvey Hahn for helping me to manage an inherently unmanageable place. And to Dr. Daniel Garfinkel and Barbara Pratt.

Steve Saunders, Wanda Finney, Sandy Hickland, and Jeremy Shapiro of A&J Agway provided patient counsel and helped me and my farm survive the winter.

The sheep, dogs, donkeys, and I have many reasons to be grateful to Drs. Mary Menard, Jen Steeves, and Whitney Pressler and the staff of the Borador Animal Hospital in Salem, New York: Kiersten DeDeo, Katie Hahn, Laura Newton, Melissa Wicks, Jon Nelson, Laurie Lourie, Melissa Rushinski, Laura Periard, Pat Albrecht, Penny Saddlemire, Suzanne Benjamin, Karen Washburn, Derrick Keath, and Maria Sherman. And I deeply appreciate Drs. Amanda Alderink and Kirk C. Ayling and staffers Rose Smith and Kathy McGraw at the Granville Large Animal Veterinary Service. All these men and women define the very notion of compassionate care for animals. Thanks also to Danny Thomas of Thomas Farms and to Ken Norman.

I am grateful to Cindy Barnes of the Sykes Hollow Kennels in Dorset, Vermont, for the wonderful care she gave my dogs.

I'm beholden to Margaret Waterston for first suggesting that I write about dogs.

Many thanks to Sharon, Hank, Max, and Eva Hersch.

I salute the late Julius and Stanley, as excellent a pair of dogs as any human can live with, and Homer, who finally got what he deserved.

And I am forever grateful to Carolyn Wilki for her friendship and insights into the true nature of dogs, guidance that finally set me on the path to understanding and doing right by these amazing creatures.

Jon Katz with Jane and Rose

JON KATZ has written thirteen books—six novels and seven works of nonfiction—including *A Dog Year* and *The New Work of Dogs*. A two-time finalist for the National Magazine Award, he has written for *The New York Times, The Wall Street Journal, Rolling Stone, Wired,* and the *AKC Gazette*. A member of the Association of Pet Dog Trainers, he writes a column about dogs for the online magazine *Slate* and is cohost of *Dog Talk,* a monthly show on Northeast Public Radio. Katz lives on Bedlam Farm in upstate New York and in northern New Jersey, with his wife, Paula Span, who is a *Washington Post* contributing writer and a teacher at Columbia University, and their dogs. He can be e-mailed at jonkatz3@comcast.net or at jdkat3@aol.com.